PSYCHOANALYTIC
THEORY
and the
RORSCHACH

D1066766

PSYCHOANALYTIC
THEORY
and the
RORSCHACH

PAUL M. LERNER

MSP Hahnemann University
Hahnemann Library

THE ANALYTIC PRESS

1991   Hillsdale, NJ   London

Copyright © 1991 by The Analytic Press., Inc.
All rights reserved. No part of this book may be reproduced
in any form, by photostat, microform, retrieval system, or any
other means without prior written permission of the copyright
holder.

Published by The Analytic Press, Inc.
365 Broadway, Hillsdale, NJ

Library of Congress Cataloging-in-Publication Data

Lerner, Paul M.

Psychoanalytic theory and the Rorschach/Paul Lerner

p.   cm.

Includes bibliographical references and index.

ISBN 0-88163-122-1

1. Rorschach test.   2. Psychoanalysis.   3. Borderline
personality disorder—Diagnosis

I. Title

RC473,R6147   1991
155.2'842—dc20

90-43856
CIP

Printed in United States of America
10 9 8 7 6 5 4 3 2 1

Acknowledgment

I wish to thank my brother, Dr. Howard Lerner, for his assistance with several of the chapters, in particular, Chapter 11, "The Rorschach Assessment of Object Representation."

Contents

v

Preface

The past decade has witnessed a significant resurgence in the use of the Rorschach for the study and understanding of people. Two streams have contributed to this renewal of interest: an empirical one based on the work of John Exner (1974) and his comprehensive system and a conceptual one based on ongoing developments in psychoanalytic theory. This book represents an attempt to review and summarize the current status of contributions arising from the psychoanalytic stream. The relatively recent integration of modern object relations theory, a broadened psychodynamic developmental theory, and a systematic psychology of the self into the mainstream of traditional psychoanalytic theory is now providing the conceptual basis for a more comprehensive, systematic, and clinically useful Rorschach theory.

Psychological testing from a psychoanalytic perspective is rooted in the work of David Rapaport. Rorschach did not wed his procedure to a specific theory of personality—Rapaport did. The marriage forged by Rapaport between the Rorschach and psychoanalysis was a perfect one of technique and theory. In blending test responses with a comprehensive theory of personality, he provided the clinical tester with a bedrock of conceptualizations that allowed test inferences of remarkable scope and range. As Mayman (1976) put it, "Rorschach inferences were transposed to a wholly new level of comprehension as Rapaport made a place for them in his psychoanalytic ego psychology and elevated psychological test findings from mundane, descriptive, pragmatically useful statements to a level of interpretation that achieved an incredible heuristic sweep" (p. 200).

This book is an extension of this tradition. More specifically, in Part 1 I attempt to update clinical testing from the perspective of psychoanalysis by integrating the contributions of Rapaport and his immediate followers (Schafer, Holt, and, especially, Mayman) with more recent concepts and formulations emerging from an evolving psychoanalytic theory.

Part 1 is organized in the following manner. In Chapter 1, I describe what is meant by a clinical approach to testing and contrast it with a psychometric perspective. In Chapter 2, an outline for a psychological test report is presented. The outline serves as an organizational and interpretive framework for the remainder of the book.

A psychoanalytic approach to the Rorschach involves an integration of test theory, personality theory, and psychopathology. Groundwork for that integration is laid in Chapter 3 with the presentation of a psychoanalytic diagnostic scheme. The scheme calls for evaluating a patient along two dimensions: one a descriptive assessment of the patient's character structure and the other a structural consideration of the patient's level of personality organization.

In my view, Rorschach administration, scoring, recording, and interpretation are all part of the same process. With this in mind, in Chapter 4 a method of administering the test is outlined, the need for recording as verbatim as possible is noted, and a scoring system is presented.

The Rorschach examiner has available several sources of information about the patient, including the nature of the interaction with the patient, the formal scores and their interrelationships, the thematic content of the responses, and the sequence of responses. Each of these sources is discussed respectively in Chapters 5, 6, 7, 8, and 9.

The final section of Part 1, Chapter 10, relates to the inferential process. It is at this point that practice and theory converge. In this chapter rules of judging the validity of an inference are offered and the steps involved in moving from test data to a psychological test report are detailed.

In general, Part 1 is intended for students and practitioners alike who are interested in the clinical applications of the Rorschach. It combines an introduction to the psychoanalytic approach to the Rorschach with an attempt to update that approach by integrating recent theoretical and research advances.

In Part 2 of the book, I extend Rapaport's legacy in a different direction. For Rapaport, the relationship between psychoanalytic theory and psychological testing was a two-way street. In one direction he saw theory as providing the clinical examiner with an array of concepts and propositions that could remarkably broaden the range and clinical relevance of test-derived inferences. In the other direction, Rapaport also saw how the tests themselves provided a means for operationalizing concepts that were hazy, elusive, and highly abstract. In his view, conceptualizing tests could facilitate the testing of key psychoanalytic formulations and thus, in time, could add to the evolving scope of psychoanalytic theory.

The purpose of the second part of the book is to review and bring together in one collection those research endeavors which have sought to translate core psychoanalytic concepts and formulations into test-related terms and then, in the tradition of Rapaport, to employ these as tools for evaluating hypotheses generated from the theory. It is my hope that such a collection can serve as a useful reference for clinical researchers who are concerned with selecting scales for assessing specific psychological variables. As well, I hope that this part of the book contributes to the theoretical basis of the Rorschach while stimulating further research.

The selection of material for inclusion in Part 2 was based on several criteria. First, I have attempted to focus on basic and timely psychoanalytic concepts such as defense, object relations, narcissism, and so on, as opposed to concepts that are peripheral and dated. Second, I have chosen concepts for which investigators either have devised their own conceptually based, systematic scoring systems or have applied well-established existing scales. When possible, the scoring manuals have been included. Lastly, recognizing that psychoanalysis is not static but rather constantly evolving, I have tended to emphasize research based on more recent developments in psychoanalytic theory.

This part of the book is organized into two major sections. Chapters in the first section cover attempts using the Rorschach to assess specific concepts. The concepts discussed include object representation, defense, and developmental object relations. The second section is divided into chapters related to clinical syndromes. The syndromes reviewed include borderline disturbances, variants of borderline disturbances (or what have been referred to as primitive mental states), and narcissistic disorders.

It is important to keep in mind that psychoanalysis is not a closed, tightly knit, well-integrated personality theory. Rather, it is a loose-fitting composite of several complementary, internally consistent submodels, each of which furnishes concepts and formulations for observing and understanding important dimensions of personality development and functioning. The submodels I have identified include drive theory, structural theory, object relations theory, self psychology, and developmental theory. Psychoanalytic theory continues to be in a state of evolution. From an early concern with an identification of the instincts and their vicissitudes and a subsequent emphasis on studying the ego, interest has now shifted to a systematic exploration of the early mother–child relationship and its impact on the development of the self and the quality of later interpersonal relationships. The concepts and syndromes that constitute the approach taken in this book reflect these shifts in theory.

I

Clinical Applications

1

Clinical Testing: An Approach and An Attitude

In this chapter I outline an approach toward clinical psychological testing that is based on the work of David Rapaport in particular and the intimate relationship he established between psychoanalytic theory and test theory. Rapaport accorded thought processes a central role in this union. He conceived of thinking as bridging test responses and psychic structures on the one hand and as reflecting these structures on the other. From Rapaport's theoretical contributions there evolved a way of viewing and using tests distinctively different from the more traditional psychometric perspective: patient-centered, rather than test-centered. The examiner is valued and his role is maximized, as opposed to seeing him or her as a source of error with a concomitant tendency to standardize the role. In psychometric testing, test responses are scored and the scores are treated as signs whose meaning is based on empirical findings. By contrast, in clinical testing, although test responses are scored, the scores are regarded as only one part of the broad array of data. The examiner also empathically and analytically sifts through the responses with the intent of gaining an understanding of the underlying psychological process. Rapaport's initial theoretical contributions have been extended in several clinically relevant directions. Based upon his notion of relative structure, one direction has been the insistence on using a battery of tests rather than relying exclusively on one test. A second direction has entailed the increased interest accorded the patient-examiner relationship. From this interest have emerged such suggestions as encouraging the patient to be an active participant in the assessment, sharing findings during testing and not afterward, thoughtfully planning the broaching and implementing of recommendations, and testing over time rather than in one lengthy and tedious session. Finally, the expanding scope of psychoanalytic theory has served to increase dramatically the predictive power of thought processes.

TEST RATIONALE

As noted in the preface, psychoanalytic approaches to the Rorschach test are based on the writings of David Rapaport. Of Rapaport's many contributions, the two that are most directly relevant to the Rorschach test are his theoretical rationale for test inference—the organization of thought—and his unique view of how testing ought to be conducted in the clinical situation.

Rapaport based his theoretical rationale for the validity of psychological tests, including the Rorschach test, on the construct of "thought processes." Accordingly, the study of projective test responses and the exploration of thought processes were considered synonymous. He conceived of thinking, together with its organization, as the mediating process connecting behavior with its psychodynamic underpinnings on the one hand and with test performance and test responses on the other. It was from this organization of thought, including such subprocesses as concept formation, anticipation, memory, judgment, attention, and concentration, that Rapaport derived inferences with regard to other facets of personality functioning. This conceptualization of the inferential power of the assessment of thought processes is especially well stated by Schafer (1954):

> A person's distinctive style of thinking is indicative of ingrained features of his character make-up. Character is here understood as the person's enduring modes of bringing into harmony internal demands and the press of external events, in other words, it refers to relatively constant adjustment efforts in the face of problem situations. The modes of achieving this harmony are understood to consist essentially of reliance on particular mechanisms of defense and related responsiveness to stimulation associated with these defenses [p. 17].

Rapaport (1950) also noted that psychiatry, like other clinical disciplines, requires objectivity. That is, procedures are needed to supplement its methods, which are often considered subjective and judgmental. Psychiatrists rely on case histories and psychiatric examinations as sources of information. Material gathered from both, however, is manifold and requires selectivity. In the taking of a case history, the examiner must not only organize his data but must also subjectively select those aspects felt to be most relevant. In the giving of a case history the patient and informant both introduce selective factors: an unconscious one, rooted in the organization of their memory; an involuntary one, rooted in the limitations of their knowledge; and a deliberate one, rooted partly in judgments based on their attitudes and partly in intentions to conceal. As a consequence, different case histories are likely to contain different categories of data; thus, no point-to-point comparison is possible between case histories. Also, as quantification of the data is not possible, organizing the material into a meaningful whole so as to yield a diagnosis, prognosis, and treatment plan involves further subjective judgment and selection.

The psychological test response represents a limited behavior segment. Therefore, the first advantage toward objectivity over other clinical procedures is the relative completeness with which the behavior segment can be recorded.

Because the same categories of behavior, or reaction, are obtained from all patients, a second advantage of testing lies in one's being able to make comparisons between recorded data. Such comparisons are made interindividually and intraindividually—one compares different individuals' performances and at the same time different aspects of a single individual's performance.

Basic to psychological testing is the assumption that every behavior segment bears the imprint of the organization of the behaving personality and permits a reconstruction of the specific organizing principles of that personality. To be revealing of personality, the behavior segment must meet certain criteria: its meaning must be unknown to and not consciously manipulatable by the subject, and the subject matter should in part be unstructured so as to allow maximal expression of the structuring principles of the individual personality. A lack of structure or multiple possibilities of structuring permit an expression of intrapsychic choices.

For Rapaport, clinical investigation constructs the structure of the personality out of observed or reported behavior while psychological testing constructs it from the organization of thought processes as inferred from test data. Inferences from thought process to personality organization are based on the formulation that the development of thought organization is an integral part of and reflects the development of personality organization.

TEST USAGE

In addition to elaborating a rationale for psychological tests, Rapaport also proposed a particular view of how testing ought to be conducted, a view systematized and extended by Mayman (1964a).

Because diagnostic testing is typically one part of a broader clinical examination of a patient, it should be conducted in a manner and style consistent with clinical purposes. As with every clinical encounter with a patient, testing calls for sensitivity, an accepting and nonjudgmental attitude and an empathic attunement to the emotional nuances of the relationship. For example, if in the initial testing session the patient's heightened and painful anxiety is creating inordinate distress and interfering with his or her capacity to fully engage in the testing, then it is incumbent upon the examiner to deal with the patient's immediate distress rather than insensitively pushing ahead with the testing.

As Mayman (1964a) has suggested, testing should be automatic and familiar enough to the examiner (including the administration of a WAIS or WISC without needing the manual) that he or she feels free to engage with the patient rather than the tests. It is important that the examiner be tactful and come to trust and rely upon his or her own clinical judgment and sense of appropriateness. There are occasions when the examiner will depart from standard test procedures by, for example, slightly revising the precise wording of instructions or inquiring about an especially jarring response. When the examiner does depart from standard procedures, the reasons prompting this and the impact of such departures on the patient's subsequent responses should be understood.

In the administration, inquiry, scoring, and interpretation of the tests, the tester maintains what Mayman has referred to as a "patient oriented" attitude as contrasted with a "test oriented" attitude. The patient-oriented attitude is reflected in a variety of ways, ranging from an awareness of the nature of subtle transactions between examiner and patient to a consideration of the types of questions the examiner asks of himself or herself.

For example, the clinical tester needs be concerned with such seemingly inconsequential issues as how he or she and the patient are to refer to each other. With adults and older adolescents, I use titles and last names as a way of establishing that we are involved in a professional, and not a social relationship, or friendship. As well, the questions I pose to myself are not psychometric ones like "Is this a borderline sign?" or "How much scatter is there?" Rather, I ask myself more clinically oriented questions, such as "What does this patient make of me in this testing encounter, how rigid is he in his attitude, and as the examiner, can I assist him to relinquish it for a more open and collaborative attitude?"

The patient-oriented perspective distinguishes a clinical approach from a psychometric one. As Mayman (1964a) noted, "In testing a patient for clinical purposes, we are not simply measuring; we observe a person in action, try to reconstruct how he went about dealing with the tasks we set for him, and then try to make clinical sense of this behavior" (p. 2). Certain aspects of the patient's behavior are reflected in test scores, but many are not. Although scores are helpful in identifying with greater accuracy significant characteristics of the response process, there are other aspects of the response that are not scored and yet should be considered.

Accordingly, the examiner should make as exact and complete a record as possible of all that transpires between examiner and patient, including the patient's verbatim responses, the direction of the examiner's own comments, and the patient's spontaneous, evaluative, and emotional expressions. Thus, such offhanded remarks as "This test really makes me feel stupid" or "I knew the answer to that in the past, but I can't think of it now" can have much diagnostic import, being sensitively reflective of characterological dispositions and ongoing affective states.

In clinical testing, then, the examiner takes stock of and records all aspects of the patient's behavior, including the careful avoidance of blackness on the Rorschach cards, carelessness and impatience in solving math problems, excessive precision and conciseness in developing TAT stories, and undo harshness and criticalness in self-evaluating performance.

Psychometric and clinical testing differ dramatically with respect to the role accorded to and value placed on the examiner. In psychometric testing the examiner is seen as a source of bias and error, therefore, his role is standardized and minimized, if not eliminated. By contrast, in clinical testing the role of the examiner is maximized: the examiner's skill, judgment, and intuitive sensitivity are not only valued but are also regarded as the most sensitive and perceptive clinical tools available. The variety of interactional reactions that arise in the patient–examiner relationship are neither avoided nor acted upon; rather, they are identified and observed and then used as valuable aids in bringing greater meaning and understanding to the patient's behavior and attitudes.

According to Mayman, throughout testing the examiner should remain attentively alert and open-mindedly receptive to any deviant or idiosyncratic aspect of a response. In this way and with experience, the examiner then accumulates anticipations of what a patient may say or do on each test and against which each new response is matched. In time, a deviant response will immediately seem out of tune, jarringly at odds with the examiner's anticipatory set. The examiner's sensitivity is the most important clinical tool. How effectively one's self is used as a clinical tool depends in part upon one's attunement to such off-key responses.

Sensitivity and intuition are important, but they are only the first steps of the clinical inferential process. Clinicians should be able at all times to point to the data from which they drew their conclusions and also to trace out explicitly the chain of inferences that led to those conclusions.

GENERAL TESTING CONSIDERATIONS

Based upon Rapaport's theoretical contributions, others have extended his work along various practical clinical lines. One line has involved the repeated insistence among psychoanalytically oriented examiners on using a battery of tests as a basis for clinical inferences, as opposed to relying exclusively on one particular test.

The importance of a test battery derives from Rapaport's notions regarding the concepts of projection and levels of structure. It has become commonplace among psychologists to distinguish between projective and nonprojective tests. Accordingly, in nonprojective tests the questions asked (such as "At what temperature does water boil?") have a single, verifiable answer. Likewise, the tasks set, such as copying a block design, have a confirmable solution. In projective tests, by contrast, there is no single, verifiable, correct response; rather, the person's answer will be based on intrapsychic determinants and not on an external criterion of validity. In accord with Rapaport, however, I believe that such a sharp distinction does not exist. Projective tests also elicit responses that approach objective verifiability, such as the popular responses on the Rorschach test, while nonprojective tests may have some projective features.

On the issue of projective versus nonprojective responses Rapaport (1950) has cogently argued

> Any organization of the external world according to a principle of organization of the subject's private world is considered projection. From this vantage point then all the nonprojective tests, in so far as they reflect something about the personality, should be considered projective [p. 348].

The distinction between projective and nonprojective responses takes cognizance of the degree of structure in the test material and the task involved. From this perspective, "a hierarchy of structuring principles emerges; these principles not only organize unstructured material, but also bring structured material into an even more embracing organization. We are facing the issue of substructures . . ." (Rapaport, 1950, p. 342).

Viewed in this context, a battery of tests permits the examiner to observe the patient in a variety of situations that differ in their relative degree of structure. One is familiar with those patients who function effectively and efficiently on the more structured Wechsler's Adult Intelligence Scale (WAIS) but experience severe difficulties, including highly regressive responses, on the less structured Rorschach test. Noting the nature of the patient's reaction to differing levels of structure often has important diagnostic and treatment implications.

A second direction in which Rapaport's work has been extended is the exploitation of the patient–examiner relationship as a rich source of clinical data. While Rapaport had much to say about test material and test responses, he had comparatively little to say about the nature of the patient–examiner relationship and the impact of the examiner on the test response process. That is not so surprising, for Rapaport's interest was in drives, defense configurations, and the interplay between the two, and not in self, relational experiences, and the import of early object relations.

The most extensive and thorough discussion of the patient–examiner relationship as a basic aspect of the testing process is to be found in the work of Schafer (1954); his more specific contributions will be detailed in Chapter 5 (Sources of Information). In overview, Schafer poignantly discussed the impact of the tester's personality and professional pressures on the test relationship, the constraints in the patient's psychological position, and the defensive aspects of the patient as manifested in test behavior. Schafer pointed out that some part of the patient consciously accepts the notion of being tested; that is, he or she accepts on faith its helpfulness and the tester's intent of being a helpful agent. If this be the case, Schafer wondered, how and why would an ostensibly positive and cooperative conscious attitude toward testing and the examiner be disrupted? For Schafer, testing in part involved an attempt to understand the patient and his or her difficulties by identifying and clarifying disruptive forces within the clinical relationship.

On the basis of Schafer's (1954) writings and mindful of the dangers involved in regarding the patient as a passive participant in the testing experience, Shevrin and Shectman (1973) have stressed the importance of the patient's active involvement in the testing process. For these authors, if testing is seen as a way of "getting at the problem," then, indeed, the patient is placed in the role of a passive object. On the other hand, if the examiner repeatedly seeks the patient's active engagement in a cooperative relationship, then patient and examiner together are in a position to observe and assess the patient's functioning. The patient becomes a participating partner in his or her own assessment.

Typically, if test findings are reported to the patient, the reporting is done after the testing has been completed and the examiner has had the opportunity to analyze and integrate the mass of test data. While this common practice meets the professional needs of the tester, it also serves to maintain the patient in a passive position and the examiner in a position of omnipotence. To ensure the patient's active participation, my practice has been to discuss findings with the patient not at the conclusion, but on an ongoing basis as they emerge throughout the course of the testing. In doing this I attempt to be particularly sensitive to the patient's own understanding of his or her difficulties, the dangers involved in premature insight, and the impact of the shared information on the patient's self-esteem. Others might argue that such practice could affect patients' subsequent responses as well as their attitude toward the testing. I too recognize this but contend that a patient's reactions to the examiner's interventions may usefully be viewed as additional information, to be understood as one would any other type of information. What is important here is not that the patient's reaction may be altered, but that the examiner recognize the impact of his or her intervention and be prepared to understand later responses within that context. Herein, I am in agreement with Shevrin and Schectman (1973), who maintain that "if the diagnostician ignores his impact on the situation, he is ignoring the only instrument on which he can rely" (p. 494).

The stance being suggested here, of attempting to elicit the patient's active participation in the testing process, has been extended by Shevrin and Shectman (1973) to the issue of recommendations. Aware that the same resistances evoked by the testing will also be evoked by the recommendations offered, this writer suggests that the examiner must consider how the recommendations should be broached and implemented. That is, one aspect of the diagnostic task is to subject the recommendations to the same kind of scrutiny, understanding, and planning that are involved in understanding the patient and his or her difficulties. Shevrin and Shectman propose that the patient should become gradually aware of what is needed by what has already taken place. In this regard, the diagnostic process itself should prepare the way for accepting the recommendations.

If one of the examiner's functions is to use himself or herself as an agent of change, and in the process to understand the nature of and resistances against that change, then it is imperative that ample time be accorded the testing. Cramming testing into one lengthy session lasting half a day represents an insensitivity to the patient's physical and emotional stamina. Equally important, it prohibits the unfolding of a process in which change is possible and therefore potentially observable. I have found three appropriately spaced one-hour sessions optimal for providing a testing structure in which neither patient nor examiner feels harried and in which sufficient time is available to facilitate and then understand alterations in the patient's attitude, manner of responding, and mode of relating.

In addition to the importance of using a battery of tests rather than one specific instrument and of striving for a greater attunement to vicissitudes of the patient–examiner relationship, a third clinically relevant direction in which Rapaport's initial contributions have been extended involves the predictive power of an assessment of thought processes. As noted previously, Rapaport viewed thinking as a conduit to understanding specific aspects of personality, including character structure, defense patterning, and organization of the drives. His range of inferences, however, was limited by the state of knowledge at the time, as well as by his own interests and proclivities.

The relatively recent integration of a modern object relations theory, a broadened psychodynamic developmental theory, and a systematic psychology of the self into the mainstream of traditional psychoanalytic theory is now permitting us to make inferences from thought processes to a far greater range of psychological phenomena. For example, if Loewald

(1973) is correct in asserting that the ego as a psychic structure and its subprocesses of thinking and perceiving originate in the interaction of the child and its early human environment and that the level of structuralization achieved is dependent on the quality of object relations, then it is equally correct to suggest that a careful appraisal of the ego by means of an assessment of thought processes should allow one to reconstruct that early human environment, comment upon such basic psychic structures as the level of self- and object relations, and draw further inferences regarding the level and nature of contemporary object relations. In essence, then, one can now view the predictive value of assessing thought processes within the context of an evolving psychoanalytic theory. Representative of this line of theorizing are Mayman's (1977) thoughtful discussion of the human movement response (M) of the Rorschach test, P. Lerner's (1986) clinical findings regarding the color response (C), Blatt and Lerner's (1983) comprehensive and systematic appraisal of the human figure response (H), and Arnow and Cooper's (1988) application of Kohut's selfpsychology to a variety of Rorschach contents.

2

The Psychological Test Report

In most settings the vehicle for communicating test findings is the psychological test report. Because the psychologist is typically one member of an interdisciplinary team, the test report should attempt to describe the patient in ways that are likely to lead to interventions beneficial to the patient. In this regard the test report is more than a scientific or technical document; it is or ought to be political and diplomatic, strategic and persuasive.

The organizing points of a report should be the clinical issues that prompted the request for the tests as well as those issues that arose in the course of testing. Without such foci a report lacks purpose and direction. A test report must have organization in another respect as well: the use of an internally consistent theory of personality and psychopathology. Naturally, that theory must be understood in all of its complexity by the examiner so that he or she can explicate the layering and interconnections among the data and achieve a synthesis of initially disparate observations.

A frequently discussed problem in test report writing is the depth at which the report should be written. I have found that test reports are especially appreciated and used when they are written at a descriptive, experiential level, free of psychological jargon and technical terms. I attempt to avoid mechanistic phrases, to explicate more abstract concepts, and—with a sprinkling of illustrative test responses—to remain empathically close to the patient's subjective experience.

In what follows, one type of test report is described. This example is presented as a way of illustrating in part the variety of clinical inferences that can be drawn, as well as a way of organizing those inferences. In addition, this proposed testing report serves as an organizing and interpretive framework for the remainder of this part of the book. That is to say, the subheadings in the report, while serving as organizational points of reference also correspond to psychological structures and processes that I bear in mind in analyzing and interpreting test data.

INTRODUCTION

The introduction should supply enough information regarding the clinical context to enable the reader to understand the report even if little else is known about the patient. It should include a statement of the patient's major difficulties, the circumstances of the testing, and the specific questions to which the testing is addressed. All questions raised in the introduction should be answered in the report. All the issues dealt with, however, need not be based on the referral questions; there may be issues, based on the ongoing testing, that the examiner independently raises. For example, a question frequently asked of the tester involves the presence of thought disorder. If, after several responses to the Rorschach test, the bizarreness of the patient's thinking becomes obvious, the examiner might choose to change his or her focus. Then, in the test report, rather than simply elaborating on the nature, quality, and context of the patient's disturbance, the examiner may feel it is also important to comment on the issue of control, that is, the quality of the patient's control over the disturbed thinking.

CHARACTER STRUCTURE

This section of the test report should include a description of the patient in terms of character traits, organized along the lines of distinct character types.

The concept of character has lately become more central in personality theory. Interest in character stems from the observation that the concerns of patients now seeking treatment differ from the concerns described in the literature of 25 years ago. In the classical neurosis, an integrated personality was painfully disrupted by alien impulses, thoughts, and feelings. Currently, we seldom confront a uniform, coherent personality but, rather, one that is disturbed and chaotic to such an extent that it is often difficult to distinguish between personality and symptoms.

Character was slow to emerge as a central concern in psychoanalysis. It was first treated by Freud as a unitary structure of minor import and peripheral to the major thrust of his theories. In his 1908 paper "Character and Anal Erotism," he noted empirically a relationship between a cluster of three character traits—parsimony, orderliness, and obstinacy—and the vicissitude of the anal drive.

Reich (1933) focused on character as a defense. Character, for Reich, was an enemy of treatment, an armor against insight and cure. Defining character as the sum total of an individual's modes of reaction, he drew attention to such specific manifestations as posture, facial expression, and manner of speaking.

Several early authors, most notably Alexander (1930), focused on the pathology of character as a whole, highlighting the maladaptive aspects of large segments of typical behavior. More recently writers have emphasized the adaptive function of character and have shifted their interest from the interplay between id and ego to that between ego and reality.

Character involves the notion of habitual modes of behavior and refers to constant, stereotyped modes of response the ego makes in mediating the demands of internal and external reality. Character traits are descriptive attributes ascribed to a person. They are necessarily an amalgam, a synthesis that expresses under one heading a combination of psychic factors that includes drive derivatives, defenses, identifications, superego aspects, modes of object relating, attitudes, values, and moods. Character structure refers to a cluster of character traits that typically go together to form a particular personality structure.

A psychoanalytic diagnostic scheme would include the following typical character structures: the hysterical character, the obsessive–compulsive character, the depressed character, the masochistic character, the narcissistic personality, the infantile personality, the paranoid personality, and the schizoid personality. Each of these character structures will be described and discussed in the next chapter.

The various character types just described represent ideals based on the assumption that there is an intrinsic logic whereby certain traits tend to coalesce to form certain typical characters. In clinical practice, therapists seldom confront a pure character type; rather, we more commonly find persons with a mixture of character traits in which certain ones predominate while others are present but play a lesser role. Therefore, in offering a characterological diagnosis, instead of simply stating, "The patient presents as an obsessive–compulsive character," therapists are more apt to say, "The patient presents as an obsessive–compulsive individual with narcissistic and masochistic features." This statement would then be followed by a description of the obsessive–compulsive, narcissistic, and masochistic features observed in the patient, together with their respective roles within the overall personality.

Also included in this section of the test report, and considered an aspect of character, is the patient's array of self-experiences. By self-experiences I mean the variety of conscious and unconscious roles and identities, whole or fragmented, that determine the patient's experience of himself or herself and that direct the patient's behavior. This array constitutes the person's overall self-image and includes what he or she wishes or fears about himself or herself; the degree to which the self-image is accepted as part of the person and its relative consciousness. Closely related to one's self-experience is one's experience of others. I speak here of relational predispositions or transference paradigms. These are repetitive playlets in which the patient assumes a particular role and assigns to others roles that fit, in a complementary fashion, his or her ingrained expectations. These relational tendencies may themselves be viewed and described in structural terms entailing such considerations as the extent to which self and others are differentiated, as opposed to fused, and the extent to which relationships are seen as stable and enduring as contrasted with conflict-laden and transitory.

THOUGHT ORGANIZATION

Associated with each character structure is a distinct style of thinking, and in this section that style is described and discussed. For example, whereas the thinking of the obsessive–compulsive tends to be rigid, dogmatic, highly precise, factual, and overly concerned with detail, the thinking of the hysteric is subjective, impressionistic, affectladen, nonspecific, and susceptible to that which is immediate, impressive, and obvious.

The most comprehensive and illuminating discussion of various styles of thinking and perceiving is represented in the work of David Shapiro (1965). With particular clarity Shapiro outlines the ways of thinking and perceiving, the modes of subjective experience, and the modes of activity associated with the following styles: the obsessive–compulsive, the paranoid, the hysterical, and the impulsive. For Shapiro, these styles of thinking, which are more generally used to infer defenses, character traits, and personality makeup, are in themselves psychological structures of importance and thus worthy of independent appraisal.

Included in the description of cognitive style are the patient's approach to various tasks (i.e., systematic, deliberate, halting, impatient), the patient's reaction to his or her own performance, and the patient's capacity to reflect and think psychologically (psychological mindedness). In evaluating cognitive style we also assess various ego functions, such as capacity for delay, tolerance for frustration, judgment, and quality of reality testing.

Intelligence, obviously, has a bearing on cognitive style. Despite the recognized dangers, including a statement of the patient's IQ scores can be helpful. The IQ scores should not stand alone but should instead be extended to include an assessment of whether such scores are an accurate reflection of the patient's capacities and, if not, why not. Factors interfering with performance should be noted.

In this section of the report I also address the issue of thought disorder. Too often, without recognition that different types of thought disorders are related to different forms of psychopathology, thought disorder is regarded as a unidimensional entity. For example, the fluidity and associative quality of thinking in the manic patient is distinct from the relational thinking of the paranoid patient or the fusion of thoughts in the schizophrenic. Therefore, one attempts to describe disturbances in thinking along several lines, including the specific nature of the disorder; the conditions, internal and external, within which it occurs; the patient's attitude toward the disturbance; and his or her capacity for control.

ORGANIZATION OF AFFECTS

Organization of affects refers to feelings and, more specifically, to the way in which they are experienced, expressed, and managed. For example, one may describe a patient variously as constricted, labile, explosive, or able to integrate various feeling states into the mainstream of his or her mental functioning. The organization of affects also includes the range of affects as well as the capacity to differentiate among affective states. The tester is also concerned here with predominant affects, be they fleeting or long-standing, as well as with the degree to which and manner in which they are experienced. To describe a person as depressed is important yet insufficient; the tester should be able to go further and describe the depression more emphatically and phenomenologically (e.g, the patient feels tired, depleted, or dead inside; or, the patient perceives the world as dark and barren and senses needs cannot be met). A phenomenological grasp of an affective state is especially useful not only for treatment planning but also for inferring the level of personality development. Blatt (1974), for example, has identified two distinctly different forms of depression and related each form to a different level of personality organization.

A term that has only recently appeared in the testing literature is "affect capacity" (Thompson, 1986); by this is meant a person's openness and receptiveness to various feeling states. With the integration of an expanded object relations perspective into psychoanalytic theory, the importance of assessing "affect capacity" has increased substantially. For instance, Melanie Klein (1935) proposed a developmental model consisting of two positions (paranoid-schizoid and depressive) distinguishable on the basis of the predominant anxiety and the level of object relations. One feature distinguishing the two positions is the capacity to feel depressed. For Klein, implicit in depression is a capacity for concern and genuine care for another; thus, depressive feelings are not regarded as simply symptomatic but also as signs of developmental achievement.

The notion of managing affects raises the issue of the individual's defensive structure. Here too one finds a correspondence between specific defenses and certain character structures. Whereas the hysterical character has been found to rely mainly on repression and the paranoid personality on projection, the obsessive–compulsive character employs intellectualization, isolation of affect, and reaction formation. In writing a report one attempts to comment upon the effectiveness of the defenses and to layer them hierarchically, moving from those that are most characteristic and preferred to those that emerge only when others have faltered.

Because of its close tie to anger and depressive affect, if suicide is an issue, it would be included in this section of the test report. When presented with the possibility of suicide, I attempt to address the following factors: the likelihood of occurrence and under what conditions, the structural and dynamic features involved, and the patient's willingness to alert and make constructive use of others. The following excerpt is taken from the test report of a young adolescent who was referred for testing in connection with an impending court hearing. Although the question of suicide had not been raised by the referrer, the examiner brought the issue to the fore.

> To avoid experiencing depressive feelings, this young man tends to act out. One form of acting out, given his current circumstances, that others should be alert to is suicide. On several of his TAT cards death was in the air and on one specific card with suicidal import, he blocked. He sees death as a way out, a viable alternative in situations in which he feels trapped and without options. Fueling the danger at this time is his sense that the alleged incident has permanently alienated him from others, especially those whom he loves and is dependent upon. He is in much pain and accessible to therapeutic intervention. To judge from his willingness to discuss his fleeting suicidal thoughts with the examiner, the possibility of suicide would be appreciably reduced were he involved in treatment.

CORE DYNAMICS

Included under the heading of core dynamics are the motives, urges, desires, and conflicts that are prominent in the patient and underlie his or her actions, character traits, dysphoric affects, and symptoms. While it is a truism that most conflicts can be found in most patients, certain conflicts are considered dominant in that they inhibit solutions to other, often developmentally later, conflicts and color much of present behavior. In this section of the test report one attempts to outline conflicts related to the vicissitudes of sexuality and aggression, disturbances in object relations, and impairments in self-cohesion. Statements included here relate to dynamic and/or genetic issues. An example is the following:

> Underlying the patient's difficulties in establishing long-term, satisfactory relationships with men is a view of her father as overly exciting and seductive, highly dangerous, and as having violated essential and needed boundaries.

Within psychoanalysis new models of personality development and psychopathology are beginning to appear. Whereas earlier models were derived from theories of psychic conflict, these newer models issue from theories of structure and structure formation in development. In the newer models development consists of the growth and differentiation of psychological functions that crystalize into more stable structures. Although conflict can occur among these structures, as conceptualized in earlier views as well, the structures themselves can be pathological as a result of faulty development.

I attempt in this section of the report to outline the dynamics of instances of structural impairment and their historic antecedents. If, as various theorists have suggested, structures arise from the gradual internalization of early object relations, then in these cases it is important that the psychologist attempt to understand and describe the nature of the early object relations and the factors that may have interfered with the process of internalization. The following example illustrates these points:

> One is struck by the patient's inability to humanize her world. Her Rorschach percept of a "robot" nicely captures her sense of self as empty, mechanical, not totally human, and vulnerable to control by others. Developmentally, these more primitive feelings and concerns are rooted in a disrupted symbiotic relationship. Consequent to this disruption, she struggles with separation, dreads aloneness, and is unable to conceive of others as separate and complete.

TREATMENT PLANNING

If in previous sections of the report inferences have been couched in terms that are relevant to disposition or treatment planning, then this section should summarize and logically follow from all that has preceded. Nonetheless, there often are treatment issues that require a more pointed discussion. I have found that therapists are particularly interested in such topics as the following: specific problems that may interfere with the establishment of a therapeutic alliance; the patient's capacity to think psychologically and to envision a role for himself or herself in treatment; and potential therapeutic levers. The following inference was found useful by the referring psychotherapist:

> Treatment could be of benefit to this patient by assisting her to get in touch with that which is good in her ... to help her define for herself an ego ideal, an ideal that could bring greater order to her life and greater control over her chaotic and self-harmful behavior.

With the emergence in psychoanalysis of new models of personality formation and psychopathology, there have also come new models of the psychotherapeutic process. Earlier theories of treatment emphasized interpretation and insight, with therapy being seen as a unique type of education and the therapeutic relationship as a special laboratory for exploring and experiencing the critical dynamic configurations as they emerged in the transference. By contrast, as Michaels (1983) has noted, new models of treatment

> emphasize the psychological substrata and nutriments necessary for growth and development, with therapy being construed as a special kind of parenting, the interpretive process as a model of growth promoting interaction, and the therapeutic relationship as a substitute for the nuclear family as a matrix for individuation and growth [p. 5].

The psychological tester has long been called upon to address the issue of the patient's treatability and to comment upon the most appropriate type of treatment. In the past, treatability was viewed rather narrowly and types of treatment were put on a continuum ranging from intensive and insight oriented at one end to supportive at the other extreme. The level of external structure required by the patient to maintain adaptive functioning was a critical factor underlying assignment within the spectrum. The evolving scope of psychoanalytic treatment has lately changed this, however, and presents new challenges for the examiner. First, the examiner must redefine and broaden the limits of treatability. Second, commenting on the degree of structure needed is not enough; the tester should also be able to detail the quality and type of structure required.

The following is taken from the testing report of an older adolescent who was initially considered untreatable by his referring psychiatrist.

> Despite his chaotic history and tendency to depreciate adults, I believe that this patient can benefit from treatment. He requires much support, structure, and containment, more than can be provided on a once-per-week basis. Repeatedly confronting his tendency to depreciate will help provide the containment by demonstrating to him that his therapist can withstand his aggression. This is to say that there is an object-seeking quality to his aggression, more specifically, an object he cannot destroy. He himself recognizes that he has more potential than he can now realize, and this, for him, is a powerful motivation for treatment. What he requires from therapy and has never had is a "good holding environment."

SUMMARY

The summary consists of a concise restatement of the most relevant and salient aspects of the report. Like the body of the report, but in capsule form, the summary should provide an integrated, internally consistent, clinically relevant portrait of the patient. The following is such a summary:

> In summary, the patient presents a mixed characterological picture with narcissistic and depressive features most prominent and organized at a high borderline level. He is continually anxious and relentlessly restless and bored. Beneath a false-self facade, one sees a young man who feels empty, on the verge of fragmenting, vulnerable, and aggressed against. Amid superior intelligence, his ego functions are relatively impaired. He has difficulty tolerating anxiety and frustration and his impulse control is fragile. He is currently being pressured by relatively intense feelings of anxiety and depression. Based on disturbances in his early maternal relationship, major difficulties are apparent in his object relations and in his sense of self. More specifically, there is little overall sense of personal identity and he has not achieved object constancy. He cannot tolerate being alone, and separations are experienced as abandonments. Intensive psy-

chotherapy was suggested with the recommendation that contact with his subjective experience could be made around his fear of aloneness and his difficulties with separations.

Thus far, I have outlined one particular type of psychological test report. Whatever the format used, it is suggested that the report address the major clinical issues, that it be guided by a theory of personality and psychopathology, and that it be written at as descriptive and experiential a level as possible. The report was presented at this point to provide an organizational framework for the remainder of the book. Two sample reports, using the proposed framework, follow.

Psychological Evaluation

NAME: Mary Smith   Tests Given: Dates Tested:
AGE: 22 years   WAIS   4/12/88
                               Rorschach   4/19/88
REFERRER: Dr. P. Jones   TAT   5/02/88

The patient is a 23-year-old single female who is a recent college graduate with a major in elementary education. She is unclear as to her long-term career goals. Her parents have been divorced for 11 years. Her mother, whom she lives with, is a lawyer, and her father she describes as a "playboy." From the material presented, the referrer has noted struggles around separating and difficulties in establishing her own autonomous identity. To assist in determining her suitability for psychoanalysis, psychological testing was requested. This report is addressed to the issues of character structure, thought organization, organization of affects, core conflicts, and treatment planning.

In her approach to the examiner and the tests, the patient appeared as a youthful, warm, engaging individual whose relationship with the examiner was marked by particular fluctuations. She began each sesssion in a rather tight, constricted way; as the session progressed, however, she was able to relax her tight controls and be freer and more spontaneous. Yet the relative looseness did not extend across sessions. That is, each time she tightened up again. She is youthful in the sense that she has a readiness and desire to idealize; she gives the impression of being an "unfinished product." Things have not yet come together or jelled for her.

She is highly self-conscious, overly concerned with the views of others, hypervigilant, highly sensitive, and painfully thin skinned.

The patient at times adopts a false self and at other times actively defends against it. This awareness of, and upset with, her own false-self tendencies becomes evident in fluctuations between compliance and quiet rebelliousness and in a strong desire to declare a moratorium (take time out) and to genuinely find herself. Overall, the patient presents a mixed characterological picture with narcissistic, obsessiveßcompulsive, and hysteric features all in evidence.

The patient attained a full-scale IQ of 125 (verbal IQ 128, performance IQ 114), which places her in the superior range of intellectual functioning. One sees in her thinking, especially with structure, adaptive obsessiveßcompulsive controls. She approaches tasks in a deliberate, persistent, systematic way and places much emphasis on neatness and accuracy. As the structure is removed, she becomes tight and constricted and moves toward privacy. There was no evidence of thought disturbance, and in general her ego functions are well intact. I say in general, for at times she can be careless and at other times she has difficulty stepping back and maintaining perspective. That is, she is not always able to see the forest through the trees.

With respect to her affective life, she is open to various affective experiences but places great emphasis on control and regulation. Letting go is not easy or comfortable for her. She is currently being pressured by moderate feelings of anxiety and depression; however, neither feeling interferes with her functioning. Her depression becomes evident in an attunement to blackness and in long-standing feelings of low self-esteem.

With respect to her dynamic life, the referrer noted her difficulties surrounding identity. This is accurate but her struggles take a particular form. On one hand, as noted previously, she is painfully aware of her false-self tendencies and defends against them. On the other hand, she is especially fearful of being controlled and of losing autonomy over her precariously established sense of self. At this point the patient is vitally interested in becoming her own person and gaining direction from within. This theme pervades her TAT stories, as evidenced by the following story: "This little boy is looking at the violin and he doesn't know how to play it. He's quite unhappy he can't play it. Most people in his family, especially his father, were great violin players and he wants to be closer to his father by playing. Eventually he learns to play, but because the drive wasn't within himself but in the family, he doesn't play as well as others would like. Drive wasn't an appropriate drive."

Implicated in the story, and a source of extreme conflict for the patient, is her father. At one level, she idealizes him, viewing him as powerful and to be pleased. Beneath this, she sees him as malevolent, as someone who has excessive aspirations for her and yet robs and exploits her autonomy with these expectations. Currently, he is able to push her buttons, and she feels powerless to ward him off; thus, a goal of hers in treatment is to free herself from his influence.

Finally, I believe that the patient is still responding to the breakup of her family. She has vague feelings of loss, which I feel are referable to the separation, and her desire to take time out to find herself, while legitimate, has an adolescent quality.

As to treatment, I strongly support the choice of analysis. She is highly suitable for this mode of treatment and would benefit from it. She is bright, reflective, determined, and persistent; most importantly, she senses herself as unfinished. Her problems may be viewed as interferences in development, and I believe the analytic situation will permit her the milieu and opportunity to resume growth.

In summary, the patient presents as an unfinished product; hence, one sees a mixed character structure with narcissistic, hysteric and obsessive-compulsive features all in evidence. She is of superior intelligence, and in her thinking one sees adaptive, obsessive-compulsive features. While she is open to affective experiences, control is especially important to her. She genuinely longs to be her own person. She aspires to be freer, more natural, and more spontaneous. Psychoanalysis was supported as the treatment of choice.

Psychological Evaluation

NAME:	Janet Bell	Tests Given:	Dates Tested:
AGE:	33	WAIS	1/12/86
		Rorschach	1/29/86
REFERRER:	Dr. H. Fisk	TAT	2/23/86

The patient is a 33-year-old single bookeeper who lives with her mother. Because of the patent's complaints of agoraphobia, her false-self features, and an unusual relationship with her father, the referrer suspected she might be borderline. He also wondered about her capacity to benefit from a more intensive, insight-oriented treatment. Those were the questions that prompted the testing. Setting up and maintaining appointments with this patient was not an easy matter. For example, she canceled one session in anticipation of a major sleet storm. To judge from her behavior around appointments, she constantly fears being overwhelmed and her behavior is marked by blatant inconsistencies. To answer the above referral questions, this report is addressed to the issues of character structure, thought organization, organization of affects, core conflicts, and treatment planning.

The patient appeared as a petite, attractive, striking woman with a "Barbie doll" quality. She dresses fashionably, is very heavily made up, and must spend considerable time making sure everything is in place. In her approach to the examiner and the tests, she appeared as highly anxious, tightly defended, and markedly superficial. Her superficiality is defensive in that she is terrified of being penetrated. I do not mean penetrated just in the sexual sense but more broadly, in the sense of being touched and rattled. She allows only so much in and closes issues off very quickly. Because of her heightened anxiety, which she has difficulty regulating, others are put in the position of containing her anxiety for her. Prominent in her character are narcissistic and masochistic features. She is self-absorbed, hypervigilant, and defensively sensitive. Sensing the environment as dangerous, like a mine field, she uses her sensitivity to alert herself to the always present dangers. Her stance is totally one of passivity. Unable to see herself as the initiator of activity, she feels herself as completely reactive. As noted by the referrer, false-self features are prominent. Coincident with the passivity is an ease in feeling a victim. She tends to present as more helpless and inept than she is, and in part, she saw the tests as humiliating her — as making her feel "stupid." The overall diagnostic impression is of a narcissistic personality organized at a borderline level.

The patient attained a full scale IQ of 114 (Verbal IQ 111, Performance IQ 116), which places her in the bright normal

range of intellectual functioning. Despite her heightened
anxiety, she is able to pull herself together to attend. In
addition, her abstraction capacities are excellent. By contrast,
and in keeping with her self-absorption, her range of general
information is limited. While there were no signs of thought
disorder or impaired reality testing, there were impairments in
several ego functions. She has difficulty concentrating; her
persistence is limited; and when her anxiety is especially high,
she behaves impulsively and uses poor judgment. In addition,
her frustration tolerance is limited.

In general, the patient has difficulty containing and
regulating affects; she is a leaky container. She is currently
being pressured by strong feelings of anxiety that, although
variable, at times reach the point of panic. Her anxiety
becomes manifest in subjective feelings of restlessness, in a
tendency to be impatient, and in an ease in becoming frazzled.
She has a strong need for order and structure, and when
either gives way, she becomes frantic. There is test evidence
of depressive affect; however, her depressiveness is long-
standing and not especially acute or intense. Central to the
depression are lowered feelings of self-esteem and a basic
sense of emptiness. With respect to her defensive structure,
she relies heavily on avoidance and externalization. When the
externalization is combined with displacement, it sets the
stage for phobia formation, and one sees much evidence of
a phobic tendency.

As to her dynamic life, the patient has considerable
difficulty dealing with aggression, especially oral aggressive
urges. The role of envy is particularly clear in the following
TAT story. "I don't like this, I'm embarrassed. I can't do this.
Looks like it is something he always wanted, and now that he
has it, he doesn't know what to do with it. He's in awe of it."
To judge from her more spontaneous comments, she is
embarrassed by her envy, as she is by her greed. To ward off
such urges, she externalizes them onto the outside world and
sees her environment as hostile, dangerous, and exploitative.
As well, such urges are turned inward upon the self, resulting
in her masochism and sense of herself as victim. As to be
expected, along with the oral rage are intense oral yearnings.

The patient also has major problems in the areas of self and
object relations. I was somewhat struck by her inability to
humanize her world. Her Rorschach percept of a "robot" nicely
captures her own sense of self as empty, mechanical, less

than totally human, and as vulnerable to control by others. She seems to both invite and fear such external control. Developmentally, such primitive feelings and concerns are rooted in a disrupted symbiotic relationship. as a consequence of this disruption, she struggles with separation, dreads aloneness, and is unable to conceive of others as complete objects.

Growing up has been a struggle for this patient; thus, one sees an infant in a woman's body. Father's role has been that of overprotecting and infantilizing her, whereas mother has not furnished her with the nutrients necessary for growth.

With respect to treatment, the patient requires much structure. She does not have the resources to structure herself. She will view and use treatment as a container, to contain affects and desires she is unable to. While this is a legitimate and useful function, it is important that she not be infantilized. She should be taken seriously, and her therapist should ask and expect more of her than her family did. Her capacity to benefit from a more insight-oriented approach is limited. Nonetheless, being simply supportive is not enough, and therefore I would maintain a more insight-oriented stance.

In summary, the patient presents narcissistic and masochistic features organized at a borderline level. Highly defended and superficial, she is fearful of being significantly touched and possibly rattled. She assumes a totally passive stance and tends to present false-self features. She is of bright normal intelligence and, with structure, functions acceptably. She is not thought disordered but reveals impaired ego functions. Affects are poorly controlled and regulated. In her dynamic life are difficulties with aggression, impaired object relations, an estranged sense of self, and a disrupted symbiotic relationship.

3

Psychoanalytic Diagnostic
Scheme

The proposed diagnostic scheme represents an integration of more classical psychoanalytic classifications of character structure with Kernberg's
recent contributions regarding levels of personality organization.

Attempts to classify various character types go back to Freud (1908,
1931) and Abraham (1921–1925) and their understanding of different
character structures on the basis of level of instinctual development.
Fenichel (1945), dissatisfied with these earlier attempts, proposed a classification combining dynamic and structural considerations. From a dynamic perspective, he distinguished character traits that involved "subli-
mination" from those that were "reactive." In the former, instinctual
energy was discharged freely whereas in the latter a defensive operation
was evoked and that operation became part of the character trait. Fenichel
further subdivided reactive character traits into those that reflected an
attitude of avoidance and those that reflected an attitude of opposition.
From a structural perspective, he first defined character as "the ego's
habitual modes of adjustment to the external world, the id, and the
superego," and then classified character types on the basis of the modes
involved. By combining the dynamic and structural points of view, he was
able to classify the reactive character traits into those that reflected
pathological behavior toward the id (the classical oral, anal, and phallic
character traits), pathological behavior toward the superego, and pathological behavior toward external objects (e.g., pathological jealousy, social
inhibitions) (p. 467). As late as 1964 Prelinger and associates (1964), in
their review of psychoanalytic conceptions of character, noted that Fenichel's classification scheme was still the most widely accepted.

As part of an attempt to integrate the thinking of the British school of

29

object relations theory with more classical formulations emerging from ego psychology, Kernberg (1970) has proposed a classification of character pathology based on an assessment of structural features. Using the concept of levels of personality organization, Kernberg's classification involves a systematic appraisal of level of instinctual development, manifestations of ego weakness, level of defensive organization, quality of internalized object relations, level of superego development, and attainment of ego identity. Kernberg's classification schema has received wide currency in the literature related to psychopathology, and the structural variables he has identified and described have proven especially useful in investigating more severe instances of character pathology, including borderline phenomena (Kwawer et al., 1980; H. Lerner and P. Lerner, 1988).

This diagnostic scheme involves assessing patients along two relatively independent dimensions. The first dimension consists of a descriptive characterological diagnosis in terms of character structure. As noted previously, because the character types represent ideals, it is important to clarify how much the patient approximates the ideal and how much he or she differs from it. The second dimension, based on Kernberg's system, involves an evaluation of the underlying level of personality organization. The dimensions are considered only relatively independent, for, as Kernberg has noted, specific character structures tend to be organized at certain levels. For example, whereas many hysterical characters are organized at a higher level, most infantile personalities are organized at a lower level.

REPRESENTATIVE CHARACTER STRUCTURES

Hysterical Character

The hysterical character is described as subjective, highly energetic, buoyant, sprightly, and lively. Hysterics depict what may be characterized as "the emotional way of life." They manifest emotionality or, more accurately, emotional reactivity is an outward expression of the self as an involved emotional participant. Hysterics view their emotionality, as Easser and Lesser (1966) have noted, "as a jewel to be exhibited, fondled and cherished. Any attempt to move beyond it or remove it is viewed as an attack and is defended against with the total personality" (p. 72).

The emotionality lends a childlike cast to the patient and is used to sustain inhibitions and to avoid the acceptance of certain adult responsibilities. Feelings, rather than thoughts, are used in times of crisis and conflict. Hysterics, directly and actively, engage the human world. Their overt and covert need to be loved results in hypersensitivity toward others. They need to test love through interactions with others, and this accounts for the variety of emotional upheavals. There is often a pursuit of excitement coupled with a defense against realization, with both deriving from a tendency to attribute sensual and sexual meaning to environmental stimuli. While, historically, suggestibility has been considered the major trait of the hysteric, Easser and Lesser (1965) have proposed, more correctly, that "the hysteric receives (and acts on) the suggestion she has assiduously implanted" (p. 397). The hysteric dislikes and avoids the exact, the rote, and the mundane. A job is never done for a job's sake, yet superior performance is forthcoming when the task has sufficient scope to permit an expression of one's sense of drama. Finally, central to the hysteric's presentation is a sense of self as part child and part adult. For a more detailed description of the hysterical character structure, refer to Siegman (1954), Easser and Lesser (1965, 1966), and Krohn (1978).

Obsessive–Compulsive Character

Freud observed and described a cluster of character traits he found in individuals whose instinctual life was fixated and organized at the anal stage. He related these traits to early experiences centered around toilet training and to initial struggles over control with caretakers. Frugality, for Freud, represented a continuation of retention, prompted by the pleasure in holding onto and the fear of letting go. Obstinacy was seen in terms of holding one's position, and stubbornness was considered an elaboration of obstinacy. Orderliness he viewed as an extension of obedience. These character traits initially identified by Freud have been markedly extended; more current descriptions of the obsessive–compulsive include diligence, heightened conscientiousness, industriousness, punctuality, and thriftiness. The obsessive–compulsive is also considered to be perfectionistic, overly meticulous, scrupulous, rigid, dogmatic, self-critical, and pedantic. Whereas the hysteric lives in a world of feelings and avoids the mundane and commonplace, the obsessive–compulsive, by contrast, lives in a world of thoughts and ideas and welcomes that which is routine, familiar and structured. For these individuals, preoccupied with issues of control, activity has a marked driven quality. As Shapiro (1965) has noted, when the obsessive–compulsive announces an intent to play, what is actually meant is an intent to work at playing. Further and more detailed accounts of the obsessive-compulsive character are available in Fenichel (1945), Gardiner (1971), and Laughlin (1956).

Depressive Character Structure

Closely resembling the obsessive–compulsive character at a descriptive level is the depressive character. Like the obsessive–compulsive, the depressive character is somber, serious, hypercritical, conscientious, and tightly controlled. More specific to the depressive character, however, are chronic feelings of worthlessness, a pessimistic outlook, and an anticipation of disappointment.

Kernberg (1975) has suggested that the depressive character manifests three groups of character traits: vulnerability to loss of love; hypercritical attitude toward self and others; and pathological management of aggressive urges. Such patients, according to Kernberg, have an excessive need for love and approval from others. The continuous need for love makes them especially vulnerable to rejection and disappointment; repeated and accumulated experiences of disappointment eventuate in a pessimistic outlook, a sense that there isn't enough love available. The hypercritical attitude is considered a direct expression of superego pressures, a demand on oneself to be somber, serious, and reliable. In severe instances it is expressed in the conviction that "life is a fraud." Depressive patients struggle with aggression. Situations that typically evoke anger in others elicit depressive feelings in these individuals. To bolster their defenses against the expression and experience of anger, depressive characters are often ingratiating, subservient, and deferential. Comprehensive descriptions of the depressive character have been provided by Jacobson (1971) and Laughlin (1956).

Masochistic Character Structure

According to Reich (1933), masochistic features are present in most neurotic structures; however, only in the masochistic character do they converge and determine the basic tone of the personality and the person's reactions. For Reich, masochists present awkward, ataxic behavior, which is especially prominent in their mannerisms; harbor intense feelings of suffering, which become manifest in their complaints; and continually inflict pain upon themselves through self-debasement. Masochistic characters are provocative; they use their suffering to reproach and aggress against others. Masochists tend to provoke those whom they feel disappointed by; that is, behind the provocation is a disappointment in love—as well as an appeal for love. The masochistic character cannot tolerate praise and tends toward self-depreciation and self-abasement. Because praise represents an expression of exhibitionistic tendencies and, as such, a source of anxiety, it is minimized and avoided. A more complete description of the masochistic character has been provided by Reich (1933); for a more pointed discussion of the masochistic character in the testing situation, refer to Appelbaum (1963).

Infantile Personality

In many respects the infantile personality would appear to be a caricature of the hysteric, but there are important differences. Many of the same characteristics are demonstrated, but in sharper, dramatic relief. Bounds of social custom and propriety are violated and breached. The latent aggressivity of exhibitionism and competitiveness becomes blatant, insistent, and bizarre. In contrast with the hysterical character, adaptive functioning is erratic. Periods of attainment alternate with periods of serious dysfunction. Such ego weaknesses as poor impulse control, emotional immaturity, and childlike dependency are not circumscribed and limited to specific conflictual areas but are evident in all aspects of life. The hysteric has difficulty within a relationship, the infantile personality with the relationship. The infantile patient begins relationships with great hopes and unrealistic expectations and feels bitter and resentful when the relationship fails and the expectations of rescue, nurturance, and unlimited care are not fulfilled. Emotional engagement embodies the desire to engulf and incorporate the other; this, in turn, is defensively experienced as a threat of self-depletion. Quite striking in the infantile personality is the tendency either to directly act on pregenital aims or to create a fantasy world and then live within it. Often, such fantasies and fantasized relationships substitute for real relationships. For a more complete description of the infantile personality, refer to Abraham (1921–25), Easser and Lesser (1965), and Sugarman (1979).

Narcissistic Personality

Based on Freud's 1914 paper "On Narcissism," two comprehensive descriptions of the narcissistic patient have emerged in the psychoanalytic literature. Kernberg (1975) reserves the designation for those patients "in whom the main problem appears to be the disturbance of their self-regard in connection with specific disturbances in their object relations . . ." (p. 227). He describes such patients as manifesting a heightened degree of self-absorption, an inordinate need to be loved and admired, and an overinflated sense of themselves amid a desperate desire for adoration. He further suggests that their emotional life is shallow, they exhibit little empathy for the motives and feelings of others, and they feel restless and bored unless their self-regard is being nourished. In their relationships potential providers of narcissistic supplies are idealized, whereas those from whom they expect little are depreciated and treated with contempt. Kernberg sees such individuals as cold, arrogant, ruthless, and exploitative beneath a veneer of charm.

Kohut (1971) too has described the narcissistic patient, but in ways different from Kernberg. Although he has identified a specific symptom complex (including lack of enthusiasm and zest, perverse activity, subjective feelings of deadness), he sees such a cluster of symptoms as insufficient for establishing the narcissistic diagnosis. Instead, he uses the concept of the "cohesive self" as the guiding principle for the differential diagnosis.

The instability, or propensity for regression, of this psychic structure, for Kohut, is the most important diagnostic sign of a narcissistic personality disorder. In achieving a differential diagnosis Kohut places major significance on treatment considerations, particularly on the nature of the emerging transference: he has identified and described a set of atypical transference patterns which unfold in the treatment of the narcissistic patient. Referred to overall as "selfobject" transferences, specific subtypes include the mirroring transference and the idealizing transference. Despite Kohut's reliance on process considerations rather than descriptive features, it has been my experience that the type of narcissistic patient depicted typically presents as hypervigilant, hypersensitive, thin-skinned, and painfully vulnerable. Such patients attune to the cues and expectations of others and mold their actions and feelings accordingly. Their self-esteem is painfully low and the depressive affect they experience involves feelings of emptiness and hollowness.

Test scores, test responses, and test behavior characteristic of the narcissistic patient have more recently been described by Arnow and Cooper (1988), H. Lerner (1988) and P. Lerner (1988).

Schizoid Personality

With the increased currency being accorded the British school of object relations has come a renewed interest in more primitive personality structures, including the schizoid personality. Originally described by Fairbairn (1952), and elaborated by Guntrip (1961), the schizoid personality is characterized as detached, aloof, and emotionally apathetic. Beneath the facade of aloofness, however, is an intense need for a good love object, a hunger for love hidden from the outer world. Fairbairn (1952) noted that the schizoid individual keeps his love locked in because he feels that it is too dangerous to release upon his objects. He or she is afraid to want, seek, take from, or give to objects in the outer world. "Whereas the depressed person is afraid of harming and destroying his love-objects by his hate . . . the schizoid person is afraid of harming and destroying his love-objects by his love" (Guntrip, 1961, pp. 282–283). Out of a refusal to invest in objects in the outer world, the schizoid individual radically invests in his or her inner world. Hence, one finds an individual who, in addition to being detached from the outer world, is highly ideational and preoccupied with intricate fantasies and who tends to limit his object relations to the inner world. For a more detailed description of the schizoid individual, refer to Fairbairn (1952) and Guntrip (1952).

Paranoid Personality

In the paranoid personality the paranoid trends have reached a point of such intensity and a level of such pervasiveness that they themselves constitute the major descriptive element and determine the characterological diagnosis. Accordingly, such individuals are rigid, malignantly distrustful, highly suspicious, and continually embattled with persecutory objects. Central to their functioning is the process of externalization. They attribute causality idiosyncratically, assign malevolent intent, and perversely experience a sense of self-vindication and self-justification. Shapiro (1965) has compared the cognitive and perceptual style of the paranoid character with that of the obsessive–compulsive and concluded, "The paranoid is, in every instance, the more extreme, the less stable, the more tense and antagonistic, the more openly occupied with instinctual conflict, and, in a word, the more psychologically primitive" (p. 107). Although the paranoid personality has been a relatively neglected area of clinical inquiry and writing, descriptions have been offered by Shapiro (1965) and Blum (1981).

In this section I have presented a description of representative and commonly encountered character structures. The list is by no means exhaustive, for there are certain character structures from a descriptive perspective that stand out because of one salient feature (e.g., passive aggressive personality) or because they represent a fit with a well-known literary or fairy-tale figure (e.g., Don Juan).

LEVELS OF PERSONALITY ORGANIZATION

Insistent that a descriptive characterological diagnosis is necessary but not sufficient, Kernberg (1970) devised a system for classifying level of personality organization based upon a systematic appraisal of underlying psychological structures. The system calls for a placing of each structure on a three-level continuum ranging from higher level to intermediate level to lower level. The specific categories that are assessed include level of instinctual development, manifestations of ego weakness, level of defensive organization, level of internalized object relations, level of superego development, and the attainment of ego identity.

Level of Instinctual Development

The category of level of instinctual development involves the predominant level of instinctual attainment and fixation. In contrast with previous psychoanalytic classifications of character on the basis of the stages of libidinal development (oral, anal, phallic, etc.), a major distinction is drawn here between genital and pregenital instinctual strivings.

At the higher level of personality organization genital primacy has been obtained, "instinctual conflicts have reached the stage where the infantile genital phase and oedipal conflicts are clearly predominant and there is no pathological condensation of genital sexual strivings with pregenital, aggressively determined strivings in which the latter predominate" (Kernberg, 1976, p. 144).

At the intermediate level pregenital, especially oral, regression and fixation points predominate. Although the genital level of libidinal development has been reached, oral conflicts predominate, reflective of regression from oedipal struggles. The aggressive aspect of the pregenital conflicts is less intense and less pervasive than is found at the lower level of organization.

At the lower level there is a pathological condensation of genital and pregenital instinctual strivings with an emphasis on pregenital aggression. Oedipal strivings do appear; however, they are condensed with pregenital sadistic and masochistic urges. According to Kernberg (1976), the predominance of pregenital aggression is evidenced "by sadistically infiltrated, polymorphous perverse infantile drive derivatives which contaminate all the internalized and external object relations . . ." (p. 146).

Manifestations of Ego Weaknesses

Necessary for the category of manifestation of ego weaknesses is a careful evaluation of the patient's ego functions, including quality of impulse control, tolerance of frustration and anxiety, effectiveness of defenses, and quality of reality testing. Also involved here is an appraisal of the nature and extent of expressions of primary process thinking.

At the higher level of personality organization the patient's ego is somewhat constricted; however, defenses are effective and there is little instinctual infiltration of defensive character traits. At this level one sees little evidence of ego weakness; rather, controls over primary process manifestations tend to be overly excessive.

At the intermediate level the patient has fewer inhibitory character defenses available, and one begins to see character traits infiltrated by instinctual strivings. Ego weaknesses begin to appear but in a more circumscribed manner, as reflected in Kernberg's (1976) term "structured impulsivity."

Characteristic of the lower level of personality organization are severe ego weaknesses. Owing to the absence of ego organizers (e.g., integrated self-concept) and the lack of an integrated superego, patients at this level manifest poor impulse control, little anxiety tolerance, disruptions in their reality testing, and a lack of channels for sublimation. Primary process thinking infiltrates and interferes with their cognitive functioning, especially in more unstructured situations.

Level of Defensive Organization

Kernberg proposed two overall levels of defensive organization. At the lower level, primitive dissociation or splitting is the crucial defense, bolstered by the related defenses of denial, primitive idealization, primitive devaluation and projective identification. At the higher level of defensive organization, repression supplants splitting as the major defense and is accompanied by the related defensive operations of intellectualization, rationalization, undoing, and higher forms of projection and denial.

At the higher level of personality organization, repression, characteristic of the advanced level of defense organization, predominates. Augmenting repression are various character defenses and defense mechanisms, such as intellectualization and rationalization.

At the intermediate level of personality organization, repression is still the major defensive operation; however, reaction formations are more predominant. In addition, patients at this level reveal some dissociative trends, some defensive splitting of the ego in certain areas, and a greater use of projection and denial.

At the lower level of personality organization, primitive dissociation or splitting predominates with a concomitant impairment of the ego's synthetic function. The patient's reliance on splitting becomes evident in contradictory and alternating ego states. As noted previously, splitting is supported by other defenses, including denial, primitive idealization, primitive devaluation, projective identification, and omnipotence.

Level of Internalized Object Relations

In keeping with formulations arising from the British school of object relations, Kernberg viewed the defensive organization and the level of internalized object relations as intimately related. More specifically, defenses both organize the inner object world and are reflected in external object relations.

Accordingly, at the higher level of personality organization there is no pathology of internalized object relations. Object constancy has been attained, object relations have a "whole" quality, and the inner representational world is stable and accessible. Object relations at this level are deep and stable, and the individual is capable of experiencing mourning, guilt, and a wide range of affective responses.

At the intermediate level of personality organization internalized object relations are relatively nonpathological; however, external object relations tend to be conflictual. Even though pregenital urges enter into relational strivings, relationships are stable and lasting and the individual is able to tolerate ambivalent and conflictual feelings toward the other.

Severe pathology of internalized object relations is evident at the lower level of personality organization. Object relations are on a "part-object" basis, object constancy is not firmly established, and there is an inability to integrate good and bad aspects of the object. Because of the lack of integration of libidinally determined and aggressively determined object images, object relations remain on a need- gratifying or threatening basis. At this level ambivalence cannot be tolerated, there is a limited capacity to experience guilt and mourning, and relationships tend to be chaotic and transient.

Level of Superego Development

The internalization of object relations constitutes a major organizing factor for superego development. Failure to integrate all-good and all-bad self and object images interferes with superego integration by creating an excessively demanding ego ideal that insists upon ideals of power, greatness, and perfection. Sadistic superego forerunners, maintained through projective and introjective processes, are not toned down or integrated with idealized superego components. According to Kernberg (1976),

> the development of a level of integration within the ego creates the precondition for the integration of the sadistically determined superego forerunners with the ego ideal and the subsequent capacity to internalize the realistic, demanding, and prohibitive aspects of the parents [p. 150].

At the higher level of personality organization one sees a well-integrated but relatively severe and punitive superego. Superego forerunners based upon sadistic impulses are present and gain expression in a superego that is overly demanding, relatively harsh, and perfectionistic.

At the intermediate level of personality organization the superego is more punitive and less integrated. Powerful ego ideal goals for greatness and powerfulness coexist with strict prohibitions and demands for moral perfection. At this level there is partial blurring of superego–ego boundaries, some projection of superego prohibitions, contradictions in the value system, and severe mood swings.

At the lower level of personality organization there is minimal superego integration. There is little capacity for experiencing guilt and concern, paranoid trends are clearly evident, and sadistic superego components are externalized through more primitive forms of projection. The delineation between ego and superego is nonexistent, and primitive ego ideal goals are indistinguishable from narcissistic strivings for admiration and adoration.

Attainment of Ego Identity

Also related to the internalization of object relations is the attainment of ego identity. Only with the synthesis of good and bad self-images is the groundwork laid for the development of ego identity. Kernberg (1976) believed that "when 'good' and 'bad' internalized object relations (involving self-images, object-images, ideal self- images, ideal object-images) are so integrated that an integrated self concept and a related integrated 'representational world' develops, a stable ego identity is achieved" (p. 150).

At the higher level of personality organization a firm and cohesive ego identity, including a stable self-concept and a stable representational world, has been established. Values are consistent, goals are realistic, and the sense of identity provides an organizing function by guiding and directing behavior.

At the intermediate level of personality development ego identity has been attained; however, it is less stable and less firm. Values are less consistent and at times contradictory, ego ideal goals are more excessive and less realistic, and behavior is less guided by considerations of identity.

Because of the lack of integration of "all-good" and "all-bad" self and object representations and the resultant absence of an integrated self-concept, at the lower level of personality organization one sees identity diffusion. The person's inner view of himself or herself is a contradictory, chaotic mixture of omnipotent, shameful, and threatened images.

In contrast with other classification schemes that place borderline disturbances along a descriptive, characterological dimension (e.g., DSM III), such disturbances in this scheme are placed on a structural dimension and regarded as a level of personality organization. More specifically, the lower level of personality organization comprises the borderline disorders. Conceptualizing borderline functioning and organization in this manner takes into account the clinical and research finding that patients with varying character structures can manifest borderline pathology. For a more complete discussion of the conceptual and clinical controversies surrounding the borderline concept, refer to Chapter 15 (The Borderline Concept and the Rorschach Test).

SUMMARY

In this chapter I have outlined a psychoanalytic diagnostic scheme. Based on contributions to the psychoanalytic literature on character formation and Kernberg's work on level of character organization, the system involves assessing patients along two dimensions. The first dimension involves a descriptive evaluation of the patient's character structure. The second dimension is the level of personality organization, based on an assessment of the following underlying structures: instinctual development, ego intactness, nature of defenses, quality of internalized object relations, superego integration, and ego identity.

4

Administration and Scoring

ADMINISTRATION

With slight modifications, my method of administering the Rorschach test follows upon that originally developed by Rapaport, Gill, and Schafer (1945–46).

To understand and interpret the meaning of test responses, one must take into account the context of the testing, including the structure of the test and the nature of the test situation. Especially with such relatively unstructured instruments as the Rorschach test, an important aspect of the structure of the test is the instructions given. With this in mind, the examiner, seated facing the patient, shows the first card and specifically asks: "Tell me, please, what do you see? What might this be?" These directions differ somewhat from those of other approaches in which the patient is encouraged to use fantasy: "Tell me what you *imagine* this to be." By making the task more reality oriented, I am attempting to establish a structure that will enable me to better understand excessive affective embellishments and more serious reality aberrations.

After the first response, and only on the first card, if the patient indicates that he or she thinks the first response is all that is required, then I ask, "Anything else?" The examiner should repeat this question after each response to Card I until the patient indicates that he or she sees nothing else. If the patient spontaneously offers more than one response, he or she should be allowed to continue until no further responses are forthcoming. Once the patient is finished and the card removed, the examiner points out, "This is how it goes, it will be the same with the rest of the cards." If at any point the patient rejects the card and offers no response, he or

41

she should be encouraged to keep trying for at least two minutes before the card is taken back. In such cases, the examiner should repeat the directions and even consider varying the instructions and adopting a more casual stance, as has been suggested by Appelbaum (1959).

INQUIRY

Other procedures described in the literature call for inquiry to be conducted only after all ten cards have been administered. Finding that procedure burdensome, I follow Rapaport's suggestion of conducting inquiry after each individual card is finished. I conduct inquiry as far as possible, with the card removed from the sight of the subject, and I do not restrict myself to one pat question such as "What about the card . . . suggested . . . ?" Rather, holding the principle of keeping questions general and nonspecific, I vary the queries and include such questions as "Why a . . . ?" or "Why . . . rather than . . . ?" or simply repeat the response in a questioning manner.

Mindful of the potential suggestive influence of inquiry and the added pressure it places on the examinee, Rapaport has suggested that inquiry be minimal and that it be confined to clarifying the scoring of a response. My experience has been otherwise. Too often, inexperienced examiners under-inquire and, as a consequence, determinants are missed and scoring is unreliable. Administration, scoring, and interpretation are all part of the same process; unless scoring is done accurately with ample information, the inferences derived are highly tenuous.

Inquiry should be aimed at securing information that would allow the examiner to confidently answer the following questions: What exactly did the patient see? Where did he or she see it? What in the blot did the patient use in fashioning the response? With respect to inquiry aimed at scoring determinants, I believe it is important that the examiner familiarize herself or himself with the stimulus properties (i.e., color, blackness, shading, etc.) of each card and that when a response is given, the examiner consider the range of potential determinants that might have been involved. For example, if on Card V the subject sees a "bat," the likelihood of blackness being one of the determinants is greater than if he or she sees a "butterfly." When inquiring for scoring, it is important that the examiner hold these possibilities in mind.

Although inquiry should be primarily directed to help clarify scoring, there are other occasions when inquiry is recommended. I find it useful to inquire into affective elaborations. Thus, were a patient to see a "vampire bat," I would ask, "Why vampire?" Also, I believe it is important to assess through inquiry the subject's attitude toward obviously and blatantly deviant responses. One testee found the response "two bears climbing an ice cream cone" unrealistic but humorous, whereas another testee offered the same response but during inquiry asked if the examiner could see it. Although each patient offered the same response, the meaning of the response for the patients differed because of marked differences in their attitudes.

RECORDING

Ideally, all that transpires in the course of administering the Rorschach test, including the patient's complete verbalizations (not merely the response proper), the patient's off-handed remarks, and the direction of the examiner's questions, should be recorded as verbatim as possible. The time that elapses between the presentation of the card and the subject's first response should be recorded, as should the time between the presentation of the card and the subject's returning it. The testee's rotation of the card and the position in which the card is held at the time of each response is indicated by a caret (∧), with its top position in the same direction as the top of the card. The responses to each card should be numbered. Overall, recording should be so complete that if the examiner or someone else were to review the protocol at a later time, he or she would be able to accurately reconstruct all that occurred during the Rorschach testing.

SCORING

Although several scoring systems are available in the Rorschach literature, I, in keeping with the theoretical slant of this book, use Rapaport's system with selected extensions and modifications. Rapaport's system calls for the scoring of each response along five dimensions. Each dimension, or perspective, represents a set of abstractions about the formal aspects of the response offered.

The formal or more structural aspects of a response are accorded particular importance, for they provide information about the patient of which he or she is not consciously aware. The scores are considered to indicate ". . . the function patterns of his awareness, rather than its content—that is, in what way he tends to become aware of situations, or experiences his affects, or avoids or elaborates on them" (Holt, 1968, p. 284). Formal characteristics are expression of perceptual organizing and associative processes that, because they tend not to be consciously experienced, are not subject to conscious control. The formal aspects are also important in that they permit the examiner to reduce the response mate-

rial to intrapsychically and interpersonally comparable common denomi-
nators.

Each of the five major categories will be described. Included within each
category is a listing of the specific scores. All the scores will be summarized
at the end of this section. In addition to the scored categories, there are
additional scores that are not included under any specific heading. These
too will be reviewed.

AREA CHOSEN

The area of a Rorschach card chosen for comment by the testee mainly
reflects the perceptual organizing process; however, it also plays a guiding
and supporting role in the associative process. As Holt (1968) has noted:

> The relative weight of the different scores in this category indicates to what
> extent the subject's perceptual organization is geared to hold together a total
> complex impression; to what extent it is limited to larger or smaller details in
> its integrative scope; to what extent the perceptional impression remains a
> global one or becomes articulated; and how well the associative process can
> supply appropriate content for each shift in the perceptual organization [p.
> 285].

The area chosen also reveals clues as to the flexibility and stability of the
individual's perceptual organization. For example, rigid individuals with
an excessive need for control have difficulty following the naturally
articulated breaks in the blot; instead, they will arbitrarily impose their
own cutoff boundaries. By contrast, subjects who are more flexible will
move with the perceptual flow of the blot. Whole responses (defined in the
following section) are offered on those cards that lend themselves to being
seen as a total gestalt, while detail percepts are seen on the more broken
cards (Schachtel, 1966). The specific area scores include the following:

W	Whole response—The area chosen is all or almost all of the inkblot (e.g., Card I: "a butterfly"; Card IV: "a monster"; Card VI: "an animal pelt"; Card VIII: "a state emblem").
D	Detail response—The area chosen is a part of the card that is conspicuous by its isolation, relative size, and frequency of response (e.g., center of Card I: "a woman with her arms outstretched"; side areas of Card II: "two

playful bear cubs"; top orange areas in Card IX: "two wizards casting a spell").

Dd

Small detail response—The area chosen is a part of the card that is conspicuous by its isolation and relatively small size (e.g., upper extensions in center of Card I: "two mittens"; peripheral spots on Card I: "islands"; red extensions at the bottom of Card II: "two spears").

Dr

Rare detail response—The area chosen is small, perceptually unbalanced, or arbitrarily delimited (e.g., cutting in half the side area of Card II and seeing the top half as "the head of a bear"). This area score is often accompanied by the determinant Fc (e.g., carving out of the heavily shaded central portion of Card IV an "angry face" and using the nuances of shading to delineate the outline and the facial features).

S

Space response—The area chosen is the white background rather than the inkblot proper (e.g., seeing in the white areas on Card I "four ghosts"). Exceptions here are large white areas that are frequently responded to because of their size and central location (e.g., center of Card II, center of Card VII). This score can be combined with another location score, W(S), as, for example, seeing on Card I "a spaceship and white spots are windows."

De

Edge detail response—The area chosen is not really an area but part of the contour line of the inkblot. Content usually accompanying this location score includes coastlines and faces in profile (e.g., right hand edge of Card IV: "the coastline of New England").

Do

Oligophrenic detail—This does not specifically refer to an area chosen. It refers to the segregation of an area that is typically seen as part of a common W or D response of good

form level (e.g., if a subject sees only the
antennae of the bat on Card V and does not
see the wings).

DETERMINANTS

This category indicates which perceptual aspects, out of the mass of
various stimuli, initiated and determined the response. The scores reflect
the impact of each of the perceptual features of the inkblots on the testee.
The individual's openness to various experiences is also reflected in the
scores.

Because the determinants lie outside the subject's conscious experience
and typically come into awareness only through the examiner's inquiry,
for Holt (1968) they constitute the most important aspect of the response.
An exception here is the hypervigilant, highly sensitive individual who
quickly attunes to the purpose of the examiner's inquiry and defensively
brings the determinants into conscious awareness. The determinants are
as follows:

F	Form response—The response is determined solely by the outline, contour, and articulation of the area chosen (e.g., Card I: "a bird"; side D areas of Card VII: "two beavers").
M	Movement response—An entire human form is seen in motion or in some posture isolated out of a process of movement. An exception is on Card III in which simply identifying the forms as human figures warrants a movement score (e.g., Card III: "two people playing tug of war"; Card VII: "two women dancing").
FM	Animal movement response—This score is reserved for responses in which an animal is engaged in humanlike movement (e.g., "bears dancing"). It does not include animals engaged in movement inherent to their nature (e.g., "lions climbing"). Those responses are typically scored F.
FC	Form color response—Color contributes to the response but is contained within a definite form response and is only of equal or subordinate significance to the form determinant

	(e.g., center area of Card II: "a red butterfly"; center area of Card III: "a pretty ribbon, the red").
CF	Color form response—Color plays the predominant role but some form elements are included.
C	Color response—Color is the sole determinant.
FCarb	Form color arbitrary—The use of color is obviously incompatible with the content of the response, but the subject clings to its arbitrary inclusion (e.g., "red beavers," "blue monkeys."
FCc, CFc,	Cc—The texture or nuances of shading with color contribute to the response (e.g., "dried blood because in places the red is darkened and in other places lighter and transparent").
FCh	Form shading response—The light–dark (chiaroscuro) shadings of the area contribute to the response but are contained within a definite form response and are of only equal or subordinate significance to the form determinant (e.g., whole of Card IV: "an animal skin . . . its outline and it looks furry; [furry?] the shading"; large open area in Card II "two lambs; [lambs?] shape of lambs and they appeared wooly").
ChF	Shading form response—Shading plays the predominant role, but some form elements are included (e.g., whole of Card VII: "a group of clouds, they look fluffy and somewhat like the outline of clouds").
Ch	Shading response—Shading is the sole determinant (e.g., Card IV: "All I can think of is a fog. It's misty with all the shading.").
FC'	Form blackness response—The blackness of the area contributes to the response but is contained within a definite form response and is of only equal or subordinate significance to

	the form determinant (e.g., Card I: "a bat"; [bat?] "the wings, its shape and the blackness"; Card V: "a large, black raven").
C'F	Blackness form response—Blackness plays the predominant role, but some form elements are included (e.g., Card VI: "an oil spill"; [spill?] "it's dark and goes off in different directions"; Card VII: "storm clouds"; [storm clouds?] "it's dark and they have the outline of clouds").
C'	Blackness response—Blackness is the sole determinant (e.g., Card IV "black paint"; Card VI "polluted water").
Fc	This score is used for responses that are form based and in which the nuances of shading are employed, not as shading per se, but to outline and articulate the response. The response is usually seen in a heavily shaded area, and the nuances of shading are used to delineate added features (e.g., "This is an angry face, the darker area here is the mouth, and these two lighter spots are the eyes").

FORM LEVEL

Form level refers to the degree of perceptual fit between the response and the area chosen. It indicates the relative accuracy of fit, as well as how definite or vague is the response offered. The congruence of fit between response and the perceptual characteristics of the area chosen reflects a basic ego function—reality testing—and the initial control feature inherent to thinking. The following form level scores are employed and are based on Mayman's (1964b) extension of Rapaport's initial scoring categories:

F+	This score is given to the sharp, convincing, accurately perceived, well-articulated response that, when seen by the examiner, affords an empathic "aha" experience.
Fo	This score is given to obvious percepts that are commonly and easily seen. Little effort is required but the response fits the location. All

	popular and near popular responses are included here.
Fw+	This score is given to weak but acceptable responses that are reasonable but not convincing. The examiner must stretch somewhat to see the response. Commonly, two or more features of correspondence between the percept and the area are articulated.
Fw-	These responses are weak and barely fit the chosen area. They are barely plausible, are quite difficult for the examiner to see, and hinge on only one feature of correspondence between the response and the location.
F-	These are totally unacceptable responses that bear no similarity to the area chosen. Such responses may be well articulated, but they are perceptually inaccurate.
Fv	The form intrinsic to the percept is vague (e.g., clouds, smoke, oil,). This does not refer to the articulation of the response but to its inherent vagueness.
Fs	Form spoil is scored when an acceptable response is distorted or lowered either by introducing an inappropriate specification or omitting a significant detail (e.g., a large man with a hairy tail).

CONTENT CATEGORIES

These scores do not convey the specific content of each response but the conceptual category under which it may be subsumed. The scores reflect the final outcome of the perceptual and especially of the associative processes. The range of categories employed by an individual reflect the wealth, accessibility, and flexibility of conceptual realms from which he or she can draw responses.

H	Whole human figure
Hd	Part of a human figure (i.e., arm, leg, head, etc.)

A	Whole animal form
Ad	Part of an animal form
Obj	Inanimate object
Pl	Plants including trees, flowers, and so forth
Ant	Anatomical responses (e.g., lungs, heart, stomach)
Geog	Geographical responses
Arch	Architectural responses, including buildings, domes, and so forth
Cl	Clouds
Bl	Blood
Sex	Sexual responses, typically involving sexual organs
Cloth	Clothing response (It is useful, if possible, to distinguish male from female clothing.)

FIFTH SCORING CATEGORY (DEVIANT VERBALIZATIONS)

Analysis of deviant verbalizations stands out as a unique and distinctive contribution of Rapaport, Gill, and Schafer (1945–46) to Rorschach theory. Rapaport made explicit the notion that because verbalizations are a reflection of thought processes, they can convey indications of disturbance. More specifically, he noted, "From the verbalization, or from the verbalized reasoning usually elicited in inquiry, one can infer the presence of thinking which does not adhere to the reality of the testing situation as defined by attitudes, responses and verbalizations of the general normal population" (cited in Holt, 1968, p. 427).

Recognizing that the testee's thinking in the Rorschach situation must be judged in relation to the perceptual reality of the inkblots, Rapaport evoked the concept of "loss or increase of distance from the inkblot" to systematize the various forms of deviant verbalizations that may appear in the Rorschach situation.

To understand the concept of "distance," one must first understand the reality of the testing situation. On this point Rapaport and associates noted:

By and large normal subjects will understand the testing situation and the test instructions to mean that they are to give responses for which sufficient justification may be found in the perceptual qualities of the inkblot; that their responses must be completely acceptable to everyday conventional logic; and that, just as they should not give responses they cannot confirm by reference to the inkblot, so their responses should not be so dominated by the perceptual configuration of the inkblot that they are no longer subject to critical control, and thus, become absurdly combined or absurdly integrated [cited in Holt, 1968, p. 429].

Given this context, a pathological "increase of distance" is evident when the testee's responses show little regard for the perceptual properties of the inkblot or when basically good responses are overly embellished with associative elaboration. If, on the other hand, the subject's responses reveal that he is taking the inkblots too seriously or, as Holt (1968) put it, "as an immutable reality, with its own real affective and logical propensities not admitting of critical control" (p. 429), then we have an indication of a pathological "loss of distance."

Described below are the most commonly encountered deviant verbalization scores. For a complete list of all deviant verbalizations, refer to Rapaport, Gill, and Schafer (1945–46).

> Fabulized Response (Fab)—A response with undue affective elaboration or too great a specificity. The elaborations are not unreasonable and the subject is usually aware of the fanciful nature of the interpretation (e.g.,"an angry wolf's face").

> Fabulized Combination (Fab-Comb)—Two accurately seen percepts are combined in an unrealistic, arbitrary, illogical way. The relationship is made on the basis of temporal or spacial contiguity (e.g., "two beavers dancing on top of an ice cream cone").

> Confabulation (Confab)—A response that is so overly embellished with fantasy and affective elaboration that the subject loses the reality of the test and replaces it with the created fantasy (e.g., "a big, ugly, menacing man stomping around. He's coming to get me"! Confabulatory responses carry to the extreme tendencies noted in the fabulized response; however, in the latter, reality is not lost.

> Contamination (Contam)—Two discrete concepts or ideas are fused together into one percept so that the separate identities are ignored (e.g., "a blood island," "a peppermint butterfly," "a bat rabbit"). Note how in the examples the stimulus prompted two separate ideas, and how the two ideas are fused into one.

> Autistic Logic (Aut)—A response is justified on a basis, often position, that shows little correspondence to conventional norms

of thinking (e.g., a stomach because it's in the middle"; "the north pole as it's on top").

Peculiar Verbalization (Pec)—An off-key, unusual verbalization that could conceivably pass as conventional and appropriate if used outside the testing situation but within the confines of the testing is jarring and out of tune (e.g., "part of a lady's vagina"; "two elephants on tippytoe").

Queer Verbalization (Queer)—Off key, unusual verbalization that would not be regarded as conventional or appropriate outside of the testing situation (e.g., "In response to Card IX, it still reminds me of female sex.").

Vagueness (Vague)—This does not refer to vague form but to the subject's weak hold on a definite form percept (i.e., "I can almost get a bat from this, I don't know, these might be wings.").

Confusion (Conf)—This refers to a confusion within the response itself or in the testee's experiencing and communication of the response (e.g., "These two animals look like mice. No, they are raccoons or even squirrels and they are about to step on this butterfly.")

Incoherence (Incoh)—Extraneous and irrelevant material is brought into the response and is disruptive at times to the extent of rendering the response incomprehensible (e.g., "I think of an underwater scene. The red is like my brother's shirt after his accident. What a mess, perhaps the fish are all in battle with each other.").

ADDITIONAL SCORES

Not included within any of the five major scoring categories is a group of additional scores. Like the major scores, these scores were developed to bring to the examiner's attention meaningful aspects of the response process. As with the analysis of deviant verbalizations, many of the additional scores are based on the verbalization within which the response is embedded or on more spontaneous comments.

Inanimate movement "m"—This score is added to responses in which movement is ascribed to an inanimate figure (e.g., "a spinning top," "a volcano erupting," "flowing blood").

C denial, C' denial, Ch denial—The determinant is mentioned but in the form of a negation or repudiation (e.g., "It wasn't the blackness."; "I didn't even think of the red.").

C ref, C' ref, Ch ref—The determinant is referred to but not integrated into a response (e.g., "I like the colors. The blackness is foreboding. The red areas are sea horses.").

C avoid, C' avoid, Ch avoid— In the examiner's judgment the determinant is implicit in the response; however, the determinant (e.g., blackness) is not explicitly expressed during inquiry (e.g., "two African women; [why African?] they are naked, have long necks and short hair.").

C impot, C' impot, Ch impot—The subject comments upon his or her impotence or inability to use the determinant (e.g., "I can't make anything out of the red. I see the colors but I can't work them in.").

C symbolism—Color is referred to but, rather than integrated into the response, is dealt with in a symbolic, intellectual way (e.g., "The red suggests they are angry." "Because of the colors I think of good and evil").

SUMMARY OF SCORES

AREA CHOSEN

W	Whole Response—The area chosen is all or almost all of the inkblot.
D	Detail Response—The area chosen is a part of the card that is conspicuous by its isolation, relative size and frequency of response.
Dd	Small Detail Response—The area chosen is a part of the card that is conspicuous by its isolation and relatively small size.
Dr	Rare Detail Response—The area chosen is small, perceptually unbalanced, or arbitrarily delimited.
S	Space Response—The area chosen is the white background rather than the inkblot proper.

De   Edge Detail Response—The area chosen is
                      not really an area but part of a contour line.

Do   Oligophrenic Detail—This score refers to the
                      segregation of an area that is typically seen as
                      part of a common W or D response of good
                      form level.

DETERMINANTS

F   Form Response—The response is determined
                      solely by the outline, contour, and articula-
                      tion of the area chosen.

M   Movement Response—An entire human form
                      is seen in motion or in some posture isolated
                      out of a process of movement.

FM   Animal Movement Response— An animal is
                      seen as engaged in humanlike movement.

FC   Form Color Response—Color contributes to
                      the response but is contained within a definite
                      form response and is only of equal or subordi-
                      nate significance to the form determinant.

CF   Color Form Response—Color plays the pre-
                      dominant role, but some form elements are
                      included.

C   Color Response—Color is the sole determi-
                      nant.

FCarb   Form Color Arbitrary—The use of color is
                      obviously incompatible with the content of
                      the response, but the subject clings to its arbi-
                      trary inclusion.

FCc, CFc, Cc   Color Shading—The texture or nuances of
                      shading with color contribute to the response.

FCh   Form Shading Response—The light-dark
                      (chiaroscuro) shadings of the area contribute
                      to the response and are of equal or subordi-
                      nate significance to the form determinant.

ChF   Shading Form Response—Shading plays the predominant role, but some form elements are included.

Ch	Shading Response—Shading is the sole determinant.
FC'	Form Blackness Response—The blackness of the area contributes to the response but is contained within a definite form response and is of only equal or subordinate significance to the form determinant.
C'F	Blackness Form Response—Blackness plays the predominant role but some form elements are included.
C'	Blackness Response—Blackness is the sole determinant.
Fc	Shading as Form—The response is based on form, and the nuances of shading are used to articulate and outline the response.

FORM LEVEL

F+	A sharp, convincing, accurately perceived, well-articulated response.
Fo	An accurate but easily seen response that requires little effort.
Fw+	A weak and acceptable response but not convincing. The examiner must stretch to see the response; commonly, two or more features of correspondence between the percept and the area chosen are articulated.
Fw-	A response that is weak and barely fits the chosen area. These responses are difficult to see and hinge on one feature of correspondence between the response and the location.
F-	A totally unacceptable, perceptually inaccurate response that bears no similarity to the area chosen.
Fv	The form intrinsic to the percept is vague.

Fs   Form spoil is scored when an acceptable re-
                      sponse is distorted or lowered by introducing
                      an inappropriate specification or omitting a
                      significant detail.

CONTENT CATEGORIES

H   Whole human figure

Hd   Part of a human figure

A   Whole animal form

Ad   Part of an animal form

Obj   An inanimate object

Pl   Plants, including trees, flowers, and so forth

Ant   Anatomical response

Geog   Geographical response

Arch   Architectural response

Cl   Clouds

Bl   Blood

Sex   Sexual response

Cloth   Clothing response

FIFTH SCORING CATEGORY (DEVIANT VERBALIZATIONS)

Fab   Fabulized Response—A response with undue
                      but acceptable affective elaboration or too
                      great a specificity.

Fab-Comb.   Fabulized Combination—Two or more accu-
                      rately seen percepts are combined in an unre-
                      alistic, arbitrary, and illogical way.

Confab   Confabulation—A response that is so overly
                      embellished with fantasy and affective elabo-
                      ration that the subject loses the reality of the
                      test and replaces it with the created fantasy.

Contam   Contamination—Two discrete concepts are fused without regard to their separate identities.

Aut	Autistic Logic—A response is justified on a basis that shows little correspondence to conventional norms of thinking.
Pec Verb	Peculiar Verbalizations—Off-key, unusual verbalizations that could pass as conventional or appropriate outside the testing situation.
Vague	Vagueness—The subject in his verbalizations conveys a weak hold on a definite form percept.
Conf	Confusion—Confusion within the response itself or in the testee's experiencing and communication of it.
Incoh	Incoherence—Extraneous and irrelevant material disrupts the response, at times, to the point of rendering the response incomprehensible.

ADDITIONAL SCORES

"m" inanimate movement	Movement is added to an inanimate figure.
C denial	
C' denial	
Ch denial	The determinant is mentioned in the form of a negation or repudiation.
C ref	
C' ref	
Ch ref	The determinant is referred to but not integrated into the response.
C avoid	
C' avoid	
Ch avoid	The subject implicitly uses a determinant but it is not explicitly mentioned.

C impot

C' impot

Ch impot   The subject comments upon his or her impo-
                  tence in attempting to use the determinant.

C symbolism   Color is referred to but, rather than integrated
                  into the response, is dealt with in a symbolic,
                  intellectual way.

SCORING GUIDELINES

The following guidelines have been found useful in enhancing accuracy
and ease of scoring.

1. In scoring determinants, begin by assuming the response is form
based and maintain this assumption until the testee explicitly indicates
otherwise. For example, if a subject sees "blood" in a red area but never,
even in inquiry, mentions the color, then the response is scored form (F).

2. On all responses that have a definite shape, form is either the sole
determinant or the dominant determinant; FC, FC', Fch, F(C). For another
determinant to be dominant, the percept must be inherently shapeless
(clouds, fire, blood, etc.).

3. The distinctions between CF-C, C'F-C', and ChF-Ch are based on the
testee's explicit comments.

4. Movement responses are treated the same as form responses. Thus,
"two black women dancing" would be scored (MC').

5. Form level is scored only for those responses in which form or
movement is the sole determinant or the dominant determinant. If another
determinant is dominant, the form level is vague by definition and need
not be scored.

6. In combinatory responses in which percepts are first seen separately
in separate areas and then combined, each percept should be scored and
then bracketed. For example, if on Card VIII the subject sees "two bears
climbing a mountain," the response would be scored:

D Fo A

D Fo Mountain

This differs from responses in which the subject has one overall impression and then comments upon the various details. An example here would
be the following response to Card IV: "I see a large monster. He has huge
legs, short arms, and a powerful tail." This response is scored W Fo
Monster.

7. If the content of a response does not fit into one of the content categories, then simply write out the content.

8. If the testee refers to an area by its color and then offers a response in which the color might be a determinant, clarify in inquiry if and how the color is being included. For example, if on Card III the subject responds, "The red area is a butterfly," then one might ask, "Why a butterfly?"

5

The Patient–Examiner Relationship

As an introduction to the inferential process, in this chapter I briefly review the sources of information the psychological examiner has available, and then discuss at greater length one particular source—the patient–examiner relationship. The other sources will be expanded on in subsequent chapters.

Schlesinger (1973) has identified three sources of information that arise from the testing situation: (1) the patient's behavior in the testing situation, the way in which the patient interacts with the tester, and the nature of changes in their relationship over time; (2) the content of the patient's test responses, including the patient's awareness of his or her own responses; and (3) the formal aspects of test responses, including test scores and their interrelationships. With specific regard to the Rorschach test, a fourth source may be added: sequence analysis, that is, a review of the sequence of responses. I agree with Schlesinger that the psychologist's task is to be attuned to these various sources of information and to integrate the data of one with that of another. Each source must be given its due and must be seen as having its own consistency and own relationship with the other levels of observation. The art of psychological testing then, consists of sensitively shifting attention from one to another of these sources while drawing, and checking, inferences throughout the course of testing.

With the recognition that an intricate interpersonal relationship, with realistic and unrealistic aspects, is intrinsic to testing and that this relationship has a significant impact on the patient's test productions and can also provide a wealth of information, several authors have attempted to describe and identify basic dimensions of the patient–examiner relationship.

The classic and still most comprehensive discussion of the relationship has been provided by Schafer (1954). The general dimensions he has identified include the following: the professional pressures placed upon and experienced by the examiner; the examiner's personality, including his or her character makeup, defenses, needs, and problems; the psychological constraints built into the examiner's role; the constraints implicit in the patient's psychological position; and the variety of defensive reactions available to the patient, given his or her position.

Schafer reminds us of the following constraints in the patient's role that typically are not discussed, yet exert a powerful influence on the testing: intimate communication and violation of privacy without a basis in trust; the relinquishment of control of the relationship; exposure to the dangers of confrontation and premature self-awareness, regressive temptations, and the dangers of freedom. He notes that under such challenging and anxiety-arousing conditions it is inevitable that defensive and transference reactions will be stimulated or exacerbated. Such reactions, he suggests, are not to be avoided or ignored, but rather are to be scrutinized as one would any clinical experience, for they provide one basis for understanding the patient.

Schachtel (1966) too has commented on the issues of control and freedom. He has described three reactions (he refers to them as definitions), based on formulations developed by Fromm and Sullivan and commonly encountered among patients in reaction to the unlimited freedom and feared loss of control inherent in the Rorschach situation.

The *authoritarian definition* is characterized by a fear of, admiration for, or rebellion against, authority. The testee feels that the test results will render him vulnerable to external and internal (superego) approval and condemnation. He feels he must work to meet certain demands, yet finding an absence of imposed demands and deeply frightened of the freedom, he invents his own demands. The tests are quickly transformed into a school examination. These self-imposed and ultimately self-limiting demands are then projected onto the examiner, who is then viewed as the loved and feared authority.

The *competitive definition* is also oriented toward powerful parental figures; however, this definition leads to competition with the imagined performance of others in order to defeat all rivals and have the examiner's (i.e., parent's) love all to oneself.

The *resistant definition* is distinguished by a conscious or unconscious reluctance to see anything and may even include the desire to do the opposite of assumed expectations. If the patient feels especially weak and guilty he may well react by conceiving of the test situation as a trial in which the best solution is to inhibit one's reactions lest he be found out.

With meticulous care Schafer and Schachtel have both attempted to outline the major dynamics involved in being tested, the transferential impact of these dynamics on the patient–examiner relationship, and the range of defensive reactions to be expected among different types of patients. Their emphasis, however, on "defensive reactions" reflects the prevailing structural theory of the 1950s and 1960s. With the more recent shift in psychoanalysis to a greater consideration of object relations and the self, the patient–examiner relationship has been reexamined, this time, from quite different perspectives.

Representative of these newer ways of thinking about the patient–examiner relationship is the work of P. Lerner (1988). In an attempt to find manifestations of projective identification in the testing situation, he applied Ogden's (1983) concepts of transference/countertransference to the patient-examiner relationship. Ogden has suggested that transference and counter-transference can be viewed from the perspective of the interpersonal externalization of an internal object relation. Transference, he noted, can take one of two forms, depending upon which role (i.e., self or self identified with the internal object) in the internal object relation is assigned to the other person in the externalizing process. In one instance, when the role assigned is that of the internal object (i.e., the self identified with the internal object), the patient experiences the other person as he had unconsciously experienced the internal object. Herein, counter-transference involves the examiner unconsciously identifying with that part of the patient identified with the internal object. Projective identification comes into play in terms of the interpersonal pressure on the examiner to engage in the identification and to experience himself or herself in a way congruent with the representation of the object in the internal object relation.

A 28-year-old female patient was tested approximately four years after her father's death. Most striking in the testing was her hypervigilance, heightened sensitivity, and excessive vulnerability. Aware and respectful of her vulnerability the examiner found himself relating to her at a distance in an overly cautious, at times measured, way. He made few spontaneous comments and did not confront her lateness. During the third testing session the patient complained of his distance and formality. In retrospect, she had experienced the examiner consciously much as she had experienced her father unconsciously, that is, as aloof, remote, over-controlled, and uninterested in her. In this example, the object component of the patient's internal relation with her father was projected onto the examiner and he felt controlled by it.

The second form of transference involves the patient projecting the self component of the internal object relation onto the examiner and experiencing the examiner the way the internal object experienced the self. The countertransference in this instance consists of the examiner's identification with the self component of the patient's internal object relation. Projective identification here involves the interpersonal pressure on the examiner to identify with the projected self and to comply with the fantasy by experiencing himself or herself just as the self experienced the internal object.

A 38-year-old single female patient sought treatment and was tested after the termination of an intense, conflict-laden two-year relationship with a married man five years her junior. She quickly entered into an idealizing relationship with the examiner in which she regarded his interest in her and observations about her as precious gifts, which she rewarded with offerings of adoration and flattery. By contrast, when the examiner was nonresponsive and less giving, she withdrew, looked pained, and contemplated leaving the testing situation. Pleased by the patient's adoration, pained by the patient's withdrawal, and frightened by her threats to leave, the examiner found himself becoming more active, more giving, and more controlled by the patient's praise. In time, the examiner was able to understand this interaction in terms of the patient's early relationship with a depressed mother. More specifically, the patient was actively doing to the examiner what she had unconsciously experienced her mother as having done to her. Namely, in excessively rewarding closeness and depressively withdrawing in reaction to separateness and autonomy, the patient's mother had created within the patient an addiction to adoration and praise.

As Ogden has noted, projective identification is an inevitable aspect of the externalization of an internal object relation. When applied to the testing situation, it means that there is always a component in the examiner's countertransference that represents an induced identification with a part of the patient's ego that is enmeshed in a particular unconscious internal object relation. By attuning to these transactions and his or her own countertransference reactions, the examiner is in a unique position to understand these internal object relations and then to infer the earlier object relational experiences they are derived from.

Arnow and Cooper (1988) have extended several of Kohut's formulations to the patient–examiner relationship, especially those regarding atypical transference patterns. In a series of publications, Kohut (1971, 1977) has identified and described a set of unique transference configurations that unfold in the treatment of patients with narcissistic personality disturbance. Referred to overall as selfobject transference, specific subtypes include the mirroring transference and the idealizing transference. Each of these patterns has been found to have both regressive and progressive features, and the treatment of the narcissistic patient typically consists of movement along one or the other of these developmental lines, though it may involve shifts between these transference patterns.

Mindful that the testing situation does not permit the unfolding of a full narcissistic transference, Arnow and Cooper (1988) nonetheless point out that "the interpersonal aspects of the testing situation represent an opportunity for experiencing a patient's primary needs for selfobjects and the feelings aroused when these needs are not met" (p. 54).

My own experience confirms Arnow and Cooper's assertion and supports the explanatory power of Kohut's observations. I have found that patients who need mirroring from the examiner typically enter testing with a compelling need to be treated as special, a craving to be admired, and a provocative sense of entitlement. As a consequence of such needs, these patients continuously assault the testing structure. Such routine mechanics as the setting up of appointments, adherence to session times, and ways of administering the tests become contentious and complicated. In reaction, the examiner often feels pressured to depart from standard testing procedures and to accord these patients "special" treatment. In a parallel fashion, their test responses are not offered to convey meaning, but rather, to impress the examiner and to create a product that they feel is commensurate with their grandiose sense of self.

I was asked to assess the 19-year-old son of a high-profiled local attorney. On the verge of failing his second year at university, he had been apprehended and charged with drug trafficking. Despite a filled schedule and a waiting list of other assessment cases, I found myself being harassed and pressured to begin the testing as quickly as possible. A cancellation arose and the patient was given that time. Although he reportedly was threatening suicide and was insisting upon his need to discuss his problems with someone, the patient missed the session, claiming that he had overslept. Only in a later testing session was he able to express his fury at the examiner for putting him on a waiting list and then offending him even further by fitting him into a time that had been slotted for someone else. For this patient, having to wait at a time of distress and having to comply with the needs of another (i.e., my schedule) constituted major blows to his overinflated sense of self.

In keeping with what Arnow and Cooper (1988) suggest, I too have found that the testing situation permits the examiner to explore empathic failures. Canceling a session or reacting with a trace of irritation quickly stirs in these patients hurt and pain, emotional withdrawal, and a view of the examiner as cold, detached, and uncaring. This contrasts with an empathic responsiveness in which the patient feels coherent and whole and regards the examiner as an ally.

Arnow and Cooper (1988) also recognize manifestations of an idealized selfobject relationship as it presents in the testing situation. They note that these patients look to the examiner for soothing and calming and, if these needs are not satisfied, typically react with panic and embarrassment. A second expression of the need for a powerful idealized object may take the form of using flattery or more subtle appeals to the examiner's narcissism.

SUMMARY

In this chapter I have discussed the patient–examiner relationship as a major source of information for the inferential process. Beginning with the seminal contributions of Schafer and Schachtel, I have reviewed newer conceptualizations that are emerging from the expanding scope of psychoanalytic theory. Newer models in psychoanalytic theory, with their emphases on the development of self and object relations, will increasingly contribute to our ways of understanding and formulating the patient–examiner relationship.

6

Major Scores: The Dimensions of the Rorschach

In the previous chapter I discussed the patient–examiner relationship as one source of information available to the psychologist who tests from a clinical perspective. A second source of information consists of the scores and their interrelationships. In this chapter I will consider the major scores from a particular perspective. Rather than focusing on each score individually, I will examine the basic dimensions underlying the scores. Therefore, this discussion will be organized around the following basic topics: movement, form, form level, color, shading and blackness. Certain other individual scores have been found especially helpful because of their capacity to reflect specific psychological processes; these will be reviewed in the next chapter.

I am taking this perspective for several reasons. First, unlike those who use psychometric approaches, I do not view the scores as signs nor do I believe there is a one-to-one correspondence between a specific score and a specific psychological process. Rather, in keeping with the psychoanalytic concept of multiple determination, I believe that any one score can reflect several underlying processes and that any one process can be expressed in various scores. Second, too often scores are viewed as ends in themselves and not as convenient, shorthand conventions for organizing, integrating, and representing aspects of the response process. It is the response process I wish to understand, and scores are meaningful as expressions of that process. Finally, it is my belief that if the examiner understands the basic dimensions of the test and the aspects of personality functioning they touch upon, he or she will be better able to view the scores from a broader perspective and appreciate the various psychological processes that might be at play.

67

HUMAN MOVEMENT RESPONSE

Beginning with Rorschach himself, many theorists have looked to the human movement response to assess some aspect of the interpersonal realm. Viewing the M response as a multidimensional concept, Rorschach (1942) advanced six interpretations for the response. Although Rorschach attributed meaning to the M response as a single variable, he based his analysis of personality on the comparison of movement with color. As such, those whose protocols revealed a predominance of movement were referred to as the M-experience type whereas those whose protocols emphasized color were referred to as the C-experience type. Of the six interpretations Rorschach offered for the M response, two—rapport and empathy—are directly related to the interpersonal area.

Rorschach (1942) suggested that the M-experience type reflects "more intensive than extensive rapport" (p. 78). Intensive rapport is found in individuals whose relationships are few but characterized by depth and closeness. In contrast is the extensive rapport found in the C-experience type. These people relate to others easily, but their relationships tend to be fleeting and superficial.

Following Rorschach's lead, other theorists as well have attributed interpersonal meaning to the M response. Piotrowski (1957) has suggested that from the M response one can infer an individual's conception of his or her "role in life." In a similar vein Schachtel (1966) views the M response as reflecting an individual's basic orientation and attitudes toward himself, others, and the world around him—that is, the individual's self-concept and his or her relational anticipations.

Dana (1968) concluded on the basis of on an extensive review of the experimental literature that the M response expresses an interpersonal orientation. More specifically, he suggested that the M response represents a "syndrome of potentials, capacities for reaching out into the environment in a variety of ways" (p. 144).

The most extensive and sophisticated discussion of the M response, which goes beyond description and is consistent with the thrust of this chapter, is represented in the work of Mayman (1977). On the basis of the writings of earlier theorists and of his own clinical experience, Mayman has identified five determinants of the movement response: (1) properties of the inkblot that help evoke movement percepts, (2) fantasy, (3) kinesthesia and its relation to the self-expressive character of the response, (4) object representations, and (5) empathy and identification.

The Perceptual Determinants of the Movement Response

It was Rapaport who first pointed out the purely perceptual determinants of the movement response. Basing his ideas in part on gestalt theory, he reserved the movement score for those responses in which the subject saw and associated to "an actual, demonstrable, perceptual imbalance in the inkblot" (Mayman, 1977, p. 231). Rapaport suggested that at an unconscious level the subject saw the gestalt in flux and was perturbed by the imbalance. Accordingly, without being conscious of it, the subject then sets matters right by ascribing to the image direction that gives the configuration better balance and stability.

This sensitivity to imbalance, Mayman (1977) notes, "is no mean achievement. If nothing else, it requires that one be able to transcend an atomistic survey of a blot area and pay attention, rather, to its dynamic composition" (p. 231). Mayman is suggesting here that at a purely perceptual level, in order to see imbalance one must be able to take distance and gain perspective. Subjects who take hold of an area in a piecemeal manner, tend to see simple and static forms, view details too discretely, and will not be prompted to see the more subtle perceptual properties, including the dynamic composition.

Also derived from Rapaport's notion of the actual perceptual basis of the movement response is the suggestion that to perceive movement requires a certain level of ideational activity. Rapaport himself put it more strongly; he suggested that movement responses indicated ideational potential and covaried with the intensity and range of ideational activity.

The absence of movement in a protocol, however, does not necessarily imply intellectual limitations. To achieve an M response, one must also be able to tolerate imbalance. We are all familiar with those testees who, because of their own inner imbalance and instability, find comfort in external balance. For such patients, imbalance in the inkblot cannot be tolerated, as it is too reminiscent of their inner feelings of flux. Here, then, the absence of M responses hints at inner fragility and turmoil rather than an intellectual deficit. For such individuals inner unrest may, at the same time, place limits on their capacity to fully utilize their intellectual talents.

Mayman (1977) has also observed that "the sensitivity to dynamic composition and the sense of flowing interrelatedness of certain blot areas can go awry . . ." (p. 232). For example, there are patients who are so compelled by the sense of intrinsic movement that they see relationships where none exist or they brush reality considerations aside and abandon themselves to the single perceptual impression. It has been my experience that those patients who are overly sensitive to the intrinsic movement of the blots, who spontaneously comment upon it without integrating it into a response, tend to be hyperideational and overly suspicious and distrusting.

The Fantasy Component of the Movement Response

A second aspect of the movement response identified by Mayman involves the contribution of fantasy. For Mayman, requisite to the offering of an M response is the availability of a fantasy life one can dip into to help vivify the response. More than most other Rorschach responses, the M response is distinguishable by its aliveness and vividness.

While a movement response requires and draws upon one's capacity to fantasize, it should not be regarded as the sole or necessarily the most accurate indicator of access to a rich inner life. I agree with Mayman that the fabulized response, that is, any response that is imbued with affective or descriptive elaborations, is the best overall indicator of the wealth of an individual's fantasy life.

Kinesthesia and the Self-Expressive Character of the Movement Response

In addition to its perceptual base and the requirement of the accessibility of fantasy, a third aspect of the movement response is kinesthesia, that is, the precise movement ascribed (e.g., fighting, dancing, clinging). While other Rorschach writers (Schachtel, 1966) have discussed the movement response broadly as an indication of self-experiences and self-concept, Mayman (1977), with greater specificity, has suggested that it is the "kinesthesias which find their way into a person's movement responses [that] are drawn from a repertoire of kinesthetic memories which express some of his core experiences of selfhood" (p. 240). Even though all movement responses may express some aspect of selfhood, he maintains that there is an essential difference between self-feelings that derive from one's kinesthetic action potentials and those that are based on contact with familiar and warmly personal objects.

The value of taking stock of an individual's kinesthesia was vividly demonstrated in a protocol in which the testee saw "two people *pulling something apart,*" "a person with *shattered dreams* and this is a symbol of the dream up here," "a baby *being torn away,*" and "someone *dropping* a bottle that *breaks* into a thousand pieces." Viewing the kinesthesias as an expression of self-experience, the examiner took these responses as reflective of a fragile sense of self that was highly vulnerable to fears of fragmentation.

In keeping with the earlier clinical observation of Sharpe (1940), Mayman extended his discussion of kinesthesia to suggest that kinesthesias are basic to all metaphors, not simply those conveyed in Rorschach responses. More specifically, that in any metaphor a person is expressing a kinesthetic, quasi-conscious memory with important undertones related to early self-experience.

The following clinical example illustrates this point. While interviewing a 38-year-old university history professor, I commented on his exceptional and tasteful dress. Unlike the typical college professor, he was wearing a highly fashionable Italian suit, an expensive silk tie, and brightly polished spectator shoes. He chuckled at my comment but then went on to say, "You know, that's the story of my life. It's like I am all dressed up and have nowhere to go." What he figuratively meant by this remark was that his friends and colleagues were being promoted and receiving raises whereas he felt that his request for promotion and tenure was being delayed and not acknowledged. With mild prodding, he was then able to recapture a host of earlier memories related to his early latency years of sitting by the window, gazing out, and waiting for his parents to return from work. The experience at age seven was of a lonely, mildly depressed youngster who was "all dressed up" but had "no one to take him anywhere."

The Object Representational Aspect of the Movement Response

Mayman (1977) reminds us that "there is more to a movement response than kinesthesia; there is also the figure carrying out the action" (p. 241). To understand this component of the M response he evokes the concept of "object representation." Herein, object representations are thought of as unconscious images of others that are rooted in early object relations and provide a substratum for all subsequent relationships. Given that a person brings to the Rorschach testing a large part of his or her repertoire of internalized representations of self and others, this component of the M response presents, for Mayman, a unique glimpse into the images that populate the person's inner life.

Taking note of these personal images is important but is only the first step; the examiner must push further and attempt to place these representations in the context of the person's self system and object relational organization. For example, the examiner must first determine the extent to which the figures represent an aspect of the self and the extent to which they reflect a sense of others. Those images referable to the self should be further evaluated in terms of whether they express what the testee feels about himself or herself or, alternatively, reflect what he or she admires and would like to be. The inferential possibilities implied in these projected images are vast; only by sifting through them and being able to identify their role in the patient's experience can these possibilities be realized. A fuller discussion of the clinical aspects of the object representational concept is presented in Chapter 8, The Analysis of Content.

Empathy and Identification in the Movement Response

This fifth and final aspect of the movement response involves the quality of the individual's object relations. Mayman (1977) draws a distinction between relationships that are on an empathic basis and those that are based on identification. Whereas the former includes two-way relationships in which separateness and self–other boundaries are maintained, in the latter self–other differences are blurred and there is little separateness.

The distinction Mayman draws between empathic relationships and identificatory relationships is quite similar to the earlier distinction Freud (1914) made between true object relations and narcissistic object relations. In a true object relationship, like Mayman's empathic relationship, the other is viewed as separate and distinct and as having motives and feelings distinct from one's own.

By contrast, in a narcissistic object relation, as in Mayman's relationship based on identification, the object is not regarded as separate and distinct but as an extension of the self and as necessary to fulfill functions that should, but cannot, be managed intrapsychically. In a narcissistic relationship the interest and investment is in the function being provided or the supply being offered and not in the person in the role of the provider or supplier. Typically, the individual in the provider role feels expendable, exploited, and used. One senses a tenuousness to the relationship and realizes that when the functions or supplies are withdrawn, they will be written off and then looked upon with contempt.

Mayman has identified several aspects of the movement response that distinguish these two modes of relating. Accordingly, individuals who are able to enter into true object relations in which there is no dissolving of self–other boundaries offer M responses in which (1) there is a broad and complex array of images of others; (2) the response takes into account realistic properties of the blots themselves, that is, there is objectivity; and (3) from the description of the percept it is clear that the testee is describing someone else and not himself or herself.

By contrast, individuals who relate themselves to others on a narcissistic basis, and who thus blur self–other boundaries, produce M responses in which (1) the response is reported with undue vividness and conviction; (2) the action ascribed and the attributes expressed are largely fabulized rather than inherent to the percept itself; (3) there is an intense absorption and involvement in the behavior of the perceived figures; and (4) the testee seems to infuse himself or herself into the described figure and thereby vicariously share in the other's experience.

In essence, implicit in Mayman's indices is the assumption that the nature of the relationship between the testee and his or her movement responses, in terms of such dimensions as range, objectivity, and distance, reflects and parallels the quality of relationship the testee establishes with his or her objects.

Summary of the Movement Response

In summary, Mayman (1977) has identified five essential dimensions of the movement response. An appraisal of these various lines permits the examiner to infer a vast array of structural and dynamic aspects of personality, including the capacity for perspective, the intensity of ideational activity, the availability of fantasy, the role of early self-experiences, the nature of self and object representations, and the quality of object relations.

FORM RESPONSE

Because form is the most important aspect of the visual world, it is not surprising that in most Rorschach records at least two thirds of the responses involve pure form. Form has long been recognized as the ordering, structuring principle of the universe as perceived by man. However, form is adaptive, as Schachtel (1966) points out, only insofar as it allows for transformations. When it becomes fixed and rigid, it stunts and inhibits rather than structures life. So too on the Rorschach test, form can be adaptive by giving order and structure to the unfamiliar and unstructured inkblots; however, it can be maladaptive when it becomes so overriding that it does not allow for flexibility and openness to other dimensions.

Based on an integration of perception, phenomenology, and psychoanalytic theory, Schachtel (1966) has identified six aspects of the form response. This section will be organized on the basis of these six aspects: (1) the role of form perception in the human sense of sight, (2) the perceptual attitude underlying form response, (3) the concept of perceptual hold and its relation to the form response, (4) the meaning of dynamic form responses, (5) the place of delay in the form response, and (6) the development of form perception.

Role of Form Perception

It is the role of form perception to take hold of significant aspects of the environment. Such taking hold implies an active organization of the visual field. What is required here is an active perceptual attitude, a looking attentively at something as opposed to simply being struck passively by it. Form perception structures, orders and objectifies the visual field and, as such, requires active focusing, attending, and structuring.

Schachtel (1966) has distinguished two modes of perceptual relatedness, and the distinction he has drawn rests on form perception:

> In the *autocentric mode* there is little or no objectification; the emphasis is on how and what the person feels; there is a close relation amounting to a fusion, between sensory quality and pleasure or unpleasure feelings; and the

perceiver reacts primarily to something impinging on him. . . . In the *allo-centric mode* there is objectification; the emphasis is on what the object is like; there is either no relation or a less pronounced or less direct relation between sensory quality and pleasure–unpleasure feelings; the perceiver usually approaches or turns his attention to the object actively and in doing so opens himself toward it receptively or, figuratively or literally, takes hold of it, tries to grasp it [p. 79].

Viewed in this context, the grasp of form is essential for the allocentric mode of perceptual relatedness.

Perceptual Attitude Underlying the Form Response

Rorschach described the form response from two perspectives: the clarity of form visualization as expressed in the accuracy of fit between percept and area chosen (form level), and the level of personality organization from which the percept originated. As to the latter, he viewed form as a function of consciousness and hence as subject to improvement by conscious effort. Later Rorschach theorists extended these notions. Beck (1944–45) considered form responses as reflecting intellectual, conscious control and a respect for reality, while Rapaport wrote of form responses as referable to the process of formal reasoning and as reflecting the person's adherence to the demands of reality.

Schachtel (1966), writing more phenomenologically, has described two perceptual attitudes that are involved in the form response—the "active attitude" and the "typical attitude." The active perceptual attitude, according to Schachtel, involves several steps, including an initial grasping of the inkblot features, comparing one's associations to the features of the inkblot, restructuring the inkblot features, and critically discerning the degree of likeness. Involved in these steps are various ego functions, including the processes of attention, reality testing, and critical judgment. Clearly, not all form responses are based on each of these steps; however, when the examiner notes an incompletely formulated response, it is important that he or she identify the missing step and attempt to understand the ego function impaired.

The second attitude identified by Schachtel, "the typical attitude," is "a neutral, impersonal, matter-of-fact, objective, detached quality in relation to the percept" (p. 95). Typically, not all form responses are offered with dispassionate objectivity and detachment. Were such an attitude to prevail throughout the test, it would likely reflect heightened resistance to the test and/or an individual who was inordinately and chronically inhibited, insulated, and restricted. Although the "typical attitude" represents one extreme and contrasts with the attitude underlying the dynamic form response, what Schachtel is suggesting here is that the nature of the form response may reflect the testee's attitude toward the test.

Concept of Perceptual Hold

Schachtel (1966) evokes the concept of "perceptual hold" to designate the individual's taking hold perceptually of the object world. Herein, he is referring to an experiential dimension of perception that extends from a firm, stable, enduring hold of the object perceived to one that is weak, tenuous, and vulnerable to interferences.

Schachtel views the form response as especially reflective of the degree and quality of the testee's perceptual hold. He notes that

> form perception can fulfill its abstractive, objectifying, identifying, orienting functions well only if the forms perceived are adequate; that is, if they correspond to the actual object seen and if the abstraction from the total object in the form perceived is valid and grasps the essential qualities of the objects [p. 109].

Thus, involvement in perceptual hold is a recognition of familiarity, receptive openness, and a decisive grasp; such functions are reflected in the form response.

The concept of "perceptual hold" has much clinical utility. Beyond describing the patient's typical level of perceptual hold, the examiner is in a unique position to observe which factors disrupt the hold, the severity of the disruption, and under what conditions the disruption occurs. For example, diffuse anxiety can interfere with a firm perceptual hold, resulting in percepts that are vague, indefinite, and amorphous. Recognizing this, the examiner can then determine where in the record vagueness occurred, ask himself or herself why it appeared at that point, and then note if the vagueness continued or if, the patient was able to recover.

Dynamic Form Responses

As noted previously, not all form responses are based on what Schachtel describes as the "typical attitude" of objectivity and detachment. Quite to the contrary, certain form responses can be rich, vivid, compelling, and lively. Schachtel refers to these responses as dynamic form, meaning that the percept is in a dynamic relation to the subject.

Schachtel's notion of dynamic form is quite similar to Mayman's (1977) concept of the fabulized response. Both writers are referring to responses that are embellished with affective and associative elaboration. For Schachtel, an important basis of the dynamic form response is emotion, whereas Mayman points to the availability of fantasy. Common to both theorists is the formulation that these types of responses speak to a rich inner life that is finding expression on the Rorschach test.

Dynamic form and the fabulized response are rich with meaning. For many individuals they reflect an interest and investment in the task, a willingness to go beyond merely what is called for. In contrast with a detached, intellectual stance, here one is playful and fanciful.

In addition to reflecting an attitude toward the test, such responses also express, more broadly, an openness to different types of experiences, a willingness, if you will, to relax tight controls and strict adherence to reality and to indulge in what Freud (1900) referred to as the "primary process." In judging this dimension it is important that the examiner distinguish between adaptive regression and maladaptive regression. In the former the excursions into primary process are under ego control; defenses are flexible but effective and reality testing is maintained. In the latter there is minimal ego control; tenuous defenses give way under the pressure of unconscious forces and reality testing is lost. Rorschach expressions of maladaptive regression include a weakening of form level and a sliding from fabulations to confabulations.

As Schachtel has noted, in the dynamic form response there is an affective relationship between the testee and his or her percept. That is, something of dynamic importance for the subject is being expressed in the response. This means that it is incumbent upon the examiner to take careful note of the content of these responses. While the content tends to be charged with personal meaning and must be understood on an individual basis, Schachtel has identified certain contents that he suggests have more general applications. For example, he views references to size as reflective of one's sense of his or her own importance and power, references to enclosures as expressive of a need for or a fear of protection, aggressive content as indicative of a desire to hurt or a fear of hurt and injury, and references to solidness or fragility as reflective of the individual's sense of self.

Delay and the Form Response

The steps involved in the form or form-dominated responses and their underlying processes (attending, taking hold, comparing, fitting, judging) require a higher level of mental activity than do more immediate, less reflective responses such as those involving pure color. Rapaport had this in mind when he asserted that form responses require and reflect a capacity for delay of discharge of impulses. Even when form was accompanied by another determinant, he suggested that it "indicated an ability to delay impulses until they can be integrated with the dictates of the formal rules of thinking" (Holt, 1968, p. 343). Holt amplified and refined Rapaport's initial postulation by noting that not all form responses do indicate the capacity for delay. Furthermore, he noted, certain form responses indicate quite the opposite: an inability to effect delay and an absence of the critical attitude implied in formal reasoning. Holt pointed out that because of the wide variety of form responses, what might be involved here are different levels of delay, as well as different uses of delay.

Schachtel (1966) too questions whether the form response is always expressive of an ability to delay. From a more adaptive perspective he points out that such responses can also represent the enjoyable and fluctuating tension of exploratory play in contact with the world of the inkblots" (p. 148).

It is my experience that present in most form responses, especially those involving another determinant, is an element of delay; however, this is dependent on the form level of the response and its complexity.

Development of Form Perception

With form, as with each of the other Rorschach dimensions (e.g., color, shading, blackness), it is important to maintain a developmental perspective. This is especially true when evaluating the records of children. For example, what in an adult record may be taken as an indication of disturbance might be regarded as normal in a child's protocol, given developmental considerations.

Ample evidence indicates that the perception of form is a relatively late developmental achievement that is based on a combination of maturational and experiential factors. Like other lines of development (e.g., cognition) changes in perception tend to proceed in an orderly, systematic, sequential manner with certain built-in directions. Two such directions have relevance to the perception of form on the Rorschach test. Schachtel (1966) has emphasized the gradual shift from passivity and a state of being impinged upon by external and internal stimuli to greater activity and an expanding capacity to control such impingements. The second direction, based on the work of Werner (1940), involves a progression from relative globalness and lack of differentiation to increasing differentiation and hierarchic integration.

In analyzing a protocol it is often helpful for the examiner to keep these two developmental directions in mind. For example, noting the overall proportion of form responses in a record might offer an indication of the role of activity in the patient's mental life and his or her attitude toward more passive experiences. Also, assessing the relative preponderance of vague form responses may offer clues as to the level of perceptual maturity. Level of perceptual maturity has predictive import in that P. Lerner

(1975) has found that it is related to cognitive maturity, social maturity, and symptom expression.

Summary of Form Responses

Using Schachtel's (1966) work as a framework, I have discussed form from the perspectives of the role of form perception in general, the perceptual attitude underlying the form response, the concept of perceptual hold, the meaning of dynamic form responses, the role of delay of impulse, and the developmental aspects of form perception. Each perspective has much to contribute to our understanding of the production of a form response.

FORM LEVEL

In the discussion of the form response, periodic reference was made to form level, the congruence of fit between the response and the area chosen. Historically, form level has been regarded as but one aspect of the form response; however, more recently—and especially with the contributions of Mayman (1964b)—form level has been elevated to a dimension in its own right and viewed as a source of useful inferences.

As previously noted, for Rorschach (1942) himself an important aspect of the form response was its clarity of visualization (i.e., form level). Although he conceived of clarity of visualization as related to intelligence, he provided little more than a gross distinction between "acceptable" and "unacceptable" forms. Beck (1944–45) accepted Rorschach's dichotomy but suggested that the distinction be based on normative data. Klopfer and associates (1954) introduced the notion of two cutoff points, one at each extreme of the form level continuum. Although this served to draw attention to especially good and especially poor percepts, it left almost 90% of all responses undiscussed in terms of the meaning of their form level. Rapaport, Gill, and Schafer (1945–46) distinguished good from poor form, as had Rorschach in his clinical work, and proposed two subcategories for each of the two major categories. Their criteria for scoring, however, were ambiguous and the meaning of the distinctions was unclear.

In his research, however, Rapaport did introduce a major innovation. To evaluate the quality of the perceptual–associative integration of a response, he proposed a continuum with six discrete grades: F+ for a well-differentiated, well-perceived response; Fo for an acceptable response generalized from one or two crudely seen details; Fv (vague) for responses intrinsically amorphous; F− for inadequately justified responses; special F+ for an especially well-articulated F+ response; and special F – for responses that are well differentiated but arbitrarily interpreted. In spite of the innovativeness of this system, Rapaport limited its applicability to the whole response (w).

Friedman (1953) extended the work of Rapaport and applied the system to all responses, not just the whole response (w). Friedman also placed the scoring system in a different conceptual framework. Basing them on the developmental theory of Werner (1940), he defined the scores as representing different levels of perceptual functioning.

It remained for Mayman (1964b) to reconceptualize the scoring system in such a way as to make it useful for clinicians. Although the work of Friedman generated much research (see P. Lerner, 1975), it offered little to practitioners. Mayman not only offered specific refinements but, more important, provided a rationale for reinterpreting the scores as reflecting different levels of reality testing. He proposed a system consisting of seven scores ranging from "reality adherence" at one extreme to "reality-abrogation" at the other extreme. The specific scores are as follows: F+ (good), Fo (ordinary), Fw+ (weak but acceptable), Fw– (weak and not acceptable), F– (arbitrary), Fv (vague), and Fs (spoiled). Because of its immense clinical value, each score will be discussed in terms of its meaning and scoring criteria.

F+ Response

A form good score (F+) is accorded those responses that are sharp, convincing, well articulated, and, once pointed out, clearly seen by the examiner. As Mayman (1964b) noted, "A good F+ response . . . may be hard to arrive at but is easy to grasp" (p. 8). Whereas one recognizes an Fo, one discovers an F+.

The F+ response represents a highly successful combination of imagination and reality adherence. Here the person goes beyond the ordinary but remains realistic. When embellishments and elaborations are offered, rather than detracting from the percept they bring the response into even sharper focus.

As with each of the form level ratings, the interpretive meaning of the F+ response lies in its relative proportion to the other scores. Ideally, one hopes to find in any record a sprinkling of F+, Fo, and Fw+ responses. When included with Fo and Fw+ responses, the F+ percept reflects a high investment in the task, an active perceptual attitude, a well-tuned sense of reality, and a willingness to depart from the commonplace.

The exclusive appearance of F+ responses in a record might indicate something altogether different. Reality testing is an ego function that involves a critical-evaluative attitude toward the external world. In some individuals this function may come under the sway of superego pressures so that self-scrutiny becomes an end in itself and self-correction a form of self-castigation. In these instances the individual feels considerable distress and guilt until he or she has reached the level of perfection supposedly implied in a F+ response. So too for patients with excessively demanding ego ideals whose aspirations are so exalted that only in the F+ response are they able to attain a level that they feel will do justice to their overly inflated but precarious sense of self.

The significance of the absence of the F+ response in a protocol depends on the nature of the scores that have been employed. For example, from a record with a preponderance of Fo scores, one might infer a rather superficial quality of reality testing, in which the person was satisfied with what was obvious and most easily seen. In those records in which weaker forms prevail, one might be observing either impaired reality testing or a tendency to brush reality considerations aside under the impact of highly invested urges and desires.

Fo Response

A form ordinary score (Fo) is given to those responses that are well perceived but are so obvious and readily seen that they require little effort. One does not seek out these percepts; rather, they are there to be seen. Although all popular and near popular responses warrant the Fo score, not all Fo percepts are popular responses.

The Fo responses reflect an accurate but superficial level of reality testing; the testee was able to see the obvious. Protocols with a disproportionately high number of Fo scores indicate a preference for the conventional and safe; such individuals often appear as shallow and banal. Then too, those testees not involved in the test, or those who are rigidly defending against immersing themselves in the inkblots, will produce protocols with a high Fo percentage.

Rorschach records lacking in Fo responses may indicate impairments in reality testing; however, those individuals who have difficulty tolerating the obvious and conventional also tend to provide records devoid of the Fo score. It is not uncommon for such an individual to comment, "I know other people see a bat here but I see other things."

A well-balanced protocol should include a high proportion of both Fo and F+ scores. This indicates an individual who sees and is comfortable with the conventional, yet at times can go beyond the obvious without losing his or her bearings in reality.

Fw+ Response

The form weak but acceptable score (Fw+) is applied to responses that are acceptable but require some stretching to see. The percept is not convincing but it does fit. Although the percept is justified on the basis of few details, the overall idea does not clash with the chosen area.

For Mayman (1964b), the weak but acceptable form response represents a departure from the strict reality adherence implicit in the Fo and F+ responses. He suggests that these responses do not indicate a serious departure from reality but rather that a permissiveness has entered the response process. The individual relaxes his or her more rigorous standards of reality adherence and lapses into a more lax and carefree state. Herein, fantasy is allowed to emerge without the need to maintain stringent reality testing. Optimally, records should have a few Fw+ responses, for not to allow such lapses is to have a too exacting standard of performance.

Fw- Response

Fw responses are essentially unacceptable but do have one or two redeeming features. Even though a detail may be offered to justify the fit between percept and location, overall there is little correspondence between the image and the blot area.

The distinction between the Fw+ response and the Fw- response may be viewed as a cutoff point between acceptable and nonacceptable levels of reality testing. In contrast with the Fw+ score, the Fw- score indicates a distinct lapse in reality testing. In this regard, the Fw- response shares commonalities with the F- and Fs responses. The Fw- response indicates not only a shift toward fantasy but a significant departure from reality adherence as well; forays into fantasy and whim are at the expense of reality considerations.

F- Response

The form arbitrary score (F-) is assigned responses in which there is little or no fit between the percept and the area responded to. An idea is offered to an area with almost complete disregard for the configural features of that area. In essence, the perceptual reality of the blot is lost; thus, F- responses indicate an abandonment of reality. Even one F- response may be taken as an indication of severe disturbance. While there are some individuals who readily and cavalierly brush reality aside, more often the score is suggestive of a psychotic loss of reality.

Mayman (1970) is quite explicit in pointing out that the score refers to a perceptual disturbance and not a conceptual one. For example, an individual can see two percepts quite accurately but then combine them in an illogical, unrealistic way (e.g., a child sitting on top of a pig's head). Even though this type of forged relationship is pathologic, the disturbance involved is qualitatively different from that underlying the F- response. As Mayman put it, "The F- is not a crazy thought; it is a crazy percept" (p. 14).

Fv Response

The form vague score (Fv) is reserved for those responses in which the idea applied to the blot area is intrinsically vague (e.g., clouds, abstract art, oil). Typically, vague responses are dictated mainly by determinants other than form (e.g., color, blackness, shading) and need not be scored. However, there are vague responses in which form is the sole determinant and here the form vague score is applied.

The Fv score differs from those responses in which the person is vague regarding what is seen or why he or she saw it. In the latter instance the confusion and perplexity are not reflected by the Fv score.

The Fv response is the cheapest response one can offer; it requires minimal effort. The score is not indicative of failures in reality testing. Rather, it either reflects a defensive stance toward the test in which vagueness is evoked to ward off fears of self-exposure or it indicates an impoverishment of associative processes.

Fs Response

The form spoil score (Fs) is applied when an acceptable response (i.e., F+, Fo) is distorted by either a significant omission or by the introduction of an inappropriate specification.

Mayman (1970) regards this response as indicative of a partial break with reality. As he puts it, "Something goes awry, and instead of an accurate perception of reality, the subject arrives at a surprisingly idiosyncratic misperception" (p. 12). In the Fs response the properties of the blot are not strong enough to prevent the person from losing touch with reality, and as a consequence a blatant distortion is incorporated into the organizing process.

Summary of Form Level

Although various theorists have pointed to its importance, not until Mayman has there been available a graded, clinically relevant scoring system. Based on a scale developed by Rapaport and extended to the full range of Rorschach responses by Friedman, Mayman's work represents a refinement of the scale and a reinterpretation of the scores as representing various levels of reality testing. Seven scores are proposed, ranging from "reality-adherence" to "reality-abrogation."

COLOR

In the Rorschach literature the color responses have been conceptually related to the individual's prevailing mode of affective responsiveness and expression; to the nature and degree of control over affects, impulses, and actions; and to the dimension of extroversion.

Rapaport, Gill, and Schafer (1945–46) viewed color and the relationship between color and form as indicative of the affect-discharge process and the concomitant capacity to effect delay. Thus, the pure color response reflected an absence of delay, the color–form response (CF) indicated greater delay but with minimal effectiveness, and the form color response (FC) suggested flexible control and adaptive delay. Rapaport further suggested that because the extent and modes of regulation over actions roughly parallel that of affects, one could also infer from the color response the capacity to effect delay before acting.

My own views of the color responses are more closely tied to those of Schachtel (1966), who related color more directly to affective experience, including responsiveness, range, level of differentiation, and expression. In keeping with Schachtel's more phenomenological perspective, in this section I discuss the Rorschach dimension of color in terms of the following: (1) the phenomenology of color perception, (2) the affective experience, (3) the concept of perceptual style, (4) the rationale for the relationship between color and affectivity, and (5) the role of color on the Rorschach. Finally, based on recent developments in psychoanalytic theory, I will draw relationships between the experience of affects and the experience of object relations.

Color Perception

In terms of Schachtel's (1966) notion of perceptual attitudes, the perception of color without form occurs with a passive, more *autocentric attitude*. This stands in marked contrast to the actively structuring and objectifying *allocentric perceptual attitude,* characteristic of the perception of form. Color impinges; one reacts to its impact rather than having to attentively seek it out. Whereas form commands active observation, color, if you will, takes hold. Schachtel (1966) put it this way: "Color seizes the eye, the eye grasps form" (p. 169).

The perception of color involves passivity, but other factors are also implicated. The color experience is immediate and is typically accompanied by a particular feeling tone or mood quality. Unlike the perception of form, colors are not just recognized but are felt, too. In this regard, the pleasure–unpleasure, comfort–discomfort dimension of the autocentric attitude is part of color perception.

The Affective Experience

The word *affect* derives from the Latin *afficere*, meaning "something done to" a person; something "affects" him. The word *emotion* comes from the Latin *emovere*, denoting a state in which one is "moved out of" a preceding state. Both words in derivation, then, reflect the passivity of the person.

Freud's view of affects also involved the notion of the essential passivity of the affective experience. Conceptualizing affects as drive derivatives, he described their passivity in relation to the active work of the ego in its attempts to maintain conscious control.

The affective experience is also characterized by an immediacy and directness between stimulus and response. Indeed, the stronger and more intense the affect, the less time there is for deliberation, reflection, and objectivity.

Perceptual Style

Basic to the relationship that Schachtel (1966) draws between the color experience and the affective experience is the concept of "perceptual style." This refers to enduring and pervasive perceptual attitudes that are characteristic of the person and find expression in his or her behavior and experience. The concept is akin to and closely parallels Shapiro's (1965) notion of "cognitive style."

Of the various attitudes that constitute one's perceptual style, of paramount importance, for Schachtel, is the tendency toward activity or passivity. Accordingly, the active–passive dimension is conceived of as cutting across all psychological domains. Thus, in the realm of affect discharge, extreme passivity becomes evident in being overwhelmed by affect, being swept up in it, and being unable to regulate it. Correspondingly, in the perceptual sphere, passivity is manifest in a tendency to be struck by the impact of sensory stimuli and thus to be unable to organize and take hold of it.

Rationale for the Relation Between Color and Affectivity

A brief review of the color experience and the affect experience reveals the following common features: both are experienced passively by the individual; in both the individual is affected immediately and directly; and both are closely bound to the dimension of pleasure-unpleasure. Because of these similarities, Schachtel sees the autocentric perceptual attitude underlying each experience.

Rapaport too recognized the relationship between color and affectivity; however, his acknowledgment was more grudging and was argued on a more general and abstract basis. One sees his caution in the following statement: "Dependent upon their organization of affects and impulses and their modes of control over them, people have associative processes that allow for dealing with the color impression in a specific manner characteristic of their affective life" (Holt, 1968, p. 376).

Color and the Rorschach

In the context of the Rorschach test color poses a challenge that can be tackled, avoided, denied, or solved in a variety of different ways. Its impact, the individual's general reaction, his or her reactivity, the extent to which it is integrated with form, the extent to which it interferes with perceptual articulation of form, and the ways in which its effects are limited are all aspects of the color dimension that need to be considered.

Many of the above considerations are reflected in formal scores, but several others are not. Thus, more spontaneous, off-handed comments, such as "Oh, this one is colorful" or "I find the red distracting" provide candid glimpses into how the testee is experiencing the color and, in turn, how he or she experiences affects.

Between off-handed comments and the major scores are the additional scores. These too were devised to capture specific aspects of the color experience. Thus, simply referring to the color but not making use of it in a response (Cref) indicates a passing attunement to affects without integrating them into one's experience. Color denial speaks directly to the defense of denial in managing affects whereas color avoidance indicates the tendency toward avoidance of affects. An investment in the idea and not the color, reflective of a tendency to intellectualize, is represented in the color symbolism response (Csym).

Virtually all Rorschach scoring systems provide for three major scores (FC, CF, C) to indicate the extent to which color is integrated with form. Using color as reflective of either affectivity or of a tendency to affect discharge and using form as representing the ordering, structuring, controlling factor, the three scores are thought to reflect the role of integration of affects into the person's psychological life.

It is generally agreed that the most satisfactory solution of the problem posed by color to the testee is the form–color response (FC). For Rapaport, this response reflects flexible control and a capacity for delay. For Schachtel, the response expresses an openness and receptivity to affective experiences. Color, according to Schachtel, enriches perception, much as affectivity enriches life. Both make possible a more rapid recognition and grasp of external events and objects and thus enhance one's pleasure.

There is some disagreement as to the merits of the solution provided by the color–form response (CF). While noting that this response reflects greater control and capacity for delay than does the pure color response (C), Rapaport also suggests that the control is tenuous, the delay insufficient, and a tendency toward impulsivity remains. Schachtel differs; he believes the response reflects spontaneity and an even greater openness to affects.

The absence of form in the color response (C) is typically regarded as problematic. Rapaport views such responses as indicating an absence of delay so that impulses are expressed directly and without regulation in action. For Schachtel, the response reflects heightened emotional reactivity coupled with extreme cognitive passivity, resulting in a proneness to emotional outbursts and a tendency to be overwhelmed and flooded by affects.

Several specific color responses (e.g., the form–color arbitrary response) will be discussed in the next chapter; however, here I would like to briefly mention those color responses in which shading and an attunement to the nuances of coloring play a role: FCc, CFc, Cc. While these responses too will be reviewed in greater detail later, let me note here that, in general, I have found these scores strongly indicative of the degree to which an individual is able to differentiate among various feeling states.

Affects and Object Relations

The relationships drawn by both Rapaport and Schachtel between the perception of color on the Rorschach and aspects of the organization of affects were based on Freud's view of affects as presented in his drive theory. In that theory, drives pressing for discharge were considered to be expressed and represented in consciousness by affects and ideas; thus, affects were regarded as drive derivatives.

More recent psychoanalytic conceptions of affects have tended to draw attention to their relation not to drives, but rather to object relations. Representative of this line of theorizing is the work of Modell (1975, 1978) and his formulation that affects are object-seeking. He notes that whereas the sharing and communication of affects affords closeness and intimacy, defenses against affects are also defenses against object relations. We are all familiar with those individuals who are not only emotionally constricted but self-sufficient as well. Believing that nothing is needed from others and that they alone can provide their own emotional sustenance, these people use self-sufficiency to ward off dangers associated with need and closeness. Winnicott (1960), in a similar conceptual vein, noted that individuals can keep themselves hidden by not sharing genuine feelings.

Only recently have these theoretical notions found their way into the Rorschach literature. In a series of papers P. Lerner (1979, 1981, 1986) has described the affect organization and quality of object relations of a subgroup of narcissistic patients and identified specific Rorschach indices reflective of both domains. While it is beyond the scope of this work to substantiate it here, it is my belief that from a careful study of the testee's affective experience as manifested in his or her ways of handling color on the Rorschach, the examiner should also be in a position to infer aspects of the individual's object relational experience.

A 34-year-old single woman with a history of numerous early losses sought treatment because of repeated failures in heterosexual relationships and nagging feelings of aloneness. During her assessment she provided a lengthy Rorschach consisting of 35 responses; however, only one of her responses included the use of color. The one color response ("red beavers") was scored FCarb, indicating that it involved an incompatible blend of color with content. Based on the relative absence of color and her FCarb score, a description of her affect experience included the following: "Despite her seeming warmth and outward emotional displays, to judge from her tests, the patient is affectively constricted and places much emphasis on control. Her affects are neither genuine nor spontaneous; rather, they have a play-acting quality and are based on others' expectations rather than what she truly feels." Basing his conclusions on the assumed connection between affects and object relations, he then suggested, "In keeping with her experience and expression of affects, her relationships as well are deceptive and ingenuine. She presents as cooperative but indeed is not. What passes for cooperation is either compliance or a seducing the other into going along with what she has already decided upon. Her compliance will emerge in treatment as will her strong investment in self-sufficiency."

Summary of Color Responses

Using Schachtel's phenomenological descriptions, I have related the testee's color experience in the Rorschach test situation to the experience of affects. Color poses a challenge to the testee; his or her attitude toward it and ways of dealing with it find parallels in attitudes toward and ways of experiencing affects. Basing my conclusions on the formulation that there is a close tie between affects and object relations, I have suggested that a careful appraisal of patients' color responses and references to color has inferential meaning in terms of their object relations.

SHADING

On his original inkblot cards Rorschach had the dark areas uniformly grey or black. Because of the poor printing, however, differences in shading and the relatively vague forms appeared. When Rorschach saw the proofs of his cards, he quickly appreciated the possibilities of this accidental dimension. However, he wrote little of this determinant though in his paper on the testing of Oberholzer's patient (Rorschach, 1942) he suggested that the response was related to an anxious, cautious type of affective adaption.

Since Rorschach, a great variety of shading responses have been distinguished, and the scoring involved has become especially refined. Authors have differentiated among such features as textural quality, vista effect, and diffusion. Despite the refinements in scoring, the meanings attributed to the shading responses vary considerably and have been the least validated of the scoring categories.

My scoring of shading is based on Rapaport (Holt, 1968), who adopted his scores from Binder (1932-33). Accordingly, when the shading impression is well integrated into a definite form response, the score is FCh; when the shading impression predominates but vestiges of form are retained, the score is ChF; and where shading is the sole determinant, the score is Ch.

Following Schachtel (1966) and Rapaport (Holt, 1968), in this section I will describe the perceptual experience of shading and the perceptual attitudes underlying it, the rationale for relating shading to anxiety, and problems involved in assessing anxiety.

Perceptual Experience and Attitude

Schachtel (1966) refers to the shading or diffusion response as one in which the testee perceives the shading as more filmlike and in which there is a sense of pervasiveness and a loss of clear boundaries and structures: "The blot is no longer seen as a solid object but as diffuse which offers no hold; it seems to dissolve and to have no internal stability or solidity" (pp. 247-48).

Because shading, typically, is not sufficiently impressive enough to become a determinant, when it does it suggests a susceptibility or readiness to be moved by it. In other words, there is a vulnerability to the experience and the underlying perceptual attitude presupposes that vulnerability.

Shading and Anxiety

According to Schachtel, the susceptibility to the shading experience on the Rorschach is the same as the susceptibility to the experience of diffuse anxiety. Like shading, the experience of diffuse anxiety is characterized by a lack of hold, a constant disruption of feeling secure, and a loss of clarity and stability. Schachtel (1966) put it this way: "The person prone to or actually experiencing diffuse anxiety . . . seems to be particularly susceptible to perceiving shading as diffusion, to be vulnerable to its objectless, nebulous, vague quality so similar to what he feels in himself when anxious" (p. 248). According to this rationale, then, the perception of shading and the experience of anxiety both issue from a common predisposition, and involved in both is an impairment in the capacity to hold. In addition, the individual attunes to the shading because its feeling tone resonates with a familiar internal feeling.

Rapaport also related shading to anxiety, but his rationale was quite different. He suggested that the diffuse shading and the relative lack of structure of the shaded cards contribute to the making of a response to these cards especially difficult. Because the anxious person already has difficulty integrating, and articulating, the chances of failing on these cards is particularly high. Thus, the rationale he proposes focuses on the gross articulation of the cards and emphasizes the articulation difficulty rather than the similarities between shading and anxiety.

Despite differences in rationales, there is agreement that anxiety can interfere with the capacity to give well-perceived and articulated form responses and that the more intense the anxiety, the more likely the occurrence of ChF and Ch responses.

Problems in Assessing Anxiety

Assessing anxiety on the Rorschach or on any other test is difficult, complex, and beset with both conceptual and methodological problems. First, not only does anxiety take many forms (e.g., panic attacks, lingering free-floating anxiety, constant restlessness, subjective sensations of tension), but the form it takes can have important diagnostic meaning. Kernberg (1975) regarded chronic, diffuse, free-floating anxiety as a cardinal symptom associated with borderline pathology and the anxiety found in a neurotic patient as less relenting, more focused and circumscribed, and better regulated. Second, anxiety is not always assessed or observed directly. On occasion, one infers anxiety by the defensive activity observed. For example, if on a highly shaded card the testee uncharacteristically turns to the periphery and offers edge detail percepts (De), then the examiner might infer anxiety on the basis of the avoidant behavior. Third, on the Rorschach test shading is not regarded as the only expression of anxiety. The inanimate movement response (m) and the form vague percept (Fv) are also considered reflections of anxiety.

Because of the complexities surrounding anxiety and its crucial role in personality development and psychopathology, it is insufficient for the examiner to simply describe the patient as anxious. Rather, the examiner must strive to understand how the patient experiences and expresses his or her anxiety, the defenses the patient employs to regulate it, the effectiveness of those defenses, and the impact of the anxiety on various areas of functioning. For certain patients, such as impulsive characters, infantile personalities, and highly constricted individuals, the testing report is incomplete unless it also addresses the patient's openness to experiencing anxiety and his or her anxiety tolerance.

The following excerpt from a testing report illustrates the above points:

> The patient is currently being pressured by relatively intense feelings of anxiety. His anxiety, which is long-standing and constant, becomes evident in difficulties in attending, in an inability to tolerate frustration, in motor restlessness, in an inability to stick with tasks, and in an assortment of vague physical complaints. To ward off the feeling, he first relies on the obsessional defenses of intellectualization, isolation of affect, and reaction formation. When these fail, and they often do, he then uses denial and milder forms of projection. When these falter, as now, he then resorts to alcohol.

Summary of Shading Responses

In keeping with Schachtel's experiential perspective, I have related shading responses to the experience of diffuse, pervasive, free-floating feelings of anxiety. Recognizing that anxiety is experienced and expressed in various ways and that its assessment is complicated, I have attempted to identify structural and experiential aspects of anxiety that should be addressed in a testing report.

BLACKNESS

Although an attunement to the blackness of the inkblots and the inclusion of blackness as a determinant in a response has been related to depressive affect, the presumed relationship has been based more on common sense and lore than on theoretical rationales or empirical findings. This is both surprising and disturbing, especially in light of the major theoretical advances that have been made in the psychoanalytic understanding of depression. With one exception, (Wilson, 1988), these advances have not been extended to the blackness responses but instead have found expression in newer and more systematic ways of appraising Rorschach content (i.e., Blatt et al., 1976; P. Lerner, 1988).

Schachtel (1966) has provided a rationale for the response to darkness in which he recognizes an experiential reaction to diffusion on the one hand and a perceptual attunement to colors on the other. As in the experience of diffusion, Schachtel maintains that there is a predisposition or vulnerability to be moved by the darkness. As in the color responses, the testee is impinged upon by the stimulus, the experience is immediate and direct, and a feeling tone accompanies the perception. In this instance, however, it is the darkness that impinges and the feeling tone is dysphoric. Schachtel includes under dysphoria a range of depressive feelings, including sadness, mournfulness, despair, and barrenness. In comparing the color and darkness responses he notes that "responses to overall darkness usually convey a feeling, in varying degrees, as if the testee had been plunged into or enveloped by a darkling mood, and, as Binder has shown, point to pervasive dysphoric moods that are readily triggered . . . " (p. 246). As with anxiety, dysphoric moods can interfere with the ability to give well articulated form responses; thus, the more intense the feeling, the more likely the offering of C'F and C' responses. It is suggested that involved in the depressive experience is a loss of interest in the outer world and a sense of meaninglessness and that these experiences interfere with the individual's perceptual hold and are reflected in a decrease of form-predominant responses.

Schachtel's rationale for relating the perception of darkness to dysphoric feelings is sound but must be regarded only as a starting point. With more recent theoretical advances, we are now in a position to identify those more specific dysphoric feelings expressed in the C' responses.

There is a growing consensus (Blatt, 1974; Kohut, 1977) that there are two distinct forms of depression: a developmentally later, guilt-ridden form characterized by the sense that something bad has occurred and an earlier, empty form characterized by feelings of depletion and helplessness, intense object seeking, and difficulties in self-regulation.

Wilson (1988) has noted that with the dichotomizing of depressive affect into empty and guilt-ridden forms, the traditional equation between C' black and depressive affect is no longer adequate. The C' scores, he suggests, do not take into account the empty forms of depression. What is implied in the C' response, he notes, is a capacity for guilt, a time perspective, an ability to distinguish right from wrong, and a signaling capacity. Thus, according to Wilson, the dysphoric feelings expressed in the C' responses are at a higher developmental level and include conscious feelings of despair and guilt-tinged depressive affects.

While Rorschach indices of the anaclitic forms of depression have been developed by Ludolph, Milden, and Lerner (1988) and Wilson (1988), P. Lerner (1988) in particular has attempted to translate phenomenological aspects of these developmentally earlier types of depression into Rorschach-related terms. One feature common to these depressions is feelings of emptiness. For Lerner, patients who feel empty provide enfeebled records in which there is a sparseness of responses. He suggests that in fashioning a response few dimensions (such as movement, color, shading) are used, and even when such properties are employed, they lack vividness and impact. One's overall sense of the protocol is that it is muted, drab, and meaningless. A second feature described by Lerner is a sense of hollowness. Here he notes that when these patients attune to the white areas (space response), such attunement points to a sensitivity to themes of hollowness. Finally, Lerner notes that while these patients are reality bound, the contents they perceive typically have a quality of injury or deadness. Therefore, throughout their protocols are found such percepts as skeletons, deserts, faceless creatures, and dead trees.

The assessment of depression on the Rorschach test is complicated, requires a familiarity with theory, and is fraught with many of the same difficulties as the assessment of anxiety.

Depression lacks a clear definition or reference point; it has alternately been used to refer to a basic affect, a more transient mood, a symptom, a syndrome, and a character style. Owing to the greater attention accorded to the writings of Melanie Klein, it has also been usefully conceptualized as a developmental achievement with important prognostic implications.

As discussed, depression takes various forms and the form it takes is intimately related to level of object relations, cohesiveness of the sense of self, and the overall nature and level of psychopathology.

In assessing depressive affect, as with anxiety, it is imperative that the examiner attempt to understand the nature of the depressive experience, the defenses used to control it, the effectiveness of the defenses, and the effect of the depression on aspects of personality functioning. Not all patients present with depressive affect; nonetheless, for informed treatment planning, it is helpful that the therapist be apprised of the patient's capacity to experience depressive feelings.

The following excerpt from a testing report was found quite useful by the referring therapist.

> Amid affective constriction, the patient is now experiencing relatively se-
> vere feelings of depression. Her depression becomes manifest in a marked
> sense of loss, especially a loss in functioning, in a concern with her waning
> sexuality, and in an attunement to subjective feelings of coldness. As well,
> she is tired and depleted and stirs in others the sense that they are asking too
> much of her. She is concerned with death and abandonment. Finally, she has
> much difficulty concentrating and this contributes to her sense of lowered
> functioning.

Summary of Blackness Responses

In keeping with a rationale developed by Schachtel and Rorschach tradition, I have related the perception of darkness to dysphoric affects. However, basing my beliefs on the recent formulations of Wilson, I suggest that
the C′ responses are related to developmentally later depressive feelings

(i.e., despair, guilt-tinged depression) and not the entire range of dysphoric affects. In assessing depressive feelings and their vicissitudes, it is especially important that the examiner be theoretically informed and cognizant of the role of depression in personality development.

SUMMARY

In this chapter I have discussed the major dimensions of the Rorschach test, including movement, form, form level, color, shading, and darkness. I have equated each dimension to an area of personality functioning and development and have attempted to provide a theoretical rationale for this. The rationales have relied extensively on the earlier contributions of Schachtel, Rapaport, and Mayman. When applicable, the rationales have been refined in the light of more recent developments in psychoanalytic theory. Ultimately, it is through a conceptual understanding of the basic test dimensions and the aspects of personality functioning they touch upon that the examiner is able to derive meaning from the scores.

7

Specific Scores and Their Meaning

While all the determinant scores are based upon the basic dimensions outlined in the previous chapter, there are select scores that I have found especially useful and a rich source of data for inference drawing. My understanding of the meanings of these scores derives from clinical observation, the existent Rorschach literature, and newer formulations arising from psychoanalytic theory. In particular, Kohut's (1971, 1977) notions regarding the development of the cohesive self, Winnicott's (1961) sensitively evocative concept of the "false self," and Modell's (1975) careful description of narcissistic defenses are all woven into the ensuing discussion.

Fc RESPONSE

The Fc score is given to those responses in which variations in shading are used like form to delineate and articulate the percept. For example, the testee might see a face in a heavily shaded area and then use the nuances of shading to outline the eyes, nose, mouth, and hairline. These variations in shading are subtle; therefore, to achieve an Fc response one must seek out, discover, and attune to fine nuances, as well as feel one's way into something potentially dangerous and not readily apparent. To do this requires perceptual sensitivity in addition to a searching, penetrating, and articulating type of activity. Schachtel (1966) has referred to this mode as a perceptual attitude "of a stretching out of feelers in order to explore nuances" (p. 251). While such an attitude of heightened sensitivity and penetrating activity can reflect and underlie an adaptive capacity for achieving highly differentiated responses, attuning to subtleties of feeling, and empathizing with the nuances of another's experience, it can also go awry. We are all familiar with persons who have their antennae out, as it were, to feel out an assumedly hostile, cold, and unfriendly environment. In such persons one observes a constant state of hypervigilance, heightened sensitivity, and excessive vulnerability.

In a large subgroup of narcissistic patients I have found this state of unremitting hypervigilance, defensive sensitivity, and excessive vulnerability to be related to an identifiable self-system, mode of object relatedness, defensive structure, manner of experiencing affects, line of cognitive regression, and manner of entering treatment.

Before these features are described in greater detail, it should be noted that, like Gabbard (1989), I believe the narcissistic personality disturbance can be conceptualized as occurring on a continuum between two extremes. At one end of the continuum is the more hypervigilant, vulnerable, narcissistic patient, characterized by a heightened sensitivity to the reactions of others, a tendency toward shyness and self-effacement, a painful self-consciousness, and a vulnerability to feelings of shame and humiliation. At the other end of the continuum is what Gabbard refers to as the "oblivious narcissist." These individuals, by contrast, tend to be self-absorbed, arrogant, haughty, impervious to the needs and feelings of others, and exploitive in their relationships. Whereas the hypervigilant patient corresponds closely to those narcissistic patients described by Kohut (1971), the oblivious narcissist closely approximates the narcissistic patient described by Kernberg (1975). For a more detailed discussion of this conceptualization of narcissistic disturbances, refer to Chapter 17 (Rorschach Measures of Narcissism and the Narcissistic Patient). The patients described in the following paragraphs correspond to the hypervigilant type.

The hypervigilant narcissistic patient presents a passive attitude toward the environment, with an unspoken willingness to be influenced. Their vigilance and sensitivity, like radar, constantly scan the outer milieu in search of potential dangers or cues to guide and direct their desires, values, and behaviors. Like chameleons, they sensitively attune to the expectations of others and mold themselves and their behavior accordingly. This sensitivity and ready accommodation, however, is defensive and in the service of warding off threats to a rather fragile self-esteem. In this regard they differ from the "as if" character (Deutsch, 1942), whose compliance and imitative behavior are related more to a search for identity. The hypervigilant narcissist has attained a sense of identity but feels it must be kept private and hidden. Nonetheless, the accommodating is without investment; consequently, the other is left with a sense that something is amiss. In like manner, the patients themselves are painfully and helplessly aware of their compliance and are left feeling ungenuine and despairing. Intimately related to the compliance is a presentation of fragility and vulnerability. The fragility is disarming, for one quickly senses that the wrong word, the forgotten act, or the slightest hint of disapproval will strain an already strained relationship to a point beyond repair. Thus, relationships are tenuous and fleeting.

The affective life of the hypervigilant narcissist is characterized by feelings of low self-esteem, a particular type of anxiety, and an empty form of depression. Reich (1960) has suggested that because of the archaic nature of their ego ideal, these patients are especially prone to continuous feelings of low self-regard and little sense of self-worth. Their anxiety is similar to what Tolpin and Kohut (1978) refer to as "disintegration anxiety," meaning an intense fear associated with the potential loss of self. Associated with the anxiety is a subjectively experienced tension state that, when felt as intolerable, initiates a series of ego maneuvers directed toward lowering this state (Easser, 1974). The depressive affect of these patients is distinctive and involves unbearable feelings of deadness and nonexistence and a self-perception of emptiness, aloneness, and hopelessness.

Hypervigilance and hypersensitivity are used to ward off affects, especially those feelings that could lead to greater closeness and intimacy (Easser, 1974). With an increase in tension, minor forms of acting out become prominent, and if these escape outlets are cut off, then withdrawal, compliance, and suspiciousness ensue. There is a marked tendency to use projective identification.

These patients also reveal a particular line of cognitive regression. They have a tendency to lapse into concrete, stimulus-bound thinking in which there is a loss of perspective. That is, there is a nearsighted clarity with an attendant loss of the backdrop.

As Easser (1974) has noted, these patients begin treatment under a cloak of vigilance, with a readiness to be distrustful. They are there but with one foot out the door, so to speak. Upon beginning treatment a rapid and at times massive regression occurs, involving feelings of terror and panic, outbursts of affect toward the therapist, and a rush of activity directed away from, but laden with meaning regarding, the treatment. Easser offered an example of such activity involving a twenty-year-old male who, upon agreeing to psychoanalysis, took out a large life insurance policy. In keeping with the hypersensitivity, all aspects of the therapist came under careful scrutiny. If the therapist recalled an incident or experience mentioned several sessions before or responded in a particularly empathic way, the patient felt held together and considered the therapist an ally. However, if the therapist canceled a session or responded with a trace of irritation in his voice, then the patient reacted with pain and regarded the therapist as hostile, distant, and uncaring.

The therapist's experience with the hypervigilant narcissistic patient is one of being viewed under a microscope. Not only is every movement of the therapist closely monitored, but his or her comments are carefully scrutinized and regarded as evidence to weigh before allowing the relationship to continue and possibly deepen. This stance evokes a countervigilance and hypercaution on the part of the therapist. Realizing that interpretations will be met with an overreaction and taken as an attack, the therapist finds himself or herself less spontaneous, less relaxed, and more careful with his or her interventions.

The patient's heightened attunement to visual, gestural, and emotional aspects of the therapist may be likened to the young infant's early experience with the mother. Because of this reenactment, one can reconstruct that earlier experience. Genetically, the perception of emotional tones and of tension by the young child precedes the learning of language and the understanding of spoken content (Schachtel, 1966). It develops from the infant's perception of his or her own sense of comfort or discomfort with the mother, including her moods and tensions. As development progresses, with "good enough" mothering (Winnicott, 1960), attention to the obvious and to verbal content gradually overshadows the need for perceiving finer visual and emotional nuances of the outer world. In the absence of such mothering this transition is tenuous and incomplete. While several authors (Kohut, 1971; Winnicott, 1960) have pointed to a defect in empathy in these mothers, I have been equally impressed with the extent and depth of their depression and how this has interfered with their capacity to freely and continuously attend to and minister to their infants, as well as to allow their offspring to fully separate.

Illustrative of the situation was a 38-year-old divorcée, the mother of three, who was referred for psychoanalysis by her family physician amid a depressive episode precipitated by a psychiatric resident who had confronted her with his belief that she was psychosomatic. She took his comment as a severe moral condemnation and soon thereafter became highly self-punitive and self-reproachful, felt inordinately ashamed, and was convinced, more than ever, that she was basically "bad."

Following her divorce some eight years earlier, she worked as an office manager for two years and then took a leave of absence because of a host of disabling symptoms, including vertigo, headaches, nausea, intense pain throughout her body, and continuous feelings of tiredness and depletion. At times her symptoms reached the point that she would be confined in bed for up to a week. While positive findings had been reported on various lab tests, a definitive diagnosis was not established because of the inconsistency of results. Lupus and encephalitis were considered but not conclusively substantiated.

Most vivid in her early memories was her sense of the family home. She recalled the house as grey, dingy, often in need of repair, and a place to which she felt embarrassed to bring friends. Her father, a real estate broker, suffered from a severe alcohol problem. Although he worked without interruption, on weekends, she recalled, he repeatedly drank himself into a stupor. Her mother worked full-time as a bookkeeper. With shame and disgust, she reported how each morning her mother would awake for work, eat breakfast, and then become nauseous and vomit until it was time to leave for work. Because both parents worked, the patient was expected to perform numerous household tasks. In general, she felt her parents robbed her of her childhood and that from an early age she was expected to mother her mother and ask for little caretaking in return.

During the two-week hiatus between the end of the evaluation and the beginning of her analysis and in anticipation of treatment, the patient devoted considerable time and effort to the preparation of a log that chronicled in meticulous detail the array of events and experiences in her life. She then began her analysis and spent each session of the next nine months reading from her log. Overtly, the patient appeared to be complying completely with the demands of the analytic situation, yet her analyst felt quite the opposite. He felt trapped and controlled by her behavior. On one hand, he felt like an ignored bystander watching his patient conduct her own analysis; on the other hand, he also felt like a captive audience continually being monitored (by the patient's hypervigilance) to ensure that his attention did not wander. Beneath the feeling of being controlled, her analyst also experienced himself and the treatment as a protective container into which the patient was pouring the hardships life had visited upon her.

There are two other aspects of the Fc response that I would like to mention. Appelbaum and his colleagues (Appelbaum and Holtzman, 1962; Appelbaum and Colson, 1968) found that an attunement to the nuances of shading when combined with and in a colored area (FCc, CFc, Cc) was indicative of suicidal tendencies. Because many of the patients I assessed offered the Fc response indiscriminately to both achromatic and colored areas, I was not surprised to find that one form of potential acting-out behavior was suicide. While Appelbaum and Holtzman sensitively describe the experiential state that might lead a person offering the response to consider suicide, they are less clear as to precipitating motives or circumstances. Among these patients I have found that precipitates leading to suicide typically relate to the nature of their self-experience and the quality of their object relations. More specifically, experiences that prompt fear of the loss of a sense of self, that involve a dramatic or cumulative loss in self-esteem, and that deny a yearned-for symbiotic attachment with a lost object are the types of events that trigger suicidal thoughts or behavior.

Finally, P. Lerner and H. Lerner (1980) found that the Fc determinant, when combined with the Dr location score (rare detail) and possessing content involving distorted part or full human forms, was a reliable and valid measure of projective identification. Lerner and Lerner reasoned that involved both in projective identification and in this combination of scores is a sense of the environment as dangerous, an attempt to defensively empathize with the sources of danger, and a reliance on such preverbal modalities as putting parts of oneself into another in order to communicate with and control the other.

FORM-COLOR ARBITRARY (FCarb) RESPONSE

The FCarb score is reserved for responses in which the use of color is obviously incompatible with the content (blue monkeys, pink beavers, etc.) but the testee clings to its arbitrary inclusion. Rapaport, Gill, and Schafer (1945–46) discussed the response as indicative of difficulties integrating affects into one's mental life. While I agree with this formulation, I also find it narrow and overly restrictive. In reexamining this response, especially in light of the writings of Winnicott (1960), I believe the score also reflects compliance, cognitive passivity marked by a loss of detachment and perspective, fears of loss of selfhood, and the development of a particular defensive structure—the false self.

The FCarb score as an expression of compliance has been noted by Schachtel (1966). He suggests that one gets

> the impression that the testee had felt it incumbent on him to include the color in his response even though no natural combination occurred . . . The color is not experienced as particularly striking or stimulating but it is noticed and then endowed by the testee with the same exaggerated demand quality that he attributes to the whole test situation [p. 181].

In addition to compliance, also involved in the response is a relinquishment of parts of the self (i.e., judgment, knowledge) and an acceptance as real something the testee knows to be unreal. This aspect of the score touches on Winnicott's (1960) discussion of the relationship between self-development and symbol formation. According to Winnicott, with the mother's repeated success in greeting the infant's spontaneous gestures, experiences become imbued with realness, and an inchoate capacity to use symbols begins. Here Winnicott envisions two possible lines of devel-

opment. In the first, with "good enough" mothering and empathic responsiveness to spontaneous gestures, reality is introduced almost magically
and does not clash with the infant's omnipotence. With a belief in reality,
omnipotence can be gradually relinquished: "The true self has a spontaneity, and this has been joined up with the world's events" (Winnicott, 1960,
p. 146). An illusion of omnipotent creating and controlling can be enjoyed,
and the illusory element can be gradually recognized through play and
imagination. The basis for the symbol, then, is both the infant's spontaneity
and the created and cathected external object. That is, symbol formation
evolves from actions and sensations joining the infant and the mother.
Conversely, when the infant's actions and sensations serve to separate
rather than join subject and object, symbol formation is inhibited. In this
second line of development, which involves mothering that is "not good
enough," the mother's adaptation to the infant's spontaneous gestures is
deficient, and symbol formation either fails to develop or "becomes
broken up" (p. 147). In this case the infant reacts to environmental demands *passively*, through imitation and with accompanying feelings of
unreality. The passivity and the feelings of unreality observed by Winnicott are quite similar to what Rapaport conceptualized as a loss of ego
autonomy with a resultant enslavement to environmental stimuli. While
Rapaport would conceive of this condition in terms of the ego and drive
forces and Winnicott in terms of the self and inner experience, what both
theorists appear to be describing is a state of affairs in which the development of selfhood has been critically interfered with and in which the
individual is therefore unable to maintain distance from the environment.

The color arbitrary response also reflects a loss of detachment and
perspective. It is as if in fashioning such a response the testee has suspended a more objective, critical, and judgmental attitude. For individuals
in whom there is a loss of perspective, life events are not critically
examined or placed in context, but rather are seen and experienced only
in terms of their most obvious and immediate qualities. The present
dominates and the significance of the past and of the future fades.

Involved in the color arbitrary response, then, is compliance, a relinquishment of parts of the self, cognitive passivity marked by a loss of
detachment and perspective, and nagging feelings of unreality. These
same processes that underlie the color arbitrary score are also involved in
the "false self."

Winnicott (1961) conceived of the false self as a defensive structure
aimed at hiding and protecting the true self by means of compliance with
external demands. Its origins are found in the infant's seduction into a
compliant relationship with a nonempathic mother. When a mother substitutes something of herself for the infant's spontaneous gestures (e.g.,
her anxieties over separation in response to the infant's need to search and

explore), the infant experiences traumatic disruptions of his developing sense of self. When such impingements are a core feature of the mother–child relationship, the infant will attempt to defend himself by developing a second reactive personality organization—the false self. The false self vigilantly monitors and adapts to the conscious and unconscious needs of the mother and in so doing provides a protective exterior behind which the true self is afforded the privacy it requires to maintain its integrity. The false self, as such, thus becomes a core feature of the personality organization and functions as a caretaker, managing life so that an inner self might not experience the threat of annihilation resulting from excessive pressure on it to develop according to another's needs.

False-self features were especially prominent in the following case. A 37-year-old, married, and childless woman was referred for an assessment and treatment following a relatively brief period of hospitalization. One month previously she had an intense and acute depressive episode involving feelings of depersonalization and frightening suicidal ideation. While the patient was moderately depressed for several years, this acute episode followed a heated confrontation with her husband in which he admitted his unwillingness to have a child but then refused to discuss the issue further. She experienced his reluctance as banishing her to a life of emptiness and meaninglessness.

The third oldest of four children, the patient described her childhood in terms of hardships, sufferings and unhappiness, emphasizing her sense of herself as a large, ugly child, her sense of being saddled by family responsibilities, and her overriding fear of her father's violence.

She graduated from teachers' college and accepted a position in a small community teaching learning-disabled children. Although an accomplished and well-regarded teacher, she experienced her work as demanding and depleting. Unable to tolerate aloneness, she dated constantly but felt that male interest in her was exclusively sexual. In her sixth year of teaching she began to see her husband-to-be. He was a married, successful businessman, 23 years her senior, with three adolescent youngsters. They saw each other on a regular basis for several years, and in contrast to her previous relationships, she felt loved and not used by him and genuinely loving toward him. One year following his wife's death from cancer, at his insistence, they were married.

She perceived her marriage as a new start in life and went about disclaiming and disowning previous aspects of her life. Despite valuing her job, she stopped working, converted to her husband's religion, and broke off contact with old friends, electing instead to move entirely into her husband's circle of relationships. In essence, she attempted to forge a new identity, one totally different from and independent of her past.

Throughout the five years of marriage she found herself becoming progressively more depressed and increasingly dissatisfied with her husband. As her earlier feelings of loneliness returned, she experienced a rekindling of her desire to have a baby and conceived of having a child as her one salvation in life. As noted previously, her husband's grudging refusal to have a child precipitated her hospitalization.

Psychological testing revealed a depressive personality organized at a high borderline level. Basing his assessment, in part, on three FCarb responses on her Rorschach test, the examiner highlighted her false-self features.

The opening phase of treatment was dominated by her depressive affect and her unrelenting preoccupation with having a baby. Without a baby or the hope of having one, she felt that life was meaningless, she was worthless, and suicide was a viable alternative.

In time, the patient's depressiveness began to abate and give way to more focused anger and disappointment with her husband. Mobilized by the anger, she could then introduce changes into her life, including the decision to pursue further training in music. Despite these gains and her greater sense of control over his life, her singular insistence with having a baby persisted.

In the seventeenth month of treatment an assignment in one of her music classes had a profound impact on treatment and highlighted the pervasiveness of her false self. She was asked to select an old photo with important personal meaning and then compose a series of musical pieces that conveyed that meaning. She chose a photo of herself, taken when she was four, in which she was sitting contentedly in a rocking chair gazing affectionately at a favorite doll. She brought the photo to several sessions. While recalling earlier experiences and feelings prompted by the picture, she mentioned, without affect and almost in passing, that when she was twenty-one years old, during her first year of teaching, she had a baby out of wedlock and soon after delivery had given the baby up for adoption.

As that experience was reviewed in depth it became clear that the loss, both of the baby and of parts of herself related to the baby, was intimately connected with her later preoccupation with wanting a child. Specific to the false self was the patient's need to maintain in privacy and not entrust to her therapist an intimate and meaningful experience—a part of her true self, if you will—that was dynamically related to her present behavior.

INANIMATE MOVEMENT SCORE (m)

An additional score I have found quite useful, especially as a reflection of subjectively felt distress, is the m score.

Piotrowski (1947) described the score as representing a role in life the

testee desired but experienced as unattainable because of external difficulties and internal inhibitions. Piotrowski further suggested that the score
reflects self-observation, intelligence, and an unwillingness to relinquish or
alter goals originating in an earlier period of development.

Klopfer and Kelley (1942) attributed a very different meaning to the m
score. They assert that the score expressed inner promptings that are
experienced by the individual as dangerous and uncontrollable. Despite
apparent differences as to the feeling tone of the urges, both authors agree
that the response expresses drives that the subject feels incapable of doing
anything about. Schachtel (1966) refers to this experiential state as that of
the "impotent spectator."

An especially astute description of the m response, and one in keeping
with my own clinical observations, is found in the work of Mayman (1977).
According to Mayman, kinesthetic memories that contain core experiences of selfhood find their way into all movement responses, including
inanimate movement. Although most tension states expressed in animate
and inanimate movement are neither unfamiliar nor alien, there are some
that are infantile, archaic, and linked to impulses that normally would be
fully repressed. Of all the movement responses, the m score expresses
those tensions that are the least ego syntonic. Thus, for Mayman (1977),
"the little m is a metaphoric expression of forces which seem impersonal,
not subject to personal control. These forces intrude on the self, they come
at one from outside" (p. 240).

Viewing the m response as reflective of a failure in repression, with the
unrepressed impulse spilling over into awareness in the form of subjective
tension, has much inferential meaning. Because the testee offering the
response to some degree feels out of control, he or she typically is
accessible to therapeutic intervention. Further, contact with the individual's subjective experience can often be established around these feelings of
inner tension. The content within which the inanimate movement response is included usually reflects the sense of failing defenses or else
depicts the nature of the impulse the individual is struggling with. Thus,
there are references to "collapsing," "coming apart," and "breaking
apart," which express faltering controls, and such responses as "dripping
blood," "exploding flames," and "erupting lava," which may be taken as
indicative of difficulties with aggression.

REFLECTION AND MIRROR RESPONSES

Although I have not included these types of responses under formal
scoring, the reflection and mirror responses (e.g., a bear seeing its reflection in the water, a woman standing in front of a mirror) are an important

source of information. With the increased attention accorded both the concept of narcissism and the narcissistic patient, Rorschach theorists are looking to these responses as expressions of some aspect of narcissism.

Basing his work on a series of studies with acting out and narcissistic personalities, Exner (1974) developed an index for assessing egocentricity. The index,/ which consists of the proportion of reflection and pair responses to the total number of responses, was found to relate to intense self-absorption and either overly high or excessively low self-esteem (Exner, Wylie, and Bryant, 1974).

Other authors (Urist, 1977; Kwawer, 1980; Ipp, 1986) have conceptualized reflection and mirroring responses as indicating a relatively early stage of relatedness in which the other exists as an extension of the self for the sole intent of confirming and enhancing the self. Relatedness, at this level, is defined as an extension of one's need state.

These two conceptions of the reflection and mirror responses are quite compatible, for as Freud (1914) noted, there is an intimate relationship between level of self-esteem and quality of object relation. I have observed that patients with compelling needs to be confirmed and validated, who relate themselves to others on a narcissistic basis, tend to establish in treatment what Kohut (1971) refers to as a "mirroring transference." In my experience, Kohut's recommendations for the technical handling of these patients are most useful.

SYMMETRY REACTIONS

Not to be confused with the reflection responses are those remarks directed toward the symmetry of the blots. These are not responses per se, but simply comments in which the testee expresses his or her attunement to the symmetry. In this instance, symmetry may be viewed as part of an overall feeling regarding a sense of balance or imbalance in the card. Noting symmetry introduces a sense of balance, but it is a premature balance. Possibilities generated by the imbalance or by providing balance through the response (e.g., the movement response) are excluded. Therefore, individuals who comment about the symmetry tend to have an excessive need for external order and clarity, struggle with ambiguity and unfamiliarity, and are characterologically inhibited and restricted.

A 29 year old account executive with an MBA applied for a position as head of the advertising department in a newly formed electronics company. The position required an individual with much creativity who could work in a relatively unstructured situation. In part because of the testee's continued attunement to the symmetry of the cards and his concomitant tendency to become hypercritical unless he found perfect forms, the examiner questioned his having the requisite capacities for the position. The examiner further questioned as to whether he would be comfortable and satisfied in such a position.

PERSPECTIVE REACTIONS

On occasion, patients in describing a percept will introduce the notion of a perspective in which they assume a particular position in relation to their percept. Examples include the following: "Oh my goodness, what an ugly creature. He's standing over me and I'm looking up at him"; "From above, it looks like a bat in flight"; "An insect being looked at from a top view." In some instances, such as Card IV, introducing perspective makes for a better-fitting response; it accounts for slight incongruities and minor distortions in the stimulus. More often, however, it is my observation that perspective indicates a defensive maneuver and an object relational stance. Thus, individuals who view their percepts from above tend not only to maintain others at a distance but do so by placing themselves above others. Conversely, those patients who view their percepts from below tend to demean and degrade themselves and place themselves in a lesser, subservient position.

SUMMARY

In this chapter I have reviewed select scores and their meaning. The scores were selected because of their relevance to more recent formulations and concepts issuing from psychoanalytic theory. In addition to specific scores, I also discussed the testee's reaction to the symmetry of the cards and the introduction of perspective to a response.

8

The Analysis of Content

There is no area of Rorschach analysis that has been more misused and more underused than content. For too many years Rorschach interpretation meant the interpretation of content, and so-called content analysis consisted of a poorly trained, beleaguered examiner unsystematically offering his or her own associations to the patient's responses and then regarding the personal associations as meaningful inferences. The resultant testing report would thus consist of a series of loose-fitting, internally inconsistent impressions, presented as facts, from which one could not disentangle the examiner's preferences, values, and dynamics from those of the patient. Members of the academic and scientific communities, already distrustful of and antagonistic toward the Rorschach test, seized upon these practices and pronounced the instrument unreliable, invalid, and lacking in scientific respectability.

In an attempt to restore respectability to the Rorschach test, many theorists and investigators tended to shy away from assessing content of responses. With the Rorschach test viewed as an instrument best suited to assess formal variables (scores, ratios, etc.), content was either ignored or approached exclusively in terms of categories that could be scored. This counterreaction too was unfortunate. The content categories are important; however, their usefulness is limited in that they are abstractions that are a step removed from the response and the person offering the response.

To exclude content altogether, in the service of psychometric refinement, is to ignore an immensely rich and valuable source of information. Even though more structural approaches to the Rorschach test have clearly proven their mettle, this does not mean that the Rorschach test cannot be viewed from an experiential perspective too.

The rationale for a more experiential perspective has been well stated by Mayman (1977).

> When a person is asked to spend an hour immersing himself in a field of impressions where amorphousness prevails and where strange and even alien forms may appear, he will set in motion a reparative process the aim of which is to replace formlessness with reminders of the palpable real world. He primes himself to recall, recapture, reconstitute his world as he knows it, with people, animals and things which fit most naturally into the ingrained expectancies which he has learned to structure his phenomenal world" [p. 17].

Schachtel (1966) has also written of the experiential dimensions of the Rorschach test; however, because of his interest in perception, he focused his attention exclusively on the various stimulus properties of the cards (color, form, wholeness of the card, etc.). To assess not only the structure but also the substance of the testee's phenomenological world, as Mayman has elucidated, requires a consideration of the content of the responses.

I was especially impressed with the potential richness of content as a vehicle for expressing meaningful experiential themes when I had the opportunity to review a set of Rorschach protocols obtained from a group of individuals who had immigrated to North America within the past five years. Although they had emigrated from various countries and represented different personality makeups, striking among this nonpatient group was a compelling need to create and then find in the blots images and percepts that conveyed a sense of familiarity. For this group, familiarity involved offering percepts that were clearly and explicitly linked to their country of origin. Representative responses included the following: "I can see the roof of a church like the church I attended as a child back home in Poland;" "A leaf I remember from Viet Nam that has been eaten by some insect. It still has its basic shape;" "Back home in Pakistan I saw a volcano. This reminds me of the volcano and the lava is coming out."

A review of the structural qualities of these percepts (i.e., roof of a church, a leaf, a volcano) and their respective locations indicates that each was of acceptable form level and that each, in part, was prompted by the particular configuration of the stimulus. Yet, to judge from the nature of the elaborations and embellishments, something of more personal meaning and significance was also at play, and this added feature found expression in the contents of the responses.

If content is to be considered as a basic source of information and a viable springboard for the inferential process and if we hope to avoid the plaguing misuses and abuses of the past, then it is imperative that it be approached in a thoughtful and systematic way. With content data, issues of reliability and validity cannot be disregarded; nonetheless, such issues need not exclude or minimize the clinical richness of the material.

Clearly, a middle path is needed and groundwork for such a path is to be found in the work of Mayman (1977). Respecting empathic intuitiveness as a valid source of information and insisting on theoretical soundness, Mayman has outlined a more systematic approach to content that combines an appreciation of the fruitfulness of the data with general principles of validity that fit the clinical situation. As noted in Chapter 4, Administration and Scoring, he has proposed a conceptual structure consisting of five dimensions, including content, for evaluating the human movement response. Three of these dimensions or components—the contribution of fantasy, kinesthesia and its relation to self experience, and object representation—can be extended to the content of nonmovement responses as well.

In addition to Mayman's contributions, a review of such well-established research scales as those of Holt (1977) and Blatt and associates (1976), as well as more recent ones, including those of Kwawer (1980), P. Lerner and H. Lerner (1980), Coonerty (1986) and Ipp (1986), reveals that investigators have employed content indices to operationalize more abstract and elusive theoretical concepts. Interestingly, these newer scales have been devised, in general, with the intent of investigating more experiential concepts. That content rather than formal scores have been used suggests that many theorists are viewing content as an especially sensitive expression of experiential themes.

The analysis of content is presented here in the following manner: I first present general guidelines for approaching content analysis; then I integrate the work of Mayman with that of various researchers. More specifically, I will use Mayman's three dimensions, as specified earlier, as an organizational framework within which I will place particular content indices that have been found useful in research. Several of the research scales from which the indices are taken, together with a review of the studies in which the scales were employed, are presented in Chapters 13 (Rorschach Assessment of Defense: II Recent Measures) and 14 (Developmental Object Relations).

GENERAL GUIDELINES

1. Although the content categories do yield important information, a complete analysis of content involves systematically scrutinizing a proto-

col, response by response. In using content the entire verbalization, not just the response proper, constitutes the basic data, therefore, content analysis is particularly dependent on obtaining as verbatim a transcript as possible.

2. A particularly rich source of data and useful place to begin content analysis are the elaborations and specifications added to a response that are not intrinsic to the blot. Such embellished responses are potentially rich with meaning.

3. The criteria applied to inferences drawn from content are no different from those applied to all other inferences (see Chapter 10); however, here it is particularly important that the criteria be applied stringently. I have found the following criteria especially helpful: (a) the examiner is able to trace the inference back to the basic data from which it arose and explicate each step of the inferential process; (b) the inference is supported by other test data; (c) the inference is internally consistent with the overall picture of the patient that is emerging from the testing.

4. A useful concept to hold in mind when approaching content analysis is "internal object relation." Increasingly, psychoanalytic theorists are emphasizing the distinction between internalized object relations and relations between the self and objects in the external world. As implied in the term, an internal object relation refers to the inner representation of a relationship that had once existed in the outer world. While internal object relations derive from the internalization of early object relations, they exert, in turn, a considerable influence on current object relations. An internal object relation has three components: a self-representation, a representation of the object (object representation), and a representation of the interaction between the two.

MAYMAN'S THREE DIMENSIONS APPLIED TO ALL CONTENTS

Contribution of Fantasy

Whereas the movement response requires the availability of a fantasy life one can dip into to help enliven the response, movement is not the only response that draws upon fantasy. Certain form responses can be equally rich, vivid, compelling, and lively. Common to these responses is a prevailing tendency to embellish a percept with affective and associative elaboration.

Embellished responses are potentially laden with meaning. For many people they reflect an interest and investment in the task, a willingness to go beyond merely what is called for. As well, in the embellishment or added specification something of dynamic importance for the subject is often being expressed. For example, to see the popular bat on Card V as a "huge vampire bat in full flight ready to descend upon a helpless victim" compellingly hints at significant trends in the personality.

While the content, as illustrated in this example, may be charged with personal meaning and should be understood and interpreted on an individual basis, Schachtel (1966) identified specific elaborations that he found to have more general application. He takes references to size (e.g., "large," "enormous," "tiny,") as reflective of the testee's own sense of importance and power, to aggressive content as indicative of a desire to inflict or a fear of hurt and injury, and to solidness or fragility as suggestive of the individual's integrity of self.

The tendency to embellish responses may also express an openness to different types of experiences, a capacity to relax tight controls and strict adherence to reality, and a freedom to indulge in what Freud (1900) referred to as "primary process thinking." Holt's (1977) manual for assessing primary process manifestations and their controls is an excellent guide for conceptualizing and organizing particular contents. Holt outlines and details content reflective of and referable to the various stages of psychosexual development, draws important distinctions among forms of aggression based on specific contents, and elaborates specific defensive operations inferable solely from content.

A descriptive overview of Holt's scoring system is presented here. I am not suggesting that Holt's scale—or even the specific indices—should be used for clinical testing; rather, I am suggesting that a familiarity with the ways in which Holt has conceptualized various contents can provide the clinical tester with a way of thinking about and approaching content analysis.

Holt's (1968b) Measure of Primary Process Manifestations

Holt's system calls for the scoring of four sets of variables: content indices of primary process, formal indices of primary process, indices of control and defense, and overall ratings.

The content part of the manual is concerned with drive representations. A major distinction is drawn between responses reflecting drives with implied libidinal wishes and those with aggressive aims. The libidinal category is further subdivided into subcategories corresponding to the developmental stages of psychosexual development. The aggressive category, which includes responses with hostile or destructive ideation, is likewise subdivided; these subcategories are established on the basis of whether it is the subject (aggressor), the object (victim), or the result (aftermath) that is emphasized in the destructive action or process mentioned in the response.

Cutting across the libidinal–aggressive division is a distinction representing two degrees of closeness to the primary process pole. Level 1 is accorded those responses that are primitive, blatantly drive-dominated, socially unacceptable, and focal to a drive-relevant organ. Responses reflecting a more civilized, contained, or socially acceptable content constitute level 2 responses.

The following categories from Holt's (1977) manual rely exclusively on content and are presented with representative examples:

Libidinal Content
Level 1 (crude, direct, primitive)
   Oral receptive—mouth, breasts, sucking, famine
   Oral aggressive—teeth, cannibalism, biting, parasites
   Anal—buttocks, feces, hemorrhoids
   Sexual—sexual organs, ejaculation, intercourse
   Exhibitionistic-voyeuristic—nudity, exhibiting
   Sexual ambiguity—same sex kissing, person with breasts and a penis
Level 2 (indirect, controlled, socialized
   Oral receptive—stomach, kissing, drinking, drunks, food
   Oral aggressive—animals feared because of their biting (crabs, spiders, alligators); verbal aggression (arguing)
   Anal—intestines, toilet, disgust, dirt
   Sexual—kissing, romance, sexual organs of flowers
   Exhibitionistic-voyeuristic—undergarments, leering, peering, observing, prancing
   Sexual ambiguity—transvestism, cross dressing

Aggressive Content
Level 1 (murderous or clearly sadomasochistic aggression)
   Attack (sadistic aggression)—vivid sadistic fantasies, annihilation of person or animals, torture
   Victim of aggression (masochistic)—extreme victimization, extreme helplessness, suicide
   Results of aggression (aftermath)—decayed, putrefied, mutilated elements; catastrophe
Level 2 (more socially tolerated hostility or aggression)
   Attack—explosions, fighting, fire, frightening figures, weapons, claws
   Victim of aggression—person or animal in pain or wounded, frightened persons or animals, figures or objects in precarious balance
   Results of aggression—injured or deformed persons or animals, parts missing, blood, aftermath of storms or fires

A second part of the scoring system in which content is evaluated is the section on control and defense. Holt conceptualizes these scores as indices of the manner in which primary process is managed. Here, what is important is not only the response but also the way in which the response is delivered and any evaluative comments surrounding the response.

Remoteness

Remoteness conveys the notion of distancing. In this system the scores are considered ways of distancing impulses or wishes; however, a close look at the categories would suggest that they also reflect a tendency to distance one's objects.

Ethnic   The figure seen is depicted as part of an ethnic group different from that of the testee (e.g., "Russian dancers," "Japanese wrestlers").

Geography The figure seen is depicted as coming from a different and distant location (e.g., "African women," "a space man from Mars").

Time   The figure seen is distanced by placing him or her in the past or in the future (e.g., "A man from the 21st century," "a court jester").

Depiction The main figure seen is depicted as in a painting, drawing, or sculpture (e.g., "a bust of two little girls," "a cartoon drawing of two men").

Context

The context or setting in which the response is presented is scored. The context seems to involve the subject's attempt to account for the primary process aspects of the response.

Cultural   The response is placed in the context of a ritual, custom, mythology, or other social reality (e.g., "naked women dancing who are performing a tribal ritual," "a man covered in black and red; he's a circus performer").

Intellectual With the inclusion of scientific, professional, or technical facts or knowledge, the response has a strong intellectual flavor (e.g., "a dissection of the spinal cord," "a slightly inflamed tonsil").

Humorous   Some elaborations serve to place the response in a humorous or fanciful context (e.g., "Insects at a convention," "two people with both male and female parts—I suppose a reunion of hermaphrodites").

Miscellaneous Defenses

Negation   This involves a denial of an impulse and is manifested in two ways. In one, the disavowal is smoothly blended into the response (e.g., "virgin," "angel") whereas in the other the response, or aspects of the response, are couched in negative terms (e.g., "two animals but they are not dangerous," "these figures are not angry").

Minimization   Here, drive-laden material is included in the response but in a reduced or nonthreatening way. This includes changing a human or animal figure into a caricature or cartoon figure (e.g., "the fist of a child," "a caricature of a man with a gun," "a cartoon lion").

Repudiation   A response is given and then retracted, or the individual denies having ever given the response (e.g., "Two angry people; no, no, wait a moment, they aren't angry but concerned").

Kinesthesia and Its Relation to Self-Experience

A second aspect of the movement response identified by Mayman yet applicable to a broad array of responses is kinesthesia, or the action component of a response. For Mayman, those kinesthesias that find their way into a movement response are drawn from a repertoire of kinesthetic memories, and involved in these memories are core self-experiences.

I believe that all kinesthesias on a record, not simply those expressed in human movement, are a potentially rich source of information and may provide clues to vital self-experiences, including subjective feelings of selfhood and of object relating.

In a recently obtained Rorschach record the following kinesthesias appeared: "pieces broken apart," "hanging on to," "split in the middle," "torn skin," "ripping away," "hands up," "struggling," "mouths open," and "still attached." A careful analysis of these kinesthesias indicates that they fall into two distinct clusters. One cluster (i.e., the first four kinesthesias listed), which convey a feeling state of heightened inner tension, painful distress, and excruciating discomfort, may be understood as reflecting a subjective sense of self that is experienced as split, torn, and fragmented. The other cluster (the last five kinesthesias listed) appears more object relational and seems to express a more oral mode of relating involving issues of dependency, clinging, and symbiosis.

Several investigators, independently of Mayman, have recently devised content-based developmental object relations scales and have employed specific kinesthesias, manifest in all responses, to indicate stages in the unfolding of selfhood through differentiation from a primary mothering figure. In general, these scales represent attempts to systematically apply Mahler's (1968) theory of separation/individuation to Rorschach data.

To study early disturbances in the object relations of borderline patients, Kwawer (1980) developed a scale consisting of various points that represent early stages of levels of relatedness. An initial stage, which he calls "narcissistic mirroring," is represented by responses in which mirrors or reflections play a prominent role. Responses at this level are understood as expressing a state of self-absorption in which the other is experienced solely as an extension of the self and used for the exclusive purpose of mirroring or enhancing the self. A second stage, entitled "symbiotic merger," is represented by responses that indicate a powerful push toward merger, fusion, and reuniting (e.g., "Two women, like Siamese twins, *attached* to each other."). A third stage of interpersonal differentiation includes "separation and division" responses. The Rorschach imagery here is reminiscent of the sequence of cell division (e.g., "These two things were once connected but *broke apart*," "It's an animal going from one *dividing* into two. Like it's *breaking away* into two objects."). The fourth and final stage, "metamorphosis and transformation," is the level in which there is a very early and rudimentary sense of self. The incipient selfhood of this stage is manifest in such Rorschach responses as "fetuses" and "embryos" and in themes of transformation and change (e.g., "a caterpillar *turning* into a butterfly").

Another example of the creative use of kinesthesias to reflect levels of selfhood and object relating is represented in the work of Coonerty (1986). Using Mahler's descriptions as guidelines, Coonerty devised a measure for identifying and categorizing Rorschach responses that reflect concerns and issues associated with the prestage of separation and with each of the subphases of the separation/individuation process proper. Rather than review Coonerty's scale in its entirety, I will detail here only those indices that involve kinesthesias.

For Coonerty, concerns arising from the "early differentiation subphase" are reflected in Rorschach imagery of merging (e.g., "These are two girls but they seem to be joined at the bottom"), engulfment (i.e., "A person but he's being enveloped by the fog), and hatching (e.g., "a genie coming out of a bottle").

Responses indicative of rapprochement issues include figures, human or animal, that are seen in one of the following types of struggles: separating or coming together with resulting damage to one or both (e.g., "A person drowning with her hand up. This person is trying to save her but will be pulled under."), engaged in a push–pull struggle (e.g., "Two dogs facing each other but pointing in opposite directions"), and enmeshed or stuck and unable to separate (e.g., "Two rats stuck in the mud and they can't get their feet free."). Responses in which the form of the figure changes (e.g., "Two people talking, no, they look more like monkeys playing") are also indicative of rapprochement.

Ipp (1986) developed a scale, based on the earlier work of Urist (1977), for assessing the capacity to experience and conceive of one's self within one's own world and in relation to significant internal objects. The scale consists of five major categories and two subcategories; of particular relevance to this discussion of the use of kinesthesias is her category "catastrophic disintegration." Belonging in this category are responses in which there is a sense of annihilation by external forces greater than the self. Inanimate movement and strong agitation generally accompany these percepts (e.g., "planets exploding," "a swirling tornado destroying everything in its path").

Object Representation

A third component of the movement response, according to Mayman, is the figure carrying out the action, the object representational aspect. This component too can be applied to all contents; however, when extended to nonhuman contents, such as animals or natural forces, one has to take into account the type of content used to express the internal object relation. For example, seeing an antagonistic or hostile relationship between two insects reflects a type of interaction; beyond this, however, it also reflects a quality and level of representation.

Understanding the nature of the interaction is usually straightforward; more difficult and challenging is determining those characteristics referable to the self representation and those to the object representation. The following example illustrates this problem. On Card VIII the testee saw "A leaf chewed up by insects and pressed for display. The color shading would look different in fall." If in this response the testee's self-representation is "the leaf," then one might conjecture that he senses himself being attacked, devoured, exposed, and put on display by demeaned and depreciated others whom he experiences as less than totally human. On the other hand, if the self is represented in the "insects," then in this instance one might suggest that he senses himself as lowly, parasitic, hungry, and exploitive and perceives others as helpless victims of his exploitive nature.

Largely because of Mayman's (1967) pioneering attempts to apply the concept of object representation to Rorschach data, investigators have devised Rorschach measures aimed at evaluating personality variables theoretically related to object representation. Here again, these researchers have tended to look to content.

Representative of this line of research is the work of P. Lerner and H. Lerner (1980) on the assessment of primitive defenses. Basing their work on the theoretical formulations of Kernberg (1975, 1976), Lerner and Lerner developed a scoring manual designed to evaluate the primitive defenses of the borderline patient. Their system calls for the human figure in a Rorschach response, either static or in motion, being evaluated in terms of the action ascribed, the way in which the figure is described, and the precise figure seen. Several of the defenses were operationalized exclusively in terms of content indices, and those will be reviewed here.

One defense defined in content-related terms is splitting. Since splitting involves a variety of separations, including a division of drives, affects, and object representations, Lerner and Lerner viewed the tendency to describe human figures in polar opposite ways as the Rorschach manifestation of this defense. Thus, the following are taken as Rorschach expressions of splitting: describing parts of a human figure in opposite terms (e.g., "A giant, his lower part is dangerous but his top part, his head, is benign"); including in a response two figures described in opposite ways (e.g., "Two figures. He's mean and shouting at her. She's angelic and just standing there and taking it"); and either tarnishing an implicitly idealized figure (e.g., "a headless angel") or enhancing an implicitly devalued one (e.g., "a devil with a warm smile").

A second defense indicated by and reflected in content is devaluation. This refers to a tendency to depreciate, tarnish, or lessen the importance of one's inner and outer objects. In assessing the Rorschach manifestation of this defense, three aspects of the human figure response are evaluated. The first involves the degree to which the humanness of the figure is retained. For example, waiters or clowns are considered more human than monsters, mythological figures, or robots. A second dimension involves a temporal–spacial consideration. Contemporary human percepts set in a current and close locale are scored higher than are those figures from either the past or the future and placed in a distant setting. The final aspect of a human figure response involves the severity of depreciation as conveyed in the affective description. Figures described in more primitive, blatant, socially unacceptable ways are scored lower than are those that are described in negatively tinged but more civilized and socially acceptable ways.

To evaluate the use of the defense of idealization in a human figure response, the same dimensions used to assess devaluation are applied. In this instance, however, the investigators were concerned with the ways in which subjects enhanced or exalted their human figures. For example, distortion of human forms under the influence of this defense would involve seeing such enhanced figures as warriors, kings, or famous leaders (e.g., "Winston Churchill"). Similarly, affective descriptions are judged as to the degree to which the figure is inflated (e.g., "nice people," "the strongest warrior imaginable").

Although the scale developed by Lerner and Lerner was confined to an evaluation of the human figure, the criteria devised have been extended to all content by Cooper and Arnow (1986) and Collins (1983).

SUMMARY

A relatively neglected area of Rorschach inquiry has been the analysis of content. Historically, content had been unsystematically approached from the perspective of symbolism, and this led to gross misuses and a subsequent distrust of the analysis of content.

A more recent approach to content, based on newer and more experience-near models in psychoanalysis, is found in the work of Mayman (1977). Viewing content as a sampling of an individual's representational world, Mayman has identified five components of the human movement response that provide a conceptual structure for assessing self and object relational experiences. Three of these dimensions—the contribution of fantasy, kinesthesia and its relation to self-experience, and object representation—can be fruitfully applied to all content without compromising theoretical underpinnings.

Coincident with Mayman's work has been the emergence of several developmental object relations and defense scales that have used content indices to operationalize more abstract concepts. The approach to content taken here involves an integration of Mayman's work with that of current research. Specifically, three of Mayman's dimensions are used as an organizational framework within which research-derived content indices are placed.

9

The Analysis of Sequence

Like the content of a Rorschach record, the sequence of responses represents a relatively neglected area of Rorschach inquiry. Although more experienced examiners look to sequence as a meaningful source of information, few authors have discussed the dimension in depth. This is not surprising, for in contrast to the formal scores, the analysis of sequence is more difficult to systematize and more difficult to generalize about.

Schachtel (1966) regards the sequence of responses as an especially important dimension, noting that it is the aspect of the Rorschach test that is most reflective of the individual's understanding and subjective definition of the task. He suggests that sequence reflects the testee's approach, or lack of it, to the test and that the approach is based on how the person experiences, comprehends, and feels about the task. Schachtel places sequence on a continuum of rigid versus loose and then infers the attitude underlying various points on the continuum. For example, a more rigid approach—one in which the same sequence is employed on each card—could be indicative of an attitude of heightened conscientiousness and obedience in which excessive authority is ascribed to the tests and the examiner and in which the testee submits to this assumed authority. This approach contrasts with a looser one as indicated by several sequences. In this latter instance, one could infer that the testee ascribes less authority to the test and is then able to approach the material in a more flexible and self-directed manner. Schachtel also attempts to determine, through an analysis of sequence, the testee's typical or preferred approach. He then uses this as a base from which to judge deviations. Despite the potential richness of Schachtel's view of sequence, it should be noted that he defines sequence exclusively in terms of the location scores; thus, his perspective is somewhat limited.

Along similar lines, Klopfer et al. (1954) discusses sequence as a sample of the way in which the individual reacts to the world. While he points out that sequence analysis consists of a card by card, response by response, examination, he, like Schachtel, emphasizes formal properties to the relative neglect of thematic content.

Because of the relative paucity of literature available, in this chapter I will offer general considerations regarding sequence analysis based largely on my own clinical experience.

GENERAL CONSIDERATIONS

1. I agree with Klopfer that sequence analysis does involve an evaluation of the entire protocol, card by card and response by response; however, it should also include test attitudes and test behavior, as manifested in the complete verbalization and off-handed comments. Thus, sequence analysis, like other data sources, is dependent on recording the administration as verbatim as possible.

2. An appreciation of the stimulus properties of each card, together with an expectation of likely content to be offered to a particular card or to a specific area in a card, enhances sequence analysis. For example, certain blots (I, IV, V, VI) lend themselves to being perceived as a whole whereas others (II, III, VII, VIII, IX, X) are more "broken" and invite being seen in a more piecemeal fashion. Schachtel suggests viewing the sequence of location scores as reflective of the testee's approach to the task. For example, if a testee maintains the same approach on every card, this could well indicate rigidity; by contrast, altering the approach to reflect the differing properties of the cards would indicate flexibility.

3. Sequence analysis is especially helpful for observing progressive and regressive shifts in personality organization, and these shifts can be reflected in formal scores, content, or a combination of both. Two models of psychopathology are presented in psychoanalytic theory. The older "conflict model" emphasized impulses pressing for discharge, defenses evoked, and the interplay between the two. The more recent "developmental arrest" or "structural deficit" model focuses on impairments in the personality structure as a consequence of faulty development. Herein, the individual is thought to be vulnerable to marked fluctuations and disruptions in personality functioning.

From the perspective of the conflict model, sequence analysis provides a unique opportunity for observing the appearance of conflict, ways in which the individual attempts to resolve that conflict, and the relative degree of success or failure in the resolution. For example, if on Card II the testee first sees "two bears fighting," then in the same area sees "two lambs grazing," and finally turns to the center white area and sees a "delta winged jet plane," then one might infer that unacceptable aggressive urges are dealt with by reaction formation and regression and that such efforts are relatively successful. By contrast, were a subject to respond to the whole of Card II with "a damaged face with blood," offer several other percepts, and then say, "I just can't get that face out of my mind, it bothers me," one, in this instance, might infer ineffective defensive efforts and a failure of resolution.

In terms of the structural deficit model, sequence analysis allows the examiner a close-up view of fluctuations in functioning; to be noted are the experiences that disrupt functioning, the areas of personality affected, and the individual's ways of attempting to deal with the disruption. If for example, on Card III a testee were to say, "It's two women arguing, yelling at each other, no, wait a second. It's one woman looking at herself in a mirror, she's yawning, just woke up," one might infer that the testee tends to see relationships as hostile and malevolent and, in reaction, withdraws and retreats into self-absorption and self-isolation. Or, on Card IX, were a female patient to see the bottom reddish area as a "dead fetus with its umbilical cord wrapped around its neck" and then offer subsequent responses in which the form level was significantly poor, then one might infer that under the impact of highly charged, affect-laden material with possibly personal meaning, the patient's reality testing suffers.

As noted, shifts in personality functioning are reflected in the formal scores, the content, or in the interaction between them. Schachtel (1966) has emphasized the sequence of location scores while Klopfer et al. (1954) have called attention to the sequence of all the scores, especially the determinants (e.g., the sequential use of color). Of the various formal scores, I have found the sequence of form level scores and the sequence of responses involving a deviant verbalization of particular usefulness. Examining shifts in form level ratings assists the examiner in assessing not only reality testing considerations but also the integrity of the defensive structure. Thus, a progressive lowering of form level ratings on several cards would indicate increasingly poor reality testing as well as basic failure in defensive efforts. In contrast, marked but more random fluctuations in form level within a card would suggest weaknesses in the defensive structure with alternations between regression and recovery. The persistent instability, rapid vacillations in moods, circumscribed regressive bouts, and variations in reality testing associated with the borderline patient are reflected in their fluctuating form level scores.

Deviant verbalizations (i.e., fabulized combinations, confabulations, etc.) constitute a major departure from the reality of the inkblot; therefore, when one is offered, it is often informative to consider the preceding responses and the subsequent responses. Whereas the former may provide clues as to what factors provoked the deviant response, the latter often reveals the patient's capacity to rebound from such lapses.

Schafer (1954) has suggested that the sequential analysis of imagery, especially when it includes test attitudes, often reveals a continuity of theme from one response to another. Using the metaphor of the dream, he notes that in the continuity of theme the testee tells a story of conflict and then of the resolution of that conflict. He also points out that the sequential analysis of content is particularly illuminating when it focuses on responses that are dramatic and dynamically transparent.

A 27-year-old female patient offered the following responses to Card I: "two women, one's back is to the other," "an ugly insect," "a mask, perhaps a Halloween mask," and "a mannequin in the center." Applying the concept of internal object relations to the sequence of responses suggests the following possible inference: In reaction to a disruptive relationship with her mother, in which she felt rejected, the patient developed low feelings of self-esteem. To protect her precarious esteem and not let others observe her lowered feelings, she hid behind a false self. The false self has left her feeling empty, on display, ready to be defined from outside, and less than a total person.

4. It is often useful to begin sequence analysis with those responses that the examiner finds somewhat jarring or out of place. In reviewing a protocol, an examiner might find himself or herself moved by or drawn to a response either because of formal considerations or content. Sudden drops in form level, the appearance of deviant verbalizations, the unexpected rejection of a card, the offering of a pure color response amid form-based responses, and excessively long reaction times are all examples of appropriate starting points based upon more formal features. With regard to content, I agree with Schafer that the sequential analysis of imagery may begin with those responses in which the content is especially dramatic and compelling and dynamically transparent.

5. Sequence analysis is particularly dependent on a theory of personality and psychopathology that extends beyond and lies outside of test theory. In sequence analysis, one is attempting essentially to draw a dynamic relationship between separate observations that are offered in a temporally continuous manner. In this sense, one is regarding the stream of responses much as one views free associations. The connection drawn between the discrete observations is an inference, a hypothesis if you will. I believe that unless the hypothesis is based on theory, it is either little more than common sense or, worse, a projection from the examiner.

6. As with content analysis, it is vitally important that stringent rules of validity be applied to sequence analysis. The topic of rules of validity is discussed at greater length in the following chapter on the inferential

process; however, it is important to note here that when drawing inferences from the sequence of responses, the examiner must be prepared to identify the Rorschach data that prompted the formulation and the theoretical postulates being employed.

SUMMARY

There is no greater need in the clinical Rorschach literature than for a systematic approach to the analysis of the sequence and content of responses. At one extreme, both areas have been abused and have contributed to the offering of inferences that were little more than wild interpretations. At the other extreme, theorists have either avoided sequence analysis and the analysis of content or have approached each in a highly cautious and tentative way. I have attempted to steer a middle ground, noting that both are immensely rich sources of information but also suggesting that rigorous rules of validity be applied. More so than other aspects of the Rorschach test, the sequence of responses may reveal the dynamic interplay between various facets of the personality organization. Meaningful therapeutic intervention depends on a comprehensive and accurate understanding of the patient, including an appreciation of the latent, inference-based dynamics underlying more observable behavior. In contrast with more structured, static, clinically removed personality inventories and instruments, the Rorschach test potentially can provide a unique glimpse of these underlying forces.

10

The Inference Process

The inferential process consists of the various interpretive steps the examiner takes in transforming the raw material from the Rorschach test (and other tests) into a complete, well-organized, clinically meaningful, informative testing report. It is the most difficult and challenging aspect of the testing, requiring that the examiner have an understanding of test theory, personality theory, and psychopathology. Theory and practice converge at this point. It is important that the examiner develop for himself or herself a testing report outline with implicit subheadings that can serve as reference points for organizing the welter of test data. One possible report format was presented in Chapter 2 and will be applied in this chapter.

In general, the inference process has been neglected in the Rorschach literature. Much has been written of interpretation, but little of the systematic integration of interpretations. Exner (1988, personal communication) is currently developing a computerized decision-making program that details the sequence of steps to be taken in systematically interpreting a protocol; however, his program is based on statistical and psychometric considerations, in contrast with the theoretical perspective taken here.

Inferences drawn from test data are, essentially, tentative hypotheses requiring validation and verification. Accordingly, in the following paragraphs I first review rules of validity that are to be applied to test inferences. I then outline the various steps that constitute the inference process. A Rorschach protocol will be used to illustrate each step.

RULES OF VALIDITY

Shaefer (1954) noted that the starting point for an inference should be the basic Rorschach data: images, scorees, attitudes, and behavior. He developed six criteria for judging what he refers to as the "adequacy of interpretation." His first criterion is that of sufficient *evidence*. Here he suggests that as an initial step the examiner draw as many reasonable implications from a response as possible but that the ultimately accepted interpretations be based on the convergence of several lines of evidence. By implication, the more an inference stands out in isolation from the mass of other test findings, the more cautiously and tentatively it should be regarded.

The criterion of sufficient and converging lines of evidence is illustrated in the following example. To Card IV the patient responded, "It's marshmallow man. Get the sense of you being small and it being large. Can see the body and what looks like a head." The response was understood by the examiner as a self-representation indicating the patient's sense of lacking an inner core and as experiencing himself as lacking coherence, firmness, inner direction, and solidness. Consistent with this interpretation, the patient offered responses in a tentative and noncommittal manner, looked to the examiner for guidance as to what was permissible in the Rorschach situation (e.g., turning the cards), frequently asked if others saw what he saw, empathized with and accommodated to the examiner's need to write everything down, and often apologized to the examiner for his imagined lack of productivity (a projection of his exaggerated ideals).

The second criterion is that of *depth*, meaning the level of personality the inference is addressed to. Schafer suggested that the inference be as deep as the evidence allows, but he also acknowledged that the deeper the interpretation, the further removed it is from the test data.

A third criterion involves specifying, whenever possible, *manifest expressions* of the interpretation, that is, how the interpretation is likely to be expressed in overt behavior. This is a difficult criterion for, as Holt and others have noted, personality assessment and predicting behavior are not synonymous. Whereas the latter involves situational factors, personality assessment typically does not include an evaluation of situational determinants. Nonetheless, the examiner is often called upon to predict to other situations (e.g., the treatment situation, likely reoccurrence of criminal behavior, school placement), and the more he or she is able to couch interpretations in behavioral terms, the more helpful the test report will be.

The *intensity* of the inferred trend is the fourth criterion. Schafer reminds us that the personality trends we infer are widespread and typically apply to the majority of the population. Therefore, to individualize and differentiate the patient from others, it is important to specify the intensity of the inferred characteristic for that particular person. To ignore this criterion is to produce inferences that are gratuitous.

The fifth criterion involves attempting to *hierarchically* place the inference in the overall personality structure. This criterion is based on the assumption that the examiner is using a theory of personality that embraces the concept of hierarchioal layers. For example, such sets of concepts as drive-defense interplay; id, ego, and superego; and unconscious, preconscious, and conscious involve the notion of hierarchy and have a central place in psychoanalytic theory. The concept of hierarchy calls the examiner to integrate his or her inferences into a clinically meaningful whole. Here, one applies well-established dynamic principles to the findings and inferences in order to integrate them. With appropriate integration, seemingly contradictory inferences can be reconciled.

The sixth, and final, criterion relates to specifying in the inference both *adaptive* and *pathological* aspects of the inferred tendency. Too often, testing reports are directed toward demostrating pathological tendencies, to the near exclusion of presenting adaptive strengths. If the examiner outlines the patient's difficulties, he or she should also include instances of how the patient attempts to resolve them. A complete report is a balanced report, one that includes both problems and assets.

My own standards of validity are quite close to those of Schafer, so the following paragraphs simply highlight and expand on several of his criteria. Schafer noted that an inference should begin with and be based on the actual test data. I would extend this to suggest that, with each inference that is included in the test report, the examiner be able to identify the test data that evoked the inference and also be able to explicate the dynamic formulations used in constructing and connecting inferences.

The criterion of intensity was evoked to underline the importance of specifying inferences in a way that individualized the patient. One can individualize a patient in several ways. One way, which I use, is to couch inferences in terms that remain close to the patient's experience. That is, the closer the inference is to the patient's experience and the more the testing report is geared to that experiential level, the greater the likelihood of capturing that which is essential and unique to the patient.

Schafer used the concept of hierarchy to indicate the process whereby findings are first linked by dynamic principles to form first-order inferences that are then themselves interrelated, again by dynamic principles, to form second-order inferences. This progressive interrelating of inferences results in an internally consistent, theoretically sound psychological portrait of the patient. With each step a more complete, refined, and individualized picture emerges. I believe that the emergent picture of each level can be used as an overall criterion to judge the relative merit of any one inference.

STEPS IN THE INFERENCE PROCESS

Step 1—Data Gathering

If test administration, test scoring, and interpretation are all part of the same process, then the inferential process begins with the administering of the Rorschach test and includes adequate inquiry, accurate scoring, and a recording of the proceedings that is complete and as verbatim as possible. As noted previously, the examiner has several potentially rich sources of information about the patient available. One source, the formal scores and their interrelationships, is dependent on accurate and careful scoring. The other sources—thematic content, sequence of responses, the patient–examiner relationship—can best be tapped if a relatively complete transcript is provided. An illustrative scored protocol is presented in Figure 1.

Step 2—Quantitative Analysis

Several highly sophisticated and richly elaborate Rorschach systems have been developed for quantifying the formal scores. Typically, scores are weighted, then tabulated, and compared with other scores in terms of prescribed ratios. The tabulated scores and the ratios become the basic data from which inferences are drawn. Because of its atheoretical roots, strong reliance on normative data, and emphasis on descriptive rather than dynamic inferences, I have tended, despite the richness of this approach, to avoid conducting more extensive quantitative analyses.

Nonetheless, there are several quite informal tabulations that I do make and have found useful. The first involves form level. Here, I first indicate if there are any F- or Fs scores, and then I simply note the number of responses at each level of form level (i.e., Fo, F +, Fw +, etc.). Second, I list all the kinesthesias. I include all kinesthesias, regardless of whether they appear in a human movement response, an animal response, or an inanimate movement response. Finally, I compile a list of all the human figure responses. The three more informal tabulations taken from the protocol presented in Figure 1 are presented in Figure 2.

Step 3—First Order Inferences

With the preparatory work completed, step 3 constitutes the beginning of the actual interpretive work. Here, I carefully review the lists of form level

	(Response)	Inquiry	
I.	(Before beginning the testing he discussed an incident from the day before, and most striking was his vulnerability to narcissistic injury.)		
8″	1. That looks like a spider.	(Spider?) Definiteness about it. Eeriness about it.	W Fw– A
	2. Impression of two gargoyles or two angels.	(else?) (Gargoyles?) When facing away, gargoyles; when facing each other, angels.	D Fw+ (H)
II.	As a whole, a spider		
6″	1. Looks like a butterfly or a moth, like it's coming at me. A big thing, a moth.	(Moth?) Exactly what it looked like. A huge moth. The colorations. (Colorations?) The shades of blackness.	W FC′ A o Confab
III.			
7″	1. Two Africans making pots or something.	(Africans?) 'Cause they were black and figures, like people. (Sex?) I didn't notice	D MC′ (H) P o
	2. Looks like an insect's mouth and face. Very vicious mouth.		D Fw– Ad
	3. This way definitely an insect. This has a vicious mouth too.		D Fw– A

Figure 1

129

	(Response)	Inquiry	
IV. 8"	1. A spaniel dog. It has long fur.	(Fur?) Just looks furry Furry?) Not sure, I suppose the shading.	W Fw+ Ch A
	2. Also a microscopic organism.	(Organism?) Not much of a shape.	W Fv Org.
V. 9"	1. That looks like a flying insect.	(Bat Kite?) I had both ideas so a kite shaped like a bat.	W Fo A P
	2. I don't know. A kite, a bat kite. You want something else?		W Fo Obj. contam.
	3. Maybe a cloud, no, yea, a cloud.	(Cloud) Just the shape of it.	W Fv Cloud
	4. A leaf eaten up by bugs and that's what is left	(Eaten up?) Like silk worms eat a leaf. Rough edges.	W Fw+ Play
VI. 11"	1. Those things that stick to your clothes when you run through the bush. Spanish needles. They can stick you.		W Fw+ Pl.
VII. 9"	1. Now, this way, smoke or something.	(Smoke?) Grey color and it puffs up.	W C' F Smok
	2. Nuclear bomb has been dropped and this is the dark cloud afterwards.	(Cloud?) Mushroom shape and it's grey and dark.	W C' F Cloud

Figure 1 (Cont'd)

130

	(Response)	Inquiry	
VIII. 7"	1. This way a reflection. A bobtail cat and its reflection down here. (Showed it to the examiner.)		D Fo A P reflection
	2. An abstract painting.	(Painting?) Different colors. Other cards were black with a bit of red; these have colors.	W C F Art
IX. 14"	1. I can use my imagination? This is a crystal ball with wizards. This is the base and magical smoke. See their hats. You don't see it, do you? One wizard is good and the other bad. He has control over a person's life.	(Smoke?) It goes with the wizards and looks a bit puffy. (Puffy?) I don't know, it just goes in different directions.	D Fo Obj D F+ (H) D Fv Smoke
X. 8"	1. One of those bags you have confetti in. This is the cork. Here's where you pull it and the confetti shoots out.	(Confetti) The different shapes and it's all over the place	W Fv Obj
	2. Oh, a goat's head, like Satan worshipers would have. Horns, like an evil goat's head.		Dr Fw+ Ad

Figure 1 (Cont'd)

131

Form Level

F +	- 1	Fw −
Fo	- 6	spider
Fw +	- 5	insect's mouth & face
Fw −	- 3	insect
F −	- 0	
Fv	- 4	
Fs	- 0	

Kinesthesias

making pots
leaf eaten up

Human Figure Response

gargoyles
angels
Africans
wizards

Figure 2

ratings, kinesthesias, and human responses and note on the lists all possible implications (see Figure 3). For example, if two Fs scores are indicated, right next to them I would note, "The patient is vulnerable to severe
disruptions in reality testing." Or, if the list of kinesthesias includes "yelling, arguing, screaming" I would write next to these "strong orally aggressive trends."

The Rorschach record is then reviewed in the same manner. I comb
through the protocol response by response, score by score, phrase by
phrase—literally word by word—and wherever a reasonable implication
can be drawn, I write in that implication. The implication is indicated
adjacent to the actual response, score, or phrase so that I can clearly keep
track of my data sources. At this step I entertain as many reasonable
inferences as possible.

This step constitutes a convergence of all sources of information, that is,
the formal scores, analysis of content, sequence analysis, and indications
of the patient–examiner relationship. I do not isolate one score from
another or regard the score as totally independent of the content. For
example, a pure color score might indicate a capacity for affective sweeps;
however, if the content of the response was "blood" or "fire," then one
could sharpen the inference by specifying the vulnerability involved in
sweeps of anger. Likewise, if on Card I the patient saw "a damaged bat with
holes in its wings that was unable to fly" and during inquiry indicated that

Form Level

F+	- 1	*Variable Form Level*	Fw –
Fo	- 6	*Form Level*	spider
Fw+	- 5	*suffers around*	insect's mouth & face
Fw –	- 3	→ *Too great* *oral aggression*	insect
F –	- 0	*a capacity*	
Fv	- 4	*for laxness*	
Fs	- 0		

Kinesthesias

Making pots
Leaf eaten up → oral aggression, identifies with the victim

Human Figure Response

gargoyles	
angels	*distances and distorts*
Africans	
wizards	*looking for the ideal object*

Figure 3

the blackness of the card was implicated, then the examiner might make the following notations: adjacent to the FC′ score would be written "depressive affect"; above the word "damaged" would be written "sense of injury, of being damaged and flawed"; and above the "unable to fly" would be written "difficulties separating and individuating." Through a series of arrows the examiner could then indicate that the three inferences were quite likely connected.

Inferences at this stage vary in their level of depth; nonetheless, I attempt to state the inference in as experience-near terms as possible. In the above example of the bat, even though the attribution of being "damaged" may indeed indicate the testee's sense of narcissistic injury, I prefer to employ the more descriptive term "damaged" that more closely approximates the testee's experience, rather than the abstract concept "narcissistic injury." In Figure 4 is the original protocol from Figure 1 after it has been reviewed in the manner outlined. Included is the array of possible inferences together with arrows to connect inferences that, at this step, appear to be related.

Step 4—Transformation

I refer to this step as transformation to indicate that here we are beginning to transfer the findings from the protocol into what ultimately will be the

	Response	Inquiry	
	(Before beginning the testing he discussed an incident from the day before, and most striking was his vulnerability to narcissistic injury.) *vulnerable to narcissistic injury*		
I. 8"	1. That looks like a spider. *bad, engulfing, devouring, mother*	(Spider?) Definiteness about it. Eeriness about it. *externalizes malevolence*	W Fw – A *Reality testing suffers*
	2. Impression of two gargoyles or two angels. As a whole, a spider *ineffective defenses*	(Gargoyles?) When facing away, gargoyles; when facing each other, angels. *splits his objects, push-pull type of relationship, rapprochement issues.*	D Fw+ (H) *distances & distorts his objects*
II. 6"	1. Looks like a butterfly or a moth, like *it's coming at me.* A big thing, a moth. *loses inner/outer boundary, loss of distance*	(moth?) Exactly what it looked like. *A huge moth. his sense of smallness* The colorations. (*Colorations?*) The shades of blackness. *depressive affect*	W FC' A *blackness* o confab

Figure 4

134

(Response)	Inquiry	
III. **7"**		
1. Two Africans making pots or something. *distances objects (women)*	(Africans?) 'Cause they were black and figures, like people. (Sex?) I didn't notice *reality testing suffers around oral aggression*	D MC' (H) P *blackness* o
2. Looks like an insect's mouth and face. *Very vicious mouth. → intense oral aggression*		D Fw- Ad
3. This way definitely an insect. This has a vicious mouth too.	*variable reality testing*	D Fw- A
IV. **8"**		D Fw- A
1. A spaniel dog. It has long fur. *Underlying dependence & neediness*	(Fur?) Just looks furry. (Furry?) Not sure, I suppose the shading (Organism?) *Not much of a shape* He has little of an inner shape	W Fw+ Ch A
2. Also a microscopic organism *His sense of lack of firmness and cohesion. Also, sense of being examined*		W F Org.
V. **9"**		
1. That looks like a flying insect.		
2. I don't know. A kite, *a bat kite loss of boundary–very early boundary disturbance* You want something else?	(Bat kite?) I had both ideas so a kite shaped like a bat (cloud) Just the shape of it.	W Fo A P W Fo Obj. contam.
3. Maybe a cloud, no, yea, a cloud	(Cloud) Just the shape of it . . .	W Fv Cloud
4. A *leaf eaten up by bugs and that's what is left.* *Projects his oral aggression and he feels ravaged, exploited & victimized by others. Feels less than total & complete.*	(Eaten up?) Like *silk worms eat a leaf.* Rough edges. *Depreciates others*	W Fw + Play

Figure 4 (Cont'd)

135

	(Response)	Inquiry	

VI.
11"

1. Those things that stick to your clothes when you run through the bush. Spanish needles. They can stick you.

He's constantly anxious, restless, & agitated; like there is something under his skin annoying him he can't get away from.

W Fw+ Pl.

VII.
9"

1. Now, this way, smoke or something.

(Smoke?) Grey color & it puffs up *Strong depressive affect*

W C' F
Smoke

2. *Nuclear bomb has been dropped and this is the dark cloud afterwards.*
Potentially eruptive & explosive but the rage is basically turned inward & dealt with mas- ochistically.

(Cloud?) Mushroom shape & it's grey & dark.
His world, at times, is heavily grey & black.

W C' F Cloud

VIII.
7"

1. This way a *reflection.* A bobtail cat & its reflection down here. (Showed it to the examiner)
Self-centered, self-absorbed, relates on a nar- cissistic basis, early need to be mirrored.

D Fo A P
reflection

2. An abstract painting
Combined with the several vague responses suggests he can be elusive & use vagueness as a defense.

(Painting?) Different colors. Other cards were black with a bit of red, these have colors.

W C F Art
difficulty integrating

Figure 4 (Cont'd)

136

	(Response)	Inquiry	
IX. 14″	1. I can use my imagination? *Asks for & needs external structure* This is a crystal ball with wizards. This is the base & magical smoke. See their hats. You don't see it, do *you*? One wizard is good & the other bad. He has control over a person's life. *Capacity to split–fearful of being controlled* *Need for external, consensual validation*	(Smoke?) It goes with the wizards & looks a bit puffy. (Puffy?) I don't know, it just goes in different directions.	D Fo Obj D F+ (H) D Fv Smoke
X. 8″	1. One of those bags you have confetti in. This is the cork. Here's where you pull it & the confetti shoots out. *Inner chaos & fearful of fragmenting even further.* *Sense of barely holding it together* 2. Oh, a goat's head, like Satan worshipers would have. Horns, like & evil goat's head. *Externalized malevolence paranoid tendencies*	(Confetti?) The different shapes & it's all over the place.	W Fv Obj. Dr Fw+ Ad

Figure 4 (Cont'd)

137

test report. I transpose the inferences from the protocols to work sheets with headings that correspond to the same subheadings (character structure, thought organization, etc.) that implicitly constitute the testing report.

Inferences are placed under their appropriate headings; however, there is not always a convenient fit. In certain instances, the same inference may be placed under several headings. In the previous example of the damaged bat, one could include inferences from this response under several headings: under the section *character structure* in terms of a sense of self as "injured and damaged"; under the section *affect organization* as "lowered feelings of self-esteem"; and under the heading *core dynamics* as "consequent to difficulties in separating and individuating, the patient senses himself as damaged and less than a total person."

Within each section I attempt to group inferences based on the arrows indicated on the protocol and on theory. For example, if on various parts of the protocol the patient was described as "self-demeaning," "apologetic," "aggressively complaintive" and "provocative," then all would be grouped together since they indicate a masochistic streak in the patient's character structure.

After all inferences have been placed under their appropriate major headings and subheadings, I then review each of the sections separately to determine which of the inferences may be related and which specific inferences are so isolated and at variance with the others that they are best disregarded. Arrows are again used to indicate interrelated inferences. Finally, inferences between sections are examined and these connections too are indicated by arrows. At this step the inferences are related on the basis of theoretical formulations. A completed work sheet based on the sample protocol is presented in Figure 5.

Step 5—The Psychological Report

The work sheets completed in Step 4 furnish the outline and material from which the testing report is written. The headings may or may not be explicitly stated in the report; in either case, they serve as organizational points of reference. The report consists essentially of the inferences and the theoretical formulations tying them together. In general, in a testing report the inferences constitute the basic material, theory binds the material and provides tightness and cohesion, and the level of language used particularizes the report to the individual patient.

A report based on the sample protocol is shown in Figure 6. I regard this report as rather incomplete, for, as noted previously, a complete assessment should be based on a test battery.

Character Structure
Variable cohesion—falls apart & pulls himself together
Anxious, restless, pressured
Self-centered, self-absorbed, unpredictable, changeable, la-
bile, fragile, vulnerable, hypervigilant, hypersensitive, re-
lates on a need-satisfying basis—dependent
Masochism—self-deprecatory, turns aggression inward
Distrusting, suspicious, antennae are out
Sense of self-impoverished, neglected, exploited, victim-
ized

Thought Organization
Impulsive, poor judgment, loses conceptual boundaries
Variable reality testing—too lax
Fragile defenses—looks for external validation
Boundary disturbance—self/other, inner/outer
Paranoid trends

Affect Organization
Poor affect control, mood shifts, can be swept by feelings
Anxiety—restless, agitated, free-floating, diffuse,
something under his skin
Depression—parts of himself as missing, empty, hope-
less, low self-esteem, turns rage inward, world as black,
vulnerable to narcissistic slight (abandonment depression)
Defenses—splitting, devaluation, projection, omnipotence,
vagueness, avoidance

Dynamics
Core oral aggression—projects outward & senses the
world as malevolent & himself as exploited & victimized.
Early disturbance with mother—views her as engulfing &
devouring, push-pull quality, rapprochement issues.
Poor object relations—distances & depreciates
Diffuse anxiety—fear of fragmenting further, masochism,
annoyance under his skin

Treatment
Looking for external control & structure
He's aware that he loses control, this scares him and he
looks for outside control
Intense depressive affect

Figure 5

Psychological Evaluation

The patient is a 26-year-old divorced male who has been charged with three counts of selling cocaine to an undercover police officer. The patient admits that he sold the drugs knowlingly; that he knew the person as a police officer. He further claims that he believed old friends and acquaintances were spreading rumors that he was an informer and that the only way he could disprove these rumors was by having himself arrested. Psychological testing was requested to assess the plausibility of his claims and his general psychological status. This report is addressed to the issues of character structure, thought organization, affect organization, treatment, and the genuineness of the patient's personal defense.

In his approach to the examiner and the tests the patient appeared as a highly anxious, pressured, restless, somewhat desperate individual who nonetheless related to the examiner in an open and cooperative manner. Characteristically unstable, chaotic, unpredictable, and emotionally labile, at this time he is especially fragile and vulnerable. The patient is self-centered, self-absorbed, and overly concerned with what others think of him. Hypersensitive, hypervigilant and thin-skinned, he has his antennae out feeling his way through an environment he senses as hostile and dangerous. Needy and dependent, he relates himself to others on the basis of their ability to satisfy his immediate needs. In his personality one sees a strong masochistic streak. He is self-depreciatory and self-defeating, and he sets himself up to be hurt and taken advantage of. Further, when he feels excessively anxious and restless, he is likely to abuse himself or set himself up to be abused. Such abuse lessens the anxiety. He is vaguely aware of this insofar as he feels himself impoverished, exploited, and victimized. Although he feels this, he has little awareness of his role in engendering hurt and pain. Despite his openness with the examiner, in general he is suspicious and distrusting of others; in his own terms, he trusts no one. The oveall diagnostic impression is of a narcissistic personality disorder organized at a borderline level.

One sees in the patient's functioning marked ego weaknesses. He is impatient and at times impulsive, his judgment is poor, his sense of reality and reality testing are variable, and he is highly arbitrary. Beyond these impairments, he is prone to circumscribed and periodic psychotic bouts. At these times, paranoid trends intensify, he loses the boundary between

Figure 6

140

himself and others and between fantasy and reality, and he sees malevolence everywhere and likely feels persecuted.

Central to the patient's instability is his tendency to fall apart and then quickly pull himself together. When he falls apart, he senses himself as "out of control." In this context, his paranoid thinking is an effort to regain control by bringing order and structure, as inaccurate as it may be, to his broken world. By contrast, when stable, his thinking is logical, goal directed, and reality bound. Of importance here are his rapidly shifting and variable level of functioning and his reliance on external structure for stability.

The patient has much difficulty controlling, modulating, and integrating affects. He is vulnerable to intense mood shifts and affective sweeps. He is currently being pressured by relatively intense feelings of anxiety and depression. His anxiety, which is long-standing and diffuse, becomes evident in feelings of agitation and restlessness and in a sense of having a continuous annoyance under his skin that he cannot get away from. As noted previously, when his anxiety mounts to an intolerable level, he discharges it by hurting or harming himself. His depression, which has been referred to as an "abandonment depression," involves feelings of emptiness, aloneness, and hopelessness. As well, he suffers from low feelings of self-esteem. At times he feels the low self-esteem directly in terms of feeling himself to be bad, worthless, and less than totally human. At other times he defends against it and feels himself to be quite the opposite—all-powerful, psychic, visionary, and omnipotent. In any event, his self-esteem is fragile and subject to the least slight.

In line with his chaotic nature, he tends to polarize the world into either all good or all bad. There is little of a middle ground, and he is unable to tolerate different feelings toward the same individual. His feelings about himself have this same polarized good and bad quality. Bolstering this tendency toward splitting is his proclivity to either excessively depreciate or idealize both others and himself.

Basic to the patient's dynamic life are intense feelings of oral aggression. That is, he feels enraged and resentful over having been neglected and deprived. The rage is then projected outward onto the environment, leaving him with a view of the world as malevolent and dangerous—a veritable jungle, as it were. He feels he has been exploited and fears and anticipates further exploitation.

The patient's relationships are highly disturbed. Needful and

Figure 6 (Cont'd)

141

dependent, he looks to others for sustenance and nurturance. At the same time, however, he distrusts others; thus, associated with desires for closeness are fears of being controlled, dominated, and used. Caught in the competing currents of desiring nurturance yet fearing the implied closeness, his relationships have a push-and-pull quality. In a similar way, mindful of his own inner disorganization, he looks for external control and structure; yet here too he distrusts and fears such control. Hence, he is likely to seek external structure and then respond to it with both obedience and rebelliousness. Further complicating his relationships is his tendency to split.

Finally, the patient is especially fearful of fragmenting and losing the limited sense of cohesion and precarious sense of self he has achieved.

The referrer specifically questioned the patient's claim that he knew he was selling durgs to an undercover policeman and wondered if such a claim were plausible and consistent with the patient's personality makeup. To judge from his tests, the claim is consistent with his personality. Behaving as he says he did is in keeping with his strong masochism, his feelings of omnipotence, his poor judgment, and his search for external authority. That he should assume others believed he was an informer is congruent with his paranoid tendencies, and that he should counter it as he did is consistent with his lapses into irrational thinking.

Because of his inner disorganization the patient is looking for external structure and control. As such, a long-term, highly structured inpatient treatment program is the intervention of choice. Contact with his subjective experience can be established around his strong depressive feelings, his feelings of restlessness, and his discomfort with being out of control.

In summary, the patient presents as a narcissistic personality organized at a borderline level. He is chaotic, unstable, vulnerable, and labile. There is a strong masochistic streak. In addition to having marked ego weaknesses, he is vulnerable to circumscribed psychotic episodes. In keeping with his diagnosis, he quickly "falls apart" and then pulls himself together. His mood shifts are rapid and he is prone to severe depressive bouts. In his dynamic life, one sees excessive oral aggression, disturbed object relations, and fears of fragmentation. His account of why he got into his current legal difficulties is consistent with aspects of his personality. He would most benefit from a long-term, well-structured inpatient treatment program.

Figure 6 (Cont'd)

SUMMARY

In this chapter I have discussed the inference process, including rules of validity that should be applied to inferences and the steps involved in moving from the Rorschach data to a testing report. One's understanding of the dynamics of testing, of the various aspects of the Rorschach testing situation, and of personality theory come together at this point. In my view, deriving accurate, meaningful, and clinically useful inferences constitutes the most challenging yet creative aspect of the testing process.

II

Research Applications

11

The Rorschach Assessment
of Object Representation

In psychoanalysis, with the increasing emphasis on the distinction between internalized object relations as opposed to relations between the self and the objects in the external world, there is much emphasis on the concept of object representation. Broadly defined, object representation refers to conscious and unconscious mental schemata—including cognitive, affective, and experiential dimensions—of objects encountered in reality. Beginning as vague, diffuse sensory motor experiences of pleasure and unpleasure, these schemata gradually expand and develop into well-differentiated, consistent, and relatively realistic representations of the self and object world. Earlier forms of representations are based on action sequences associated with need gratification; intermediate forms are based on specific perceptual and functional features; and higher forms are thought to be more symbolic and conceptual (Blatt, 1974). There is a constant and reciprocal interaction between past and present interpersonal relationships and the development of representations. These schemata evolve from and are intertwined with the internalization of object relations, and new levels of object representations provide a revised organization for subsequent interpersonal relationships (Blatt, 1974).

RESEARCH STUDIES

Two primary research groups have contributed to the systematic study of the object representation construct by means of the Rorschach test and other projective techniques through experimental procedures. These two research groups represent different but not mutually exclusive approaches

147

to the study of object representations. Mayman and his colleagues at the University of Michigan have focused on the thematic dimension of object representations. Employing early memories, manifest dreams, written autobiographies, and a variety of projective procedures, including the Rorschach test, and developing innovative scoring systems, these investigators have studied the relationship between object representation and severity of psychopathology, type of character structure, quality of object relations, and capacity to benefit from psychotherapy. Informing their work and methods have been theoretical formulations rooted in ego psychology, including the more recent contributions of Mahler, Pine, and Bergman (1975) and Kernberg (1975, 1976).

Blatt and his colleagues (1976) at Yale University, by contrast, have emphasized the structural dimension of object representations. While this group has also developed independent projective measures and scales (e.g., parental descriptions, Thematic Apperception Test scales), they have studied the developmental level of object representations across a wide spectrum of normal and clinical populations. The work of this group too is based on ego psychology and object relations theory; in addition, and in keeping with their developmental thrust, these researchers also integrate the developmental cognitive theories of Piaget and Werner.

The Study of Object Representations at the University of Michigan

Employing the specific theoretical contributions of Jacobson and Erickson, Mayman (1967) conceptualized object representations as templates or enduring internalized images of the self and of others around which the phenomenological world is structured and into which ongoing experiences of others are assimilated. Mayman asserted that Rorschach content, like the manifest content of dreams and early memories, was more than simply an embellished screen that concealed and hinted at deeper and more profound levels of unconscious meaning. He argued that manifest content in its own right could reflect levels of ego functioning, relative capacity for object relations, and the nature of interpersonal strivings. According to Mayman (1967):

> A person's most readily accessible object representation called up under such unstructured conditions tell much about his inner world of objects and about the quality of relationships with these inner objects toward which he is predisposed [p. 17].

Mayman (1967) identified several dimensions by which to assess the content of Rorschach responses in order to answer the following questions:

What kind of world does each person recreate in the inkblot milieu? What kinds of animate and inanimate objects come most readily to mind? What manner of people and things is he prone to surround himself with? Does he put together, for example, a peopleless world of inanimate objects; if so, which objects have special valence for him? Do they hint at a certain preferred mode of acting upon the world or of being acted upon by it? Are they, for example, tooth-equipped objects? Or, phallically intrusive objects? Decaying or malformed objects? [p. 17].

In addition to psychosexual levels of the image and the degree of humanness in Rorschach responses, Mayman also considers both the extent to which conflict or rage permeates the portrayal of the other and the degree of the individual's vulnerability to separation and loss. For Mayman, the Rorschach human response is viewed as a vehicle for understanding "important personal meaning" about "a person's capacity to establish empathic contact with another human being" (1977, p. 244).

In an early study Mayman (1967), equipped with these notions and with a commitment to a clinical empathic–intuitive approach to the analysis of projective test data, selected Rorschach protocols from the Menninger Psychotherapy Research Project and distilled from each record verbatim clusters of "content-fragments" that he considered to be self-representations, object representations, and conflict representations. All patients were evaluated independently on the Health–Sickness Rating Scale, as well as on a wide range of other clinical variables. Mayman examined the extent to which ratings of psychopathology based exclusively on representational content gleaned from a Rorschach administered before treatment corresponded to clinical ratings of psychopathology. Editing out all references to traditional Rorschach scores, Mayman asked graduate students and interns to "immerse themselves" in each patient's Rorschach responses, to regard the imagery as a sample of the patient's inner world, and to assign a rating for the degree of psychopathology implicit in the representational content. Mayman found that relatively inexperienced judges could successfully predict ratings based on an independent psychiatric evaluation ($r = .86$). Beyond demonstrating that an object relations approach to Rorschach content correlates significantly with independent ratings of psychopathology, Mayman also showed that relatively inexperienced clinically trained raters can make important contributions to research.

Mayman's seminal contributions to Rorschach research have spawned a number of object representation scales and a host of construct validity studies that have further refined the concept (Urist, 1973) and have extended the thematic analysis of object representations to manifest dreams (Krohn, 1974), autobiographical data (Urist, 1973), and to studies measuring a person's capacity to enter into and benefit from insight-oriented psychotherapy (Ryan, 1973; Hatcher and Krohn, 1980). Different scales designed to evaluate object representational levels as specific points on a developmental continuum have been correlated with each other (Urist, 1973) and have been applied and correlated across various data bases, including manifest dreams, the Rorschach test, early memories and health–sickness ratings (Krohn and Mayman, 1974). These studies reflect Mayman's focal interest in thematic content, his gifted clinical approach to projective data, which emphasizes the value of empathic–intuitive skills of trained clinicians, and his abiding interest in variables related to psychoanalytic theory and treatment.

Following the methodological thrusts of Mayman and integrating the theoretical contributions of Kernberg and Kohut, Urist (1973) examined the multidimensional qualitative aspects of the object representational concept by correlating several Rorschach scale ratings of 40 adult inpatients, covering a wide spectrum of psychopathology, with independent ratings of written autobiographies. The specific scales developed by Urist were gauged to reflect the developmental ordering of stages in the unfolding of object relations along a number of overlapping dimensions, including mutuality of autonomy, body integrity, aliveness, fusion, thought disorder, richness and complexity, and differentiation and individuation. Urist found significantly high correlations among the various measures of object relations and interpreted this as indicating high consistency among self- and object representations across a wide range of sampled behavior.

Urist (1973) also demonstrated that object relations are not unidimensional areas of ego functioning. A factor analysis revealed an important distinction between two related but separate structural underpinnings of object representation: an integrity factor, related to issues of self-other differentiation, stability, and consistency (an index of secondary narcissism), and a boundary factor, related to developmental gradations in fusion–merger tendencies and in thought disorder associated with the inability to maintain a cognitive-perceptual sense of the boundary between self and other and between one object and another (an index of primary narcissism).

On the basis of this research, Urist (1977) developed a procedure, for systematically evaluating Rorschach responses that expressed interactions between people, animals, and objects—The Mutuality of Autonomy Scale. Utilizing the data from his 1973 study, Urist correlated Rorschach scale ratings with independent measures of the same dimension applied to the written autobiographies and behavioral ratings of ward staff. Urist reported a consistency across all variables and ranges of measures that points to an enduring consistency in patients' representations of relationships. He further demonstrated that the Rorschach can be utilized to systematically assess aspects of mutuality of autonomy within a patient's experiences of self and other. The Mutuality of Autonomy Scale has been validated in several independent studies (Tuber, 1983; Spear and Sugarman, 1984; Ryan, Avery, and Grolnick, 1985; Coates and Tuber, 1988).

In summary, the research findings of Mayman and his colleagues provide strong support for the importance of assessing object representations in clinical research and practice. These investigators have developed a conceptual model and assessment procedures that have implications for the study of different forms of psychopathology and for the study of the psychotherapeutic process. They have attempted to add a more experiential, phenomenological, and object relational dimension to theory, assessment, and research. Emphasis is placed on a clinically based methodology, on the development of means for capturing the complexity and unique nature of clinical phenomena, and on a qualitative approach to data collection and analysis that allows the data to maintain their clinical richness.

Research Studies at Yale University

Although Blatt shares with Mayman a commitment to bring into research the more subtle differentiations and observations of experienced clinicians, his research and that of his colleagues at Yale have focused on the assessment of structure as opposed to content. Underlying the research of this group is the assumption that the structural dimensions of object representation can be assessed with acceptable levels of reliability and that they provide valid data that have considerable generalizability for understanding various facets of human functioning.

Blatt's theoretical commitment is to a study of object and self-representations based on an integration of psychoanalytic theory with the cognitive developmental formulations of Piaget and Werner. His contribution to the Rorschach literature has revolved around the study of the development of the concept of an object both in normal and in various clinical populations.

Building on their initial investigation of boundary disturbances, Blatt, and associates (1976) developed a highly comprehensive and sophisticated manual for assessing object representations in Rorschach records. Based on the development theory of Werner (1940) and ego psychoanalytic theory, the system calls for the scoring of human responses along three developmental dimensions: differentiation, articulation, and integration. Within each of these areas, categories were established along a continuum based on developmental levels. Differentiation refers to the type of figure perceived and to whether the figure is quasi-human detail, human detail, quasi-human, or a full human figure. For the dimension of articulation, responses are scored on the basis of the number and types of attributes ascribed to the figure. The integration dimension of the response is scored in three ways: the degree of internality of the action, the degree of integration of the object and its action, and the integration of the interaction with another object. Responses are also scored along a content dimension of benevolence-malevolence. The scale is presented in Appendix A (pp. 268–277).

In an early study (Blatt et al., 1976), the scoring system was applied to the Rorschach protocols of 37 normal subjects on four separate occasions over a 20-year period. Results from this longitudinal study revealed that human responses on the Rorschach test consistently change with development. More specifically, there was a marked and progressive increase in the number of well-differentiated, highly articulated, and integrated human figures. In addition, there was a significant increase in the attribution of activity that was congruent with important characteristics of the figures and an increase in the degree to which human objects were seen in constructive and positive interaction.

Blatt and associates then extended the scale to the human responses of a sample of 48 seriously disturbed borderline and psychotic adolescents and young adults. When compared to the human responses of the normal sample, several interesting findings appeared. First, the seriously disturbed inpatients had a significantly greater number of human responses at lower developmental levels (i.e., responses that were more often quasi-human, distorted, unmotivated, incongruent, passive, and malevolent). These responses at lower developmental levels, however, occurred primarily on accurately perceived responses. Second, and quite surprisingly, patients had a significantly greater number of more developmentally more advanced responses than did normals on inaccurately perceived responses. These findings were replicated by Ritzler, Zambinco, Harder, and Kaskey (1980). According to Blatt, these results indicate that patients, as compared with normals, function at lower developmental levels when in contact with conventional reality but at higher developmental levels when they give idiosyncratic interpretations of reality. As such, the data indicate that the capacity to perceive reality adequately does not aid psychotic patients to organize their experience more effectively or to function at higher levels. The findings suggest that there are at least two aspects to the psychotic experience. First, the psychotic patient perceives the world as distorted, undifferentiated, fragmented, and destructive. The second aspect involves the psychotic patient's capacity to experience the world unrealistically but, within the unrealistic experience, to function more effectively and to perceive the world less malevolently. These Rorschach findings have implications for the treatment of severely disturbed patients (Blatt, Schimek, and Brenneis, 1980). Specifically, for psychotic patients, introducing and interpreting reality is experienced as painful and disruptive and will engender retreat and withdrawal. Thus, while it is incumbent upon the therapist to maintain a reality orientation, it is equally important that he or she recognize and empathize with the pain that accompanies this stance.

The Concept of the Object Scale has been applied to various types of psychopathology. Blatt and Lerner (1983) applied the instrument to the Rorschach records of several patients, each of whom was independently selected as a prototypic example of a specific clinical disorder. These authors not only found a unique quality of object representation for each of the clinical entities but their findings, based on Rorschach data, were remarkably congruent with clinical expectations.

In a nonparanoid schizophrenic patient the object representations in the Rorschach response were found to be inaccurately perceived and at lower developmental levels of differentiation (i.e., quasi-human rather than Blatt's full human figures). The representations were inappropriately articulated and seen as inert or involved in unmotivated activity. There was relatively little interaction between figures, and the Rorschach content was essentially barren.

In a narcissistic patient organized at a borderline level, the object representations in the Rorschach response were found to gradually deteriorate with stress or simply over time. Intact, accurately perceived full human figures gave way to inaccurate, inappropriately articulated, quasi-human representations. Early responses had a superficially intact quality, and relationships between figures were depicted as benevolent and conventional. Yet action between figures lacked inner definition and there was little meaning attributed to the action. In time, the quality of the concept of the object deteriorated as the representations changed from full to quasi-humans or part-objects. As well, the responses became progressively more inaccurately perceived and inappropriately elaborated.

Representations in a patient diagnosed as an infantile character with anaclitic depressive features were accurately perceived and well-differentiated but minimally articulated. Interaction was perceived between figures, but this typically involved an active–passive transaction in which one figure was seen as vulnerable and in a relationship with a depriving, rejecting, undependable other.

In a seriously suicidal patient with an introjective depression characterized by profound feelings of self-criticism and guilt, there was an oscillation between object representations at a high developmental level and seriously impaired representations in which the activity was destructive and had malevolent intent (Blatt, 1974).

The object representations in the Rorschach record of a delinquent adolescent were conventional full human figures that were poorly articulated. Figures were accurately perceived but lacked detail, and actions ascribed were purposeless and directionless. In contrast to the narcissistic-borderline patient, responses did not deteriorate in quality nor in developmental level of representation.

Finally, in a patient diagnosed as hysteric, object representations were accurately perceived, well-differentiated, and highly articulated. The elaborations, however, involved superficial external and physical details rather than more internal or personal attributes. There was little internal sense of motivation or action between figures; rather, things seemed to simply occur.

Blatt and Lerner (1983) concluded, based on their clinical analysis of these prototypic cases, that there are significant, consistent differences in the structure and content of object representations in patients with different types of psychopathology and that one can validly assess object representations through a systematic appraisal of human responses on the Rorschach. These clinical findings have been substantiated in a number of research studies involving various clinical groups, including borderlines (Spear, 1980; Lerner and St. Peter, 1984), schizophrenics (Johnson, 1980; Spear and Schwager, 1980), depressives (Fibel, 1979), opiate addicts (Blatt et al., 1984), anorexics (Sugarman, Quinlan, and Devenis, 1982).

Other investigators have related parts of Blatt and associates' (1976) scoring manual to psychological variables conceptually linked to object representations. Johnson (1980) reported significant correlations between two scale measures, degree of articulation of the representation and developmental level of interaction, and an independent measure of field independence. He also found a significant correlation between scale measures of the integration of the object with its action and the portrayal of congruent interactions in a role playing task. Fibel (1979), in a sample of seriously disturbed adolescent and young adult hospitalized patients, found a significant positive relationship between scale scores and independent clinical ratings of quality of interpersonal relations.

Throughout his research on psychopathology Blatt has steadfastly maintained the significance of assessing impairments in object representations and the role they play in predisposing an individual to a particular form of psychopathology. There is considerable clinical and research evidence that suggests not only that the content and structure of object representations are essential dimensions in specific forms of psychopathology but, in addition, that changes in the structure of object representations parallel changes observed in treatment (Lerner, 1986). With the development of a Rorschach measure of object representations, this developmental construct is now available for systematic assessment. For Blatt, the assessment of object representation has involved an integration of psychoanalytic theory with cognitive developmental psychology. The procedures developed now provide the means for investigating a wide range of theoretical formulations, as well as for examining dimensions of the social matrix in which the developing child evolves. The representational world emerges from the interaction of cognitive, affective, interpersonal, and social forces. As such, it may be regarded as a core structure for studying the multitude of factors that influence normal psychological growth, the impairments that eventuate in psychopathology, and the changes in the psychotherapeutic process.

CONCLUSION

Whereas instinct theory and, later, ego psychology were once the conceptual centerpieces of analytic theory, psychoanalysis has increasingly become a developmental theory of self and object relations with emphasis on the processes whereby external experiences are internalized and become the basis of personality growth and functioning. With this shift in theoretical emphasis, new concepts, such as object representation and self-representation, corresponding to a clinical rather than a metapsychological level, have gained increased currency in the analytic literature. Because these newer concepts are less removed from the clinical situation and are closer to our clinical data, they lend themselves to operationalizing in a way that the older and more abstract concepts do not.

The research reviewed in this chapter indicates that there are reliable and valid methods and techniques available for the systematic assessment of object representations and internalized object relations. The combined findings further indicate that these constructs are enduring dimensions of personality organization and that they provide meaningful information about the developmental level of personality and the quality of external interpersonal relationships.

Mayman and his colleagues, basing their work on the theoretical formulations of Federn, Jacobson, and Kernberg, have investigated the affective-thematic aspects of human experience. Using such theoretical constructs as "affective states," "experience of self," and "sense of identity," this group has attempted to bring a more phenomenological approach to traditional assessment.

Blatt and his colleagues have also employed concepts and formulations based on ego psychology and object relations theory; however, they have also integrated these concepts with formulations from cognitive developmental psychology.

Because of different theoretical starting points, each of the two groups has emphasized somewhat different dimensions of object relations. The Michigan group has focused on the contextual and affective aspects of object representations, while the Yale group has emphasized the structural and cognitive aspects. Mayman and his colleagues have developed a more experiential approach to assessment whereby there is a close adherence to clinical data and the judgment of skilled clinicians is maximized by asking them to immerse themselves in the data and then make ratings in an "intuitive and empathic" manner. The research methodology and theoretical formulations of the Yale group represent a rich synthesis of clinical experience with a developmental perspective. Methods are devised and designed to provide quantitative data anchored in clinically relevant observations.

The findings from each research team overlap and in large measure are mutually supportive. Both groups are interested in how the individual constructs reality and the internal outcome of this process, the nature of mental representations and of their interactions, and the processes whereby experience is transformed into subjective meaning. Each group has contributed significantly to the development of a more phenomenological clinical theory derived directly from test data. Their assessment of the concept of object representation is now providing qualitative and quantitative data that has relevance for a variety of disciplines.

Using various clinical populations, both groups have studied and outlined impairments in object representations among patients differing in severity of psychopathology. More recently, both groups have begun to apply their theoretical concepts and research methodologies to aspects of the psychotherapeutic process. Specifically, research is currently under way in which the construct of object representation is being used to help predict those patients who are more likely to benefit from an insight-oriented psychotherapy. Further, other studies are being conducted in which the construct serves as a criterion measure to assess the effectiveness of long-term intensive treatment.

APPENDIX A
DEVELOPMENTAL ANALYSIS OF THE
CONCEPT OF THE OBJECT

A. Accuracy of the response (Blatt and Lerner, 1983)
    Responses are classified as perceptually accurate or inaccurate by how well they conform to the configuration of the stimulus properties of the card $(F+, F\pm, F\mp, F-)$; $F+$ or $F\pm$ responses are classified as accurate; and $F-$ responses and $F\mp$ responses are classified as inaccurate (Rapaport, Gill, and Schafer, 1945–1946; Allison, Blatt, and Zimet, 1968)
B. Differentiation
    Responses are classified according to types of figures perceived; whether the figure or subject of the action involves quasi-human details; (Hd); human details: Hd; full quasi-human figures: (H); and full human figures: H.
    1. Quasi-human details: part of a quasi-human figure is specified.
    2. Human details: part of a human figure is specified as human.

3. Quasi-human responses: figures that are whole but less than human or not definitely specified as human.
4. Human responses: the figure must be whole and clearly human.

C. Articulation

Responses are scored on the basis of types of attributes ascribed to the figures. A total of seven types of attributes are considered. These types of attributes were selected because they seem to provide information about human or quasi-human figures. The analyses are not concerned with the sheer detailing of features, and a distinction is made between appropriate and inappropriate articulation. The analyses are only concerned with articulations that enrich a human or quasi-human response, that enlarge a listener's knowledge about qualities of the figures represented. (A response that states that a man has a head, hands, and feet does not enlarge the listener's knowledge about the man; possession of these features is presupposed by the initial response, "man.") An articulation such as "a man with wings" is scored as an inappropriate articulation because it is an elaboration that adds inappropriate specification of the features of the human or quasi-human figure. There are two general types of articulation: the articulation of (1) perceptual and (2) functional attributes.

1. Perceptual characteristics:
    a. Size or physical structure. Size or structure is only scored as articulated if there is a qualitative description of aspects of body parts or of the whole body that is more than a simple enumeration of standard part features. Certain aspects of facial expression are scored as articulations of size or structure (including "eyes closed" or "mouth open," in which the description of facial expression amounts to something more than just a description of physical appearance.)
    b. Clothing or hairstyle. The qualitative description of some aspect of either clothing or hairstyle must enrich the description of the figure. Simple mention of items of clothing implied by the response does not enrich one's understanding of the figure and is therefore not scored as an articulation.
    c. Posture. Posture is scored if the description of body posture is separate from the verb describing the activity of the figure or if the description of facial expression goes beyond mere articulation of the physical appearance of features in that it contains a sense of movement or feeling. Posture is not scored if body posture is implied in the verb rather than being separately articulated or if it is simply a description of a figure's position in space (e.g., facing outward).

2. Functional characteristics:
    a. Sex. Sex is scored if specific mention of sex of the figure is made or if an assignment to an occupational category clearly implies a particular sexual identity. If the final sexual identity is not decided but alternatives are precisely considered, sex is scored as articulated. If, however, the indecision is based upon a vague

characterization of the figure with an emphasis on the sexual nature of the figure as a whole, sex is not considered articulated.

b. Age. Specific reference is made to some age category that the figure belongs to.

c. Role. When figures are human, a clear reference to the work a figure does (occupation) is scored as an articulation of role. With regard to quasi-human figures, role is scored if the manner in which the figure is represented implies that it would engage in certain activities rather than others. When sexual identity is clearly indicated in a role designation (e.g., "mother," "witch," "priest"), both sex and role are scored as articulated.

d. Specific identity. A figure must be named as a specific character in history, literature, etc. To the degree that age, sex, and occupation are clearly indicated in the specific identity, these features are also scored as articulated. Thus, in the response "Charles de Gaulle," sex and occupation are specified. Such is not the case in the response "piglet."

3. Degree of articulation. This is the total number of attributes articulated (size, clothing or hairstyle, posture, sex, age, role, and specific identity). Thus, for any single Rorschach response, a total of seven types of features could be articulated. The average number of features taken into account in human or quasi-human responses constitutes the score for the degree of articulation of individual figures.

D. Motivation of action

This is a rating of the degree of internality for the motivation of the action attributed to the figures (unmotivated, reactive, and intentional). Reactive explanations involve a focus on past events and behavior and are explained in terms of causal factors; one assumes that, for certain prior reasons, an individual had to do a certain thing. By contrast, intentionality is proactive and implies an orientation toward the present or future. The individual chooses to do something to attain a certain end or goal. The ability to choose between motives and to undertake an activity purposively implies greater differentiation between subject and action than is the case when an individual is impelled to take an action because of past occurrences. For this reason, the analysis of action considers whether or not a motive was provided and whether the motivation was reactive (causal) or intentional.

E. Object–action integration

The degree of integration of the object and its action is rated. Four levels of integration are distinguished: fused, incongruent, nonspecific, and congruent.

1. Fusion of object and action. An amorphous object and its action are fused. The object possesses no separate qualities of its own and is defined only in terms of its activity. Nothing is known about the object except what it is doing.

2. Incongruent integration of object and action. There is some separate articulation of object and action. Something is known about the object apart from its activity, but the activity is incongruous and unrelated to the defined nature of the object. The articulation of action detracts from, rather than enriches, the articulation of the object.

3. Nonspecific integration of object and action. There is some separate articulation of object and its action, but the relationship between the object and its action is nonspecific. The figures, as defined, can engage in the activity described, but there is no special fit between object and action; many other kinds of objects could engage in the activity described. Thus, although the articulation of action does not detract from the articulation of the object, neither does it enrich it.

4. Congruent integration of object and action. The object and the nature of its action are articulated separately. The action is particularly suited to the defined nature of the object. By way of contrast with the preceding category, not only must the action be something the object might do, it must be something that the object would be especially likely to do. There is an integrated and particularly well-suited relationship between the object and the specified action. The articulation of the action enriches the image of the object. In responses where the role definition of the object is nothing more than a literal restatement of the action, object and action are not considered integrated. Responses like "dancer's dancing," or "singer's singing" are scored as nonspecified (level 3) relationships. However, responses such as "ballerina dancing" or "character from a Rudolph Friml opera singing" are classified as a congruent integration of object and action.

F. Content of action
   1. Malevolent. The action is aggressive or destructive, or the results of the activity imply destruction or harm or fear of harm.
   2. Benevolent. The activity is not destructive, harmful, or aggressive. It may be neutral, or it may reflect a warm, positive quality.

G. Nature of interaction
   This analysis applies to all responses involving at least two human or quasi-human figures or where a second figure is not directly perceived but its presence is implied by the nature of the action.
   1. Active–passive interaction. Two figures are involved in an interaction in which one figure is acting upon another figure in an active-passive relationship. One figure is active and the other is entirely passive (while acted upon, it does not respond in any way).
   2. Active–reactive interaction. The interacting figures may be unequal. While one figure is definitely the agent of the activity, the second figure is reactive or responsive to the action of the first.
   3. Active-active interaction. In a third type of interaction both figures contribute equally to the activity, and the interaction is mutual.

12

Rorschach Assessment of
Defense—I: Traditional
Measures

The concept of defense has been a cornerstone of psychoanalytic theory
and a major subject of Rorschach investigation. Until recently, however,
the concept has remained relatively immune to the impact of object
relations theory. As Stolorow and Lachmann (1980) noted, "An examination of the history of the concept of defense indicates that while ideas about
what a defense wards off have evolved, the concept of defense itself has
remained static" (p. 89). Historically, several writers (A. Freud, 1936;
Jacobson, 1971; Gedo and Goldberg, 1973) have attempted to introduce
developmental schemes that rank defenses, from archaic or primitive to
higher order or advanced, yet these conceptualizations have remained
exclusively related to the vicissitudes of psychosexual development and
have excluded object relational considerations.

This is now changing. With the increased acceptance of the British
school of object relations and Kernberg's (1975) comprehensive integrative efforts, new conceptions of defense are emerging. With these newer
views comes the recognition that defense is not only limited to the
regulation of drives and affects but is also intimately involved in the
internalization and organization of object relations.

In this and the next chapter I review the various psychoanalytic theories
of defense, beginning with the conception involved in Freud's drive theory, extending through modifications proposed in structural theory, and
ending with revisions suggested by object relations theory. Following each
described stage of theory development is a discussion of Rorschach measures of defense derived from the specific conceptual formulations. More
traditional measures based upon drive theory and structural theory are

161

reviewed in this chapter, and an assessment of primitive defenses based on object relations theory is discussed in the following chapter.

FREUD'S CONCEPTIONS OF DEFENSE

Freud's various and changing views of defense have been reviewed by several authors (Rapaport, 1958; Madison, 1961; Hoffer, 1968; Leeuw, 1971). In his earliest writings, prior to 1900, he used the term *defense* to describe the ego's struggles against painful ideas and affects. In these early papers he outlined the processes of conversion, displacement of affects, withdrawal from reality, repression, and projection. Freud presented his initial concept of defense within the context of an incomplete conceptualization of the ego; nonetheless, as Rapaport (1958) has noted, the implicit notions within this early view—that drives are dammed up and displaced and that the defense, by preventing the recall or re-encountering of a reality experience, prevents or delays the experiencing of a painful affect—have remained cornerstones of most subsequent psychoanalytic conceptions of defense.

Following a period in which his interest in defense waned, Freud's interest rekindled in 1923, and with the publication of "The Ego and the Id" he made explicit his tripartite model of the personality and accorded the concept of defense a central role. Freud conceived of defense as an ego function and regarded the defense mechanisms as the executive methods of this ego capacity (Leeuw, 1971). Whereas in his earlier view he conceptualized repression as responsible for the creation of anxiety, herein he posited that it was anxiety that created the need for repression. Freud (1926) further conceived of the ego as having a range of defenses at its disposal. He outlined isolation, undoing, denial, and splitting of the ego, and reconsidered repression.

Based on the structural model as presented in "The Ego and the Id", authors subsequent to Freud drew attention to the chronology and genesis of the defense mechanisms, as well as to their relation to levels of ego and drive organization. Anna Freud (1936) systematized the concepts of the specific defense mechanisms, clarified the relationship between defense and reality relations, and investigated the role of affects (Rapaport, 1958). Reich (1933) investigated and described the defensive aspects of character formation. He conceived of character as augmenting the primary repression of instincts by way of autoplastic changes.

RORSCHACH MEASURES OF DEFENSE

In the Rorschach literature one finds two major works that have used Freud's drive and structural models as a basis for translating theoretical formulations regarding defense into Rorschach-related concepts. The two systems for systematically scoring defense, that of Holt (1977) and Levine and Spivak (1964), have each generated considerable research.

Assessment of Primary-Process Thinking and Its Control

For almost two decades Holt (1977) has been developing and refining a Rorschach scoring manual designed to measure manifestations of primary process thinking and its control. Holt's system calls for the scoring of four sets of variables: content indices of primary process, formal indices of primary process, control and defense, and overall ratings. Because ideation is considered an instinctual derivative, that is, only the idea representing the instinct rather than the instinct itself can achieve consciousness, the section of Holt's manual related to control and defense has relevance in this review of defense and its measurement.

The control and defense scores represent an attempt to assess the manner in which the primary process material is regulated and modulated and how successfully this is accomplished. There are two aspects to this scoring: an identification of the specific defensive operation being employed and a determination as to whether the operation improves or further disrupts the response. Holt devised the following scores to specify the particular defensive operation being used: remoteness, context, postponing strategies, miscellaneous, and overtness.

Remoteness involves several subcategories (remoteness-ethnic, remoteness-animal, remoteness-geographic, etc.) and is based on the principle that when an unacceptable impulse is expressed in a response, it may be rendered more acceptable if the subject distances himself or herself from the response by making the percept distant in time, place, person, or level of reality.

Context refers to the setting in which the response is presented and the extent to which this makes the primary process aspects of the response more acceptable. Four levels of context, including the cultural, aesthetic, intellectual, and humorous, are distinguished.

Two types of *postponing strategies*, delay and blocking, are scored. As implied in the name, these refer to processes by which the emergence of primary process is delayed or blocked.

Miscellaneous defenses is a catchall category that Holt uses to include an array of defensive maneuvers, such as rationalization, vagueness, projection, obsessional defenses, isolation, evasiveness and avoidance, and impotence and sequence.

Overtness refers to the distinction between potential and active types of aggression. Four types of overtness are distinguished: overtness in behavior, verbal overtness, experiential overtness, and potential overtness.

In addition to these specific defense scores, the fourth part of the scoring manual, overall scores, also includes ratings that bear on defense. The *defense demand* rating was devised to evaluate the degree to which either the nature of the idea underlying a response or the way it emerges demands that some defensive and controlling measure be undertaken in order to make the response a socially acceptable communication. This is scored on a six-point scale ranging from little apparent need for defense to increasingly greater need for defense. A second rating, *defense effectiveness*, was developed in order to evaluate the relative effectiveness of the defensive operation in reducing or preventing anxiety and in permitting a more successful and adaptive response. This score too is related on a six-point scale, with positive values indicating good control and negative values indicating more pathological defensive efforts. A final overall rating is *adaptive regression*. This score, which combines the amount of primary process material with the effectiveness of its integration, is obtained by multiplying the defense demand score and the defense effectiveness score, response by response, then summing the products and dividing the summed product by the number of primary process responses.

Reliability

In general, studies involving the reliability of the entire Holt scoring system, including the measures of defense, have investigated the agreement among judges in scoring. Overall, the level of agreement attained with the overall ratings has been satisfactory; however, the findings regarding the individual categories have been discouraging. One should view the latter conclusion with caution, however, for as Lerner and Lewandowski (1975) have noted,

> . . . the scoring system has undergone several modifications and revisions, and the degree to which two scorers agree must be considered in light of the edition of the manual used. This becomes especially relevant when one considers that many of the changes were made with the specific intent of enhancing reliability [p. 192].

McMahon (1964) tested his agreement with another experienced scorer on 20 cases randomly selected from a sample of 40 schizophrenic and 40 medical patients in a V.A. Hospital. On the mean defense effectiveness score he reported a product-moment correlation of .56.

In a study involving the Rorschach records of psychotherapists in training, Bachrach (1968) reported reliability coefficients greater than .89 between two well-trained graduate students for the ratings of mean defense demand, mean defense effectiveness, and adaptive regression.

Allison (1967) and an independent rater scored the Rorschach protocols of 20 divinity students and obtained the following reliability coefficients: mean defense demand, .99; mean defense effectiveness, .81; and adaptive regression, .67.

Benfari and Calogeras (1968), in a sample of 40 college students, reported reliability coefficients of .95 for mean defense demand and .90 for mean defense effectiveness scores.

Rabkin (1967), together with another experienced scorer, scored 25 records randomly selected from a group of 100 Rorschach records obtained from patients participating in the Menninger Foundation Psychotherapy Research Project. The reliabilities reported by Rabkin were the following: mean defense demand, .86; and mean defense effectiveness, .90.

Russ (1980), in a study involving 20 protocols selected from a group of 51 second graders, obtained inter-rater reliabilities between two experienced scorers of .76 for mean defense demand, .80 for mean defense effectiveness, and .90 for adaptive regression.

As noted previously, findings with respect to the agreement in scoring of the individual categories have been relatively unsatisfactory. Holt (1977), using raw data from two studies, found that scorer agreement was highly related to the frequency with which a specific category was used. Lerner and Lewandowski (1975), using their own scoring of protocols obtained in their clinical practice, reported that "if the content and formal variables were scored accurately, then the control and defense scoring was straightforward and afforded little difficulty" (p. 188). In summary then, while the inter-rater reliability for the overall ratings across several studies is highly adequate, data is inconclusive with respect to the reliability of the individual defense and control scores.

Studies related to the construct validity of the scoring system have involved the following: (1) attempts to link the drive and control measures to behaviors and characteristics theoretically related to primary process thinking; (2) the use of specific scores as criterion measures in studying the effects on thinking and defense of experimentally induced or clinical conditions; and (3) attempts to find differences in the expression and control of primary process thinking among groups differentiated on the basis of other variables, such as diagnosis and level of conscience development. The studies to be reviewed here will be examined exclusively in terms of the specific and overall indices of defense; for a more detailed and comprehensive review of the findings of these studies as they relate to the entire scoring system, refer to Holt (1977) and Lerner and Lewandowski (1975).

Cognitive Studies

Several investigators have attempted to relate aspects of Holt's manual to various cognitive and perceptual variables that are conceptually linked to the expression and control of primary process manifestations. The areas studied include the thought process of individuals who have undergone unusual religious experiences, the capacity to cope with cognitive complexity, the capacity to tolerate unrealistic experiences, conjunctive empathy, tolerance for perceptual deprivation, and creativity.

In a sample of 29 male college students, Maupin (1965) investigated the relationship between responses to a meditation exercise and specific ego capacities, including the capacity to regress adaptively. He reported a correlation (Tau .49, $p < .001$) between indices of the response to meditation and the measure of adaptive regression. The relative contributions of the various components of the adaptive regression score were explored in a multivariate chi-square analysis. The main contribution to the relationship with response to meditation came from the "defense effectiveness" component ($\chi^2 2 = 7.82, p < .02$).

Allison (1967) studied the thought processes of individuals who had undergone a religious conversion experience. The sample consisted of 20 male divinity students who were subdivided into three groups on the basis of an autobiographical statement as to whether or not they had undergone an unusual or mystical experience. Allison found that whereas both the defense demand ($p < .05$) and the adaptive regression ($p < .05$) scores were significantly related to the intensity of the conversion experience, the defense effectiveness score did not discriminate the subgroups.

The most direct test of the relationship between the amount and control of primary process on the Rorschach test and the capacity to deal with cognitive complexity was conducted by Blatt and associates (1969). Fifty male college students were administered the Rorschach test and the John-Rimoldi, an apparatus designed to measure the ability to analyze and synthesize abstract and logical relationships. The authors found that although the ability to handle cognitive complexity, as defined by the John-Rimoldi, was not related to defense demand, it was significantly related to defense effectiveness and adaptive regression.

Similar, but less impressive, results regarding the relationship between adaptive regression and cognitive flexibility were reported by Murray and Russ (1981) in a study of 42 college students. They found a significant relationship between the adaptive regression score and a measure of cognitive flexibility (Mednick's remote association test) for males but not for females.

A third area of investigation that has received considerable attention is that of creativity. Most researchers who have attempted to relate Holt's scores to measures of creativity have been interested in testing Kris's (1952) hypothesis that "regression in the service of the ego" is necessary for the artist. In developing this concept, Kris emphasized the relationship between creativity and adaptive regression.

Pine and Holt (1960) attempted to predict from a triad of scores (the adaptive regression score, effectiveness of defense measure, and demand for defense index) the quality of imaginative productions on a variety of experimental tasks, including a Thematic Apperception Test (TAT) literary quality score, Science Test, and Brick Use Test. In a sample of 27 undergraduate students they found that the adaptive regression score and the effectiveness of defense score were significantly related to a summary imaginative quality measure for the males. For the females the findings were weak and inconclusive.

Support for the above findings was provided by Cohen (1960), who also studied the relationship between creativity and adaptive regression. In his study, which involved college students, gender did not affect the findings.

Using a sample of 56 unemployed actors, Pine (1962) attempted to replicate the findings from the earlier study with Holt (Pine and Holt, 1960). He found, in contrast to the previous investigation, that not one of the correlations between the defense measures and creativity was significant. In explaining this discrepant finding Pine noted that the variance in the defense effectiveness scores was too small in this sample to permit a meaningful ranking of subjects.

Finally, Dudek and Chamberland-Bouhadana (1982) compared a group of mature, renowned artists with a group of young art students on the various Holt measures. They found that all three overall scores (defense demand, defense effectiveness, and adaptive regression) significantly differentiated the experienced from the inexperienced artists.

Another cognitive perceptual variable that investigators have studied with respect to its relationship to the amount and success of integration of primary process material is the capacity to "tolerate unrealistic experience." Feirstein (1967) tested the hypothesis that subjects who are able to adaptively integrate (high defense effectiveness) drive-related material into their thinking will also be able to perceive their environment in ways that contradict conventional modes of perception. Twenty male graduate students were administered Rorschach tests together with four tests of "tolerance for unrealistic experiences," including Phi phenomena, reversible figures, aniseikonic lenses, and stimulus incongruity. The author reported a significant correlation ($r = .46, p < .05$) between the Rorschach defense effectiveness score and a combined measure of tolerance for unrealistic experience. An adaptive regression score, consisting of the defense effectiveness score and an index of the amount of unrealistic thinking, also correlated significantly ($r = .49, p < .025$) with the criterion measure.

Another variable that has been related to the various defense measures is conjunctive empathy. Based on scale ratings derived from tapes of psychotherapy sessions, Bachrach (1968) found that as quality of conjunctive empathy expressed by the psychotherapist increased, there were significant increases in adaptive regression and defense effectiveness. Defense demand did not significantly relate to the empathy measure, though in reviewing the raw data Bachrach noted a curvilinear relationship with defense demand, greater at either extreme of the empathy dimension.

The final factor that investigators have attempted to relate to the expression and control of primary process is the capacity to tolerate perceptual deprivation. Wright and Abbey (1965) found that an index of control score, which consisted of the proportion of defense demand to defense effectiveness, was significantly related to success in tolerating a deprivation situation ($\chi^2 = 8.04, df = 2, p < .05$) in a sample of 21 subjects. Because in this study the Rorschach test was administered several months after completion of the isolation experiment, and therefore success or failure in tolerating the deprivation experience might have influenced the Rorschach scores, Wright and Zubek (1969) attempted to replicate the earlier study but used Rorschach tests administered prior to the experiment. The obtained results were quite consistent with those reported in the earlier study. That is to say, the index of control score was again highly related to the capacity to tolerate the perceptual deprivation situation.

Goldberger (1961) employed Holt's manual to predict as well as to study reactions to perceptual isolation. Fourteen college students were isolated for a period of eight hours and encouraged to openly discuss their thoughts and feelings. From a combination of the Rorschach test, a series of cognitive tests, clinical ratings, and overt verbal behavior during the experiment, Goldberger found the following: (1) defense effectiveness was positively related to controlled primary process thinking during isolation and to the experience of positive affect during isolation; (2) defense effectiveness was negatively correlated with poorly controlled primary process thinking during isolation, the experience of negative affect during isolation, and cognitive test impairment in the isolation situation; and (3) defense effectiveness did not predict a tendency to prematurely terminate the isolation experience.

In summary, two summary defense scores from the Holt manual have been found to be related to a host of cognitive–perceptual variables that, on theoretical grounds, are linked to the expression and control of primary process thinking. Across several studies the defense effectiveness score and a measure of adaptive regression have been related to the capacity to tolerate and adaptively cope with situations in which reality contact is temporarily suspended (Zen meditation, religious conversion experiences, perceptual isolation), the ability to tolerate unrealistic experiences, and the capacity to deal with a variety of cognitive tasks. As well, subjects who are able to adaptively regulate drive expressions and integrate logical and

illogical thoughts into appropriate Rorschach responses are more empathic in treatment relationships. The findings with respect to creativity
were somewhat equivocal; nevertheless, several investigators were able
to demonstrate a relationship between the defense scores and indices of
creativity.

Clinical Studies

A second area of investigation involves studies in which researchers
have used defense scores from the Holt manual to assess the impact on
thinking of specific clinical conditions.

Saretsky (1966) investigated the effects of chlorpromazine on the
Rorschach records of a group of schizophrenic patients. Forty hospitalized
male patients were divided into experimental and control groups with
subjects in the experimental group receiving chlorpromazine and those in
the control group a placebo. The pre- and post-drug Rorschach protocols
for each subject were scored for mean defense effectiveness. For both
groups the author reported significant increases in the defense effectiveness score, thus indicating changes in the patients' attitudes toward disturbing ideation and the manner of controlling it. Furthermore, independent ratings of clinical improvement in both groups correlated
significantly with the degree of improvement in the defense effectiveness
score.

A second study employed the Holt scoring system to assess changes in
thought processes in a patient diagnosed as having myxedema psychosis.
Because treatment of this illness with desiccated thyroid results in rapid
clinical improvement, Greenberg and associates (1969) administered three
Rorschachs over a seven-month period to a 17-year-old female patient
having the disease. The patient was tested three days after thyroxin
treatment was initiated, two months later, and during a follow-up period
five months after the second testing. Between the first and second testing
the patient's clinical condition improved dramatically, whereas between
the second and third evaluations the improved state was maintained.
Ratings on mean defense effectiveness increased and were consistent with
the improved clinical state.

Group Differences

Other studies have investigated differences in the expression and control of primary process manifestations among groups differentiated on the
basis of some other psychological variable.

Zimet and Fine (1965) investigated differences in the extent and nature
of thought disturbance between subgroups of schizophrenic patients. The
Rorschach records of 23 reactive schizophrenics and 36 process schizoph-

renics were scored using several of the Holt summary ratings. Consistent with clinical expectations, the reactive schizophrenics produced significantly more modulated and controlled primary process responses than did the process group.

Benfari and Calogeras (1968) studied differences in types of thinking between groups distinguished on the basis of conscience development. Forty college students were subdivided into two groups according to their responses to a conscience scale. The members of one subgroup, referred to as having a "nonintegrated conscience," were characterized both by a tendency to hold severe moral principles and strict prohibitions and by a compelling desire to rebel against these severe standards. These subjects revealed inner conflict by presenting such affects as guilt, self-reproach, and ambivalence. The other group, designated "integrated conscience," included subjects who held strong ethical beliefs and a disciplined acceptance of these standards. Conflict regarding values and behavior was not evident in this group. Using scores from the Holt manual, support was found for the proposition that a less well-controlled and defended ego is associated with a more punitive and conflicted conscience.

In conclusion, as part of his attempt to operationalize the concepts of primary and secondary process, Holt devised a number of individual and summary defense scores to evaluate the way in which, as well as how effectively, primary process manifestations are controlled. Unfortunately, the individual scores have received little currency in the research literature. Agreement in scoring between raters for the individual categories has not been satisfactory; however, Lerner and Lewandowski (1975) found that scoring was relatively easy if the content and formal expressions of primary process were scored accurately. While the individual scores, in general, have not been used in studies of validity, Lerner and Lerner (1982) found negation and minimization to be effective and useful indices of higher level forms of denial. By contrast, research involving several summary scores has been extensive. Highly satisfactory levels of reliability have been reported for the following scores: defense demand, defense effectiveness, and adaptive regression. Measures of defense effectiveness and adaptive regression have been related to the following: (1) a number of conceptually related cognitive and perceptual factors; (2) changes in thought organization associated with improvement in clinical states; and (3) differences between groups distinguished on the basis of either diagnosis or integration of conscience.

Rorschach Index of Repressive Style

Levine and Spivak (1964) devised the Rorschach Index of Repressive Style (RIRS) initially as an attempt to operationalize Freud's concept of repression. In his 1915 article "The Unconscious," Freud noted that "repression is essentially a process affecting ideas on the border between the systems Ucs and Pcs" (p. 180). Levine and Spivak inferred from Freud's statement that repression works through the cognitive system and has the effect of inhibiting ideational processes.

Were they to have continued conceiving of their scale of repressive style as a measure of the ideational results of repression, their line of reasoning would have been similar to that of Holt. However, over time they modified their conceptual basis and came to conceive of their scale as a measure of an ideational style that predisposes one to the use of repression. It is important to keep this conceptual shift in mind, for in the research accompanying the scale the authors do not always make explicit which view of repression they are attempting to assess. As well, this conceptual ambiguity leads to methodological weaknesses in the research itself.

Having shifted their conceptual base from a measure of repression to a measure of repressive style, Levine and Spivak (1964) operationally defined repressive style as "a consistent characteristic of an individual that is manifest in vague, unelaborated language which is lacking in integration and flow" (p. 14). Focusing not as much on the response itself as on the manner in which the response is delivered, the scoring manual represents an attempt to systematically assess the construct of repressive style.

The system calls for the scoring of each response along the following seven dimensions: specificity, elaboration, impulse responses, presence of primary process thinking, self references, presence of movement, and associative flow. Underlying these factors is the thesis that to the extent that the verbalization of a response is impersonal, lacks movement, reflects vague and unelaborated thinking, is unintegrated, and reveals an absence of associative flow, the greater is the degree of repressive functioning. Conversely, the more specific, detailed, reality bound and logical a response is, and the more it is offered with a free flow of words, the less the degree of repressive functioning.

The scale has been subjected to several types of tests of reliability. Levine and Spivak reported on four separate studies in which inter-rater correlations of .95 to .98 were obtained. The combined results led the authors to conclude that the scale could be scored with considerable consistency by different scorers across various samples.

Because it is assumed that the scale measures an enduring, characterological feature, the authors thought it important to demonstrate the measure's long-term reliability. Data obtained by both Paulsen and Ledwith (Levine and Spivak, 1964) indicate that repressive style is not only an enduring mode of response but, in addition, becomes characteristic of a child at about seven years of age.

Several studies have been conducted to assess the retest reliability of the

RIRS. Collectively, these studies found that when the conditions of administration remain constant but different inkblots are used, reliability correlations range from .50 to .67. When the same inkblots are administered under the same conditions within a relatively short interval of time, reliability correlations range between .74 and .82.

Attempts to establish the concurrent validity of the RIRS have involved investigating the relationship between the scale and other Rorschach scores, as well as between the scale and a specific Thematic Apperception Test (TAT) score. In a sample of 68 student nurses Levine and Spivak (1964) found RIRS to be most highly correlated with movement response (M), color response (c), and experience balance. Whereas subjects with high RIRS scores tended to offer a dilated experience balance, those with low RIRS scores produced constricted experience balances. The authors, using as criteria more traditional Rorschach scores, took these findings as indicating that subjects who obtain high RIRS scores tend to produce richer and fuller records. In a second study, which involved 92 college students and used the Holtzman Inkblots, Levine and Spivak (1964) substantiated the earlier findings and also found a positive and significant correlation between RIRS and the number of pure form responses.

Levine and Spivak also studied the relationship between RIRS and TAT "transcendence scores." These scores represent an attempt to assess the extent to which a subject's description of the TAT cards goes beyond the immediate stimulus properties of each card. As predicted, RIRS was found to correlate positively with several indices of transcendence.

From the foregoing studies, then, the authors concluded that subjects who produce high RIRS scores (i.e., less repressive functioning) tend, on other measures, to manifest a richness of intellectual and affective responsiveness, reveal a capacity for reflectiveness, and are able to effect delay of impulse gratification.

Further efforts to demonstrate concurrent validity have included investigations of the relationship between RIRS and questionnaire measures of anxiety and repression. In general, the findings have not been impressive. Correlations between the RIRS and various anxiety scales (Taylor Manifest Anxiety Scale, Saranson Test Anxiety Scale, Cattel IPAT) have been at a borderline level of statistical significance, and none of the relationships have been strong (Levine and Spivak, 1964). With specific regard to repression, little relationship was found in a sample of 155 college students between the RIRS score and the following MMPI scales: the repression scale, the internalization ratio, Hawley's defensive scale, the K scale, and the repression-sensitization scale.

The construct validity of the scale has been investigated in several studies that have attempted to relate RIRS scores to the ego capacity to tolerate sensory isolation and to various cognitive–perceptual dimensions, including field dependence–independence and leveling–sharpening.

Using the data obtained by Goldberger (1961) in his study of reactions to sensory isolation, Levine and Spivak (1964) rescored the Rorschach protocols employing the RIRS scale. RIRS scores were found to correlate positively and significantly with ratings of the capacity to adapt to sensory isolation ($r = .61$, $p < .05$), as well as with a rating of frequency and vividness of imagery ($r = .73$, $p < .01$). No significant relationship was found between RIRS score and a measure of maladaptive reaction to sensory isolation.

Because Witkin's (1950) description of the personality characteristics of field-dependent and field-independent individuals seemed in keeping with their own understanding of repressive style as assessed by the RIRS, Levine and Spivak (1964) investigated the relationship between the RIRS and measures of field dependence. Using a supplied group of Rorschach protocols obtained from 24 ten-year-olds for whom perceptual measures were also available, the authors reported a correlation of $-.25$ between the RIRS score and an index of field dependence. Consistent results were also obtained on data collected by Young (1959), whose sample consisted of college students. In both studies the results, although not strong, indicate that subjects who manifest repressive functioning in the Rorschach, as measured by the RIRS, tend to be field dependent.

Leveling–sharpening, a cognitive dimension investigated by Holtzman and Gardner (1959), refers to the extent to which a subject in solving cognitive tasks is guided more by internal cues (sharpeners) than by immediate, external perceptual properties (levelers). Rorschach protocols previously obtained by Holtzman and Gardner from ten extreme levelers and ten extreme sharpeners drawn from a sample of 80 female college students were rescored for RIRS by Levine and Spivak. The authors reported a mean RIRS of 2.25 for levelers and 2.77 for sharpeners, which was significant between the .05 and .10 levels of significance. This result, together with the finding that the RIRS correlated especially well with a measure of ranking accuracy, led the authors to conclude that subjects who score higher on the RIRS tend to perceive stimuli more discretely and then use the discrete impression as an internal frame of reference against which new stimuli are judged.

Based on the consistency of findings across these studies of sensory isolation, field independence–field dependence, and leveling–sharpening, Levine and Spivak (1964) interpreted the results as indicating that subjects who differ on the RIRS dimension also differ with respect to the degree to which they have available and can use their own thoughts and fantasies in interpreting experience, the extent to which they rely on the external properties of the situation, and the extent to which they respond to their surroundings in terms of an internal frame of reference. More specifically, whereas low RIRS subjects (those more globally repressive), tend to be more reliant on immediate perceptual aspects of a situation, look outside of themselves for guiding cues, and have little inner frame of reference, high RIRS subjects (those less globally repressive), by contrast, respond to given situations by interpreting them in terms of their own readily available ideas and memories.

Clinical Groups

Another group of studies were undertaken to compare RIRS scores between clinical groups who, on theoretical grounds, are assumed to differ with respect to their reliance on repression.

Clinical experience shows that the typical patient who relies on repression as a defense is the hysteric, whereas intellectualization and isolation of affect are the defenses one finds in the obsessive-compulsive. Using this clinical impression, Levine and Spivak (1964) reviewed 16 Rorschach records, 8 for each syndrome, and scored the protocols using the RIRS scale.

Whereas the mean score for the eight hysterics was 1.97, that for the obsessive compulsives was 3.55 (lower score indicates greater repression). Using the U test, this difference was found to be significant at the .001 level of significance. An investigation of the individual records indicated that the two hysterical cases with the highest RIRS scores were also described as individuals who were tested at a point in which their repressive defenses were failing.

Pursuing this latter finding in a second study, Levine and Spivak (1964) compared RIRS scores of four patients each of whom represented a different level of severity of breakdown of repressive defenses. The scores for the respective patients were as follows: well-defended hysteric with repressive trends, 1.47; hysteric with phobic and depressive features presenting precarious defenses, 1.59; hysteric with badly faltering defenses, 2.66; and a borderline psychotic with multiple phobias but with a heavy reliance on repressive defenses, 1.92. In this study of individual cases, then, lower RIRS scores were associated with well-functioning repressive defenses while higher scores seemed to be associated with failing defenses.

Based on the thesis that psychosomatic involvement is associated with a reliance on repression, a third study compared Rorschach records of a group of neurotic patients with somatic complaints with the records of a group of neurotic patients who presented with other psychological complaints. As predicted, the patients with psychosomatic disorders produced, in general, more repressed Rorschach protocols, as judged by RIRS scores.

In summary, basing their work on Rapaport's pioneering efforts to systematize the ways in which Rorschach responses are delivered, Levine and Spivak creatively quantified this dimension by devising a scale for measuring a specific mode of cognition. Although the scale has considerable face validity and has generated much research, its conceptual base is nonetheless somewhat ambiguous, and many of the supporting studies suffer from methodological weaknesses.

As noted previously, the scale was initially developed to assess the specific defense of repression; however, in time, the authors modified this conceptualization and began to conceive of the scale as measuring a more general cognitive style that predisposed one to the use of repression. As a consequence of this shift, it appears that some studies (i.e., those involving a comparison of different diagnostic groups) were designed and based on the initial conceptualization whereas other studies (i.e., those involving the relationship between the scale and specific cognitive controls) were based on the later conceptualization. Thus, it is not always clear which construct the studies are meant to validate.

Apart from suggesting that ideational style predisposes one to the use of repression, the authors did not develop as fully as possible the more general relationship between cognition and defense, nor did they fully explore and detail the repressive cognitive style. Shapiro (1965) has comprehensively described a cognitive style, which he refers to as the "hysterical style," that is strikingly similar to the one described by Levine and Spivak. Shapiro carefully delineated the relationship between this style and repression, but he also cautioned that "this mode of functioning or, specifically, of cognition decidedly *favors* the phenomenon we describe as 'repression'" (p. 117). In other words—and consistent with clinical experience—Shapiro is suggesting that there is not a one-to-one relationship between cognitive style and defense and that cognition is only one aspect of the matrix that determines the specific defense.

Because of the conceptual ambiguities and the contention of Levine and Spivak that the RIRS assesses a unitary dimension, there is much confusion regarding the meaning of higher scale scores. Although higher scores are conceived of as indicating less repressive functioning, in certain studies high scores seem to indicate the use of defenses other than repression whereas in other studies the higher scores are taken to indicate a breakdown in the defense of repression. Clearly, a preference for other defenses and the faltering of repression are quite different matters.

With respect to methodology, most of the results reported by Levine and Spivak were taken from studies in which the original data were collected by others and typically for other purposes; that is to say, Levine and Spivak secured Rorschach protocols from other projects and then rescored these records for RIRS. Thus, not only were the Rorschach records obtained under varying circumstances, but in addition, examiners differing in experience, training, and method of administration initially obtained the records. Levine and Spivak themselves found that although the correlation between RIRS scores is high when the conditions of re-examination are constant, changes in certain conditions of administration affect the scores.

Despite the above noted conceptual difficulties and methodological weaknesses, the scale does represent an attempt to systematize an important component of Rorschach testing (the delivery of the response) within an overall theoretical framework. Several of the component dimensions identified by Levine and Spivak (specificity, elaboration, impulsivity, and associative flow) are similar to indices Schafer (1954) also used as indicators of a reliance on repression. This, together with the consideration that studies involving the scale have yielded positive findings, suggests that if the conceptual ambiguities can be clarified, especially in the light of later works on repression (Shapiro, 1965; Horowitz, 1972; Krohn, 1978), then the scoring system could serve as a basis for constructing a Rorschach measure of repression. With the more recent growth of interest in primitive defenses (Lerner and Lerner, 1982), especially as they contrast with repression, the need for a valid measure of repression is particularly pressing at this time.

SUMMARY

In parallel with shifts in psychoanalytic theory, concepts of defense have shifted; yet, the notion of defense has remained a cornerstone of the theory. As part of an overall review of the construct and the ways it has been operationalized in Rorschach terms, in this chapter I have reviewed Freud's notions of defense, as conceived first within drive theory and then as reconceptualized within the structural model. I then discussed two comprehensive Rorschach scoring systems based on Freud's respective formulations.

Although both scoring systems have generated a considerable amount of research, many of the studies have suffered from methodological weaknesses. In addition, both scales have proved too cumbersome for clinical application.

Overall, the scales have attempted to operationalize a concept of defense that was abstract and somewhat elusive, couched in mechanistic terms, and embedded in a system of hypothetical energic forces. Then too, because both drive theory and structural theory have been pitched at a metapsychological level, their constituent concepts, such as defense, have been defined in ways far removed from the clinical situation and the patient's experience. It is this "experience-distant" quality that has proved troublesome to researchers and has resulted in a variety of methodological difficulties.

More recently, interest has shifted away from drive theory and structural theory and toward object relations theory and self psychology. Accordingly, the concept of defense has been reformulated in important and refreshingly new ways. These reformulations and the research they have spawned are the subject matter of Chapter 13.

13

Rorschach Assessment of Defense—II: Recent Measures

Important and innovative changes are arising in the concept of defense. These modifications have been stimulated by the British school of object relations, beginning with the writings of Melanie Klein. While anchoring her views in several of Freud's specific formulations, Klein nonetheless fundamentally reconceptualized defense by suggesting that such mechanisms not only regulate affects and drives but are also related to the effects on intimacy and cognition of the experience, organization, and internalization of object relations. For Klein, defenses not only protect the ego from overwhelming sensations but are also nondefensive organizing principles of infantile mental life.

Two such organizing principles stand out in Klein's portrait of infantile mentation: splitting and projection. Klein's view of splitting derives from Freud's (1915) use of the concept in "Instincts and Their Vicissitudes," in which he proposes the idea of an early developmental distinction between a purified pleasure ego and a collection of excessively negative object impressions (Grala, 1980). Whereas the pleasure ego represents an internalization of gratifying object relations, the latter results from a projection of feelings associated with nongratifying, frustrating object relations.

A special form of projection detailed by Klein is projective identification. Here, unwanted parts of the self and internal object are split off and projected onto an external object. Because the object is not felt to be separate but, rather, is identified with the projected parts, the process affords possession of and control over the object. Bion (1967) extended the concept of projective identification in terms of the metaphor of the container and the contained. He suggested that projective identification not

179

only allows the disavowal and projection of unwanted parts of the self but also permits the containment of such parts within the object.

An attempt to integrate the two streams of psychoanalytic formulations of defense—the ego psychological and that evolving from the British school of object relations—is represented by the work of Kernberg (1975), particularly by his structural concept of levels of defensive organization. Kernberg proposes a hierarchical organization of levels of character pathology linked to type of defensive functioning and developmental level of internalized object relation. For Kernberg, internalized object relations are organized on the basis of specific defensive structures. As part of this model, he systematically defines and coordinates the more primitive defenses described by Klein and clarifies the distinction between splitting and repression. Accordingly, while splitting is a developmental precursor of repression, it continues to function pathologically in those patients who are preoedipally fixated, as indicated by an inability to form whole object relations and by a disturbance in object constancy.

Kernberg has identified two overall levels of defensive organization of the ego, one associated with preoedipal and the other with oedipal pathology. At the lower level, splitting or primitive dissociation is the basic defensive operation, with a concomitant impairment of the ego's synthetic function. Splitting is bolstered through the related defenses of low-level denial, primitive idealization, primitive devaluation, and projective identification. At a higher developmental level, associated with oedipal pathology, repression supplants splitting as a major defense and is accompanied by the related defensive operations of intellectualization, rationalization, undoing, and higher-level forms of denial and projection.

LERNER DEFENSE SCALE

On the basis of Kernberg's theoretical conceptualizations of defense and the clinical test work of Mayman (1967), Pruitt and Spilka (1964), Holt (1970), and Peebles (1975), Lerner and Lerner (1980) devised a Rorschach scoring manual designed to evaluate the specific defensive operations presumed to characterize the developmentally lower level of defensive functioning.

The scoring manual is divided into sections on the basis of the specific defenses of splitting, devaluation, idealization, projective identification, and denial. Within each section the defense is defined, Rorschach indices of the defense are presented, and clinical illustrations are offered. The sections on devaluation, idealization, and denial call for an identification of the defense and a ranking of the defense on a continuum of high versus low order. In keeping both with Kernberg's contention that these defenses organize and reflect the internal object world and with the empirical relationship found between human responses on the Rorschach test and quality of object relations (Blatt and Lerner, 1983), the system involves a systematic appraisal of the human figure response. In assessing the human percept, attention is accorded the precise figure seen (e.g., clowns, warriors, magicians), the way in which the figure is described, and the action ascribed to the figure.

Scoring System

Rationale

Our emphasis on the structural concept of defense was prompted by several considerations. These defenses are considered intrinsic to the nature and quality of the borderline patient's object relations. In addition, because these structures have been well described and illustrated in a clinical context, they lend themselves to operationalization and, eventually, quantification. Finally, if these defenses can be reliably and validly assessed, then not only the clinical researcher but also the clinical practitioner would be furnished a tool of much explanatory and predictive worth.

General Scoring Considerations

1. In general, the basic unit to be scored is the response containing an entire human figure, either static or in movement (H response). There are two exceptions to this principle. Several of the indices for splitting involve two responses. In these instances, only one score is awarded. Also, one of the scores for projective identification involves the scoring of human detail responses.

2. Before applying the system, all responses should be scored for form level using a system devised by Mayman (1970).

3. The sections on devaluation, idealization, and denial call for an identification of these defenses, as well as a ranking of the defense on a continuum of high versus low order.

4. Any response may receive more than one score.

5. In assessing the human percept, attention should be paid to the following aspects of the response: the action ascribed to the figure, the way in which the figure is described, and the exact figure seen.

Specific Defenses and Their Scoring

Splitting

Splitting involves an admixture of separations of drives, affects, internal object representations, external object relations, and introjective mechanisms (Robbins, 1976). With regard to object relations, it refers to what a person does to and with his inner and outer objects. More specifically, it involves a division of internal and external into (1) parts, as distinct from wholes, and (2) good and bad part-objects (Pruyser, 1975). Behaviorally, splitting is manifest in a tendency to perceive and describe others in terms of overruling polarities (Pruyser, 1975). While these polarities convey the division of good versus bad, they may take several forms, including frustrating versus satisfying, dangerous versus benign, and friendly versus hostile. The tendency to polarize affective descriptions of objects underlies the indices considered indicative of splitting. To denote splitting, use the letter (S).

Score splitting in the following cases:

(A) In a sequence of responses, a human percept described in terms of a specific, nonambivalent, nonambiguous affective dimension is immediately followed by another human response in which the affective description is opposite that used to describe the preceding responses: for example, "looks like an ugly criminal with a gun" immediately followed by "couples sitting together cheek to cheek."

(B) In the description of one total human figure a clear distinction of parts is made so that one part of the figure is seen as opposite another part: for example, "A giant. His lower part here conveys danger, but his top half looks benign."

(C) Included in one response are two clearly distinguished figures, and these figures are described in opposite ways: for example, "Two figures, a man and a woman. He is mean and shouting at her. Being rather angelic, she's standing there and taking it."

(D) An implicitly idealized figure is tarnished or spoiled by the addition of one or more features, or an implicitly devalued figure is enhanced by the addition of one or more features: for example, "a headless angel."

Devaluation

Devaluation refers to a tendency to depreciate, tarnish, and lessen the importance of one's inner and outer objects. It is considered a muted form of spoiling and, as such, is closely linked to envy. Specifically, it is conceptualized as an aim of envy as well as a defense against it. Envy aims at being as good as the object; when this is felt as unattainable, however, it then seeks to spoil that goodness in the object and thus remove the source of the envious feelings (Segal, 1973). In addition to identifying the defense, devaluation is also rated on a five-point continuum. Underlying the continuum are three dimensions. The first dimension involves the degree to which the humanness of the figure is retained. For example, such percepts as waiters or clowns are accorded a higher score than are more distorted forms, such as monsters and mythological objects. A temporal–spatial consideration determines the second dimension. Contemporary human percepts set in a current and close locale are scored higher than are those percepts from either the past or future and set in a distant setting. The final dimension involves the severity of depreciation as conveyed in the affective description. Figures described in more primitive, blatant, socially unacceptable ways are scored lower than are those that are described in negatively tinged but more civilized and socially acceptable ways. To denote devaluation, use the symbol DV. Add to this score the number below corresponding to the appropriate level of devaluation. For example, "an angry man" is scored DV1.

(1) The humanness dimension is retained, there is no distancing of the figure in time or space, and the figure is described in negatively tinged but socially acceptable terms: for example, "two people fighting,"; "a girl in a funny costume."

(2) The humanness dimension is retained, there may or may not be distancing of the figure in time or space, and the figure is described in blatantly negative and socially unacceptable negative terms. This score would also include human figures with parts missing: for example, "a diseased African child,"; "a woman defecating,"; "sinister-looking male figure," "a disjointed figure with the head missing."

(3) The humanness dimension is retained, but involved in the percept is a distortion of human form; There may or may not be distancing of the figure in time or space; and if the figure is described negatively, it is in socially acceptable terms. This rating includes such figures as clowns, elves, savages, witches, devils, and figures of the occult: for example, "sad looking clowns"; "cannibal standing over a pot"; "the bad witch."

(4) The humanness dimension is retained, but implied in the percept is a distortion of human form. There may or may not be distancing of the figure in time or space, and the figure is described in blatantly negative and socially unacceptable terms. This rating involves the same types of figures as in (3); however, the negative description is more severe: for example, "a couple of evil witches"; "two people from Mars who look very scary"; "a sinister Ku Klux Klansman."

(5) The humanness dimension is lost, there may or may not be distancing of the distorted form in time or space, and the figure is described in either neutral or negative terms. This rating includes puppets, mannequins, robots, creatures with some human characteristics,[1] part-human–part-animal responses, and human responses with one or more animal features: for example, "Mannequins with dresses but missing a head"; "two people but half-male and half-animal; from outer space"; "a woman with breasts, high-heeled shoes, and bird's beak for a mouth."

---

[1]This rating does not include monsters with or without human characteristics.

Idealization

Idealization involves a denial of unwanted characteristics of an object and then an enhancing of the object by projecting one's own libido or omnipotence onto it. It aims at keeping an object completely separate from persecutory objects, which preserves the object from harm and destruction. This defensive aspect of idealization—that is, its aim is to protect the object from inner harm—is precarious, for the more ideal the object becomes, the more likely it is to arouse envy. As in the case of devaluation, idealization is also rated on a five-point continuum. Underlying the continuum are the same three dimensions. For scoring, denote idealization with the letter I. Add to this score the number below corresponding with the appropriate level of idealization. Thus, "a person with a big smile" is scored I1.

(1) The humanness dimension is retained, there is no distancing of the figure in time or space, and the figure is described in a positive but not excessively flattering way: for example, "two nice people looking over a fence"; "a person with a happy smile."

(2) The humanness dimension is retained, there may or may not be distancing of the person in time or space, and the figure is described in blatantly and excessively positive terms: for example, "two handsome, muscular Russians doing that famous dance"; "What an angelic figure; long hair, a flowing gown, and a look of complete serenity."

(3) The humanness dimension is retained, but implied in the percept is a distortion of human form. There may or may not be distancing of the figure in time or space, and if the figure is described positively, it is in moderate terms. This rating includes such objects of fame, adoration, or strength as civic leaders, officials, and famous people: for example, "Charles de Gaulle"; "an astronaut, one of those fellows who landed on the moon."

(4) The humanness dimension is retained, but implied in the percept is a distortion of human form. There may or may not be distancing of the figure in time or space, and the figure is described in blatantly and excessively positive terms. This rating includes the same types of figures as in (3); however, the positive description is more excessive: for example, "a warrior; not just any warrior but the tallest, strongest, and bravest"; "Attila the Hun, but with the largest genitals I have ever seen."

(5) The humanness dimension is lost, but implied in the distortion is an enhancement of identity. There may or may not be distancing of the distorted form in time or space, and the figure is described in either neutral or positive terms. This rating includes statues of famous figures, giants, supermen or superwomen, space figures with supernatural powers, angels, and idols. Also included are half-humans in which the nonhuman half adds to the figure's appearance or power: for example, "a bust of Queen

Victoria"; "powerful beings from another planet ruling over these softer creatures."

Projective Identification

This refers to a process in which parts of the self are split off and projected onto an external object or part-object. It differs from projection proper in that what is projected onto the object is not experienced as ego alien. Rather, the self "empathizes" (Kernberg, 1975) with the object and tries to control the object by means of the projection. A close examination of the concept of projective identification suggests the operation of at least three subprocesses: an externalization of parts of the self with a disregard of real characteristics of the external object, a capacity to blur boundaries between self and other, and an overriding need to control the other. The two indices of projective identification represent an attempt to assess these subprocesses. To denote this score, use the letters PI.

Score projective identification in the following cases:

(A) Confabulatory responses involving human figures in which the form level[2] is Fw − or F − and the percept is overly embellished with associative elaboration to the point that real properties of the blot are disregarded and replaced by fantasies and affects. More typically, the associative elaboration involves material with aggressive or sexual meaning, as in the following example: "A huge man coming to get me. I can see his huge teeth. He's staring straight at me. His hands are up as if he will strike me."

(B) Those human or detail responses in which the location is Dr, the determinant is FC, and the figure is described as either aggressive or having been aggressed against[3]: for example, "an ugly face" (with forehead and features seen in reference to the inner portion of Card IV); "an injured man" (Card VI upper, center area).

Denial

Denial in this system refers to a broad group of defenses arranged on a continuum based on the degree of reality distortion involved in the response. Higher-level forms of denial involve a minimum of reality distortion, whereas middle- and lower level manifestations of denial in-

---

[2]These scores are taken from Mayman's (1970) manual for form level scoring. The Fw-score is assigned to unconvincing, weak form responses in which only one blot detail is accurately perceived. The F- score refers to arbitrary form responses in which there is little resemblance between the percept and the area of the blot being responded to.

[3]Dr is a location score used when the area chosen is small, rarely used, and arbitrarily delimited (Rapaport, Gill, and Schafer, 1945). F(C) is a determinant used when the subject makes out forms within a heavily shaded area without using shading as shading or uses the nuances of shading within a colored area (Rapaport, Gill, and Schafer, 1945).

clude increasingly greater degrees of reality distortion. Examples of denial at the highest level include several defensive processes observed by Holt (1970) and presented in his manual for the scoring of manifestations of primary process thinking. Middle-level denial includes responses in which there is a major contradiction between the human figure perceived and the actions or characteristics ascribed to that figure. Lower-level manifestations of denial involve significant distortions of reality to the point that a segment of subjective experience or of the external world is not integrated with the rest of the experience. There is a striking loss of reality testing, and the individual acts as if he were unaware of an urgent, pressing aspect of reality. To score denial, use the symbol DN. Add to this score the number below corresponding to the level of denial. Thus, the response "I know they are not fighting" would be scored DN1.

(1) *Higher level denial*: Denial at this level consists of several subsidiary defenses manifested in responses in which the form level of the percept is F+, Fo, or Fw+.

(a) *Negation*: Negation involves a disavowal of impulse. The disavowal may be manifested in two ways. In one, the disavowal is smoothly blended into the response itself, whereas in the other the response, or aspects of the response, are couched in negative terms: for example, "virgin"; angel"; "These figures are not angry."

(b) *Intellectualization*: In this process, the response is stripped of its drive and affective charge by its being presented in an overly technical, scientific, literate, or intellectual way: for example, "two homo sapiens"; "two Kafkaesque figures."

(c) *Minimization*: With minimization, drive-laden material is included in the response but in a reduced and nonthreatening way. This includes changing a human figure into a caricature or cartoon figure: for example, "a shadow cast by an evil person"; "a child with his hand clenched in a fist"; "a funny man, more like a caricature."

(d) *Repudiation*: With repudiation, a response is retracted or the individual denies having even given the response.

(2) *Middle-level denial*: Denial at this level involves responses in which the form level is F+, Fo, or Fw+ and involved in the response is a basic contradiction. The contradiction may be on affective, logical, or reality grounds: for example, "a sexy Santa Claus"; "two nuns fighting"; "a man reading while asleep."

(3) *Lower level denial*: At this level, reality adherence is abrogated but in a particular way. Specifically, an acceptable response is rendered unacceptable either by adding something that is not there or by failing to take into account an aspect of the blot that is clearly to be seen. This corresponds to Mayman's (1970) form spoil (Fs) response.[4] In addition, this level

---

[4]The form spoil response differs from the F− response in that a basically acceptable

also includes responses in which incompatible descriptions are given to the percept: for example, "two people, but their top half is the female and bottom half male; each has breasts and a penis"; "a person, but instead of a mouth there is a bird's beak"; "person sitting on their huge tail."

Reliability

The reliability of the scoring system has been reported in various studies. Commonly, independent judges trained in scoring rate a series of Rorschach protocols and then the level of agreement among the judges for each of the defenses is determined.

In the initial investigation (Lerner and Lerner, 1980) ten Rorschach records (of five borderline and five neurotic patients) were scored independently by two well- trained raters. The percentage of perfect agreement between the raters for the major defense categories was as follows: splitting, 100%; devaluation, 91%; idealization, 87%; projective identification, 100%; and denial, 83%. For the subcategories, percentages of perfect agreement ranged from 76% to 95%.

In a second study (Lerner, Sugarman, and Gaughran, 1981), of borderline and schizophrenic groups, high levels of inter-rater reliability were also obtained. Correlation coefficients ranging from .94 to .99 were obtained for the major defense categories and coefficients between .47 and .95 for the continuum variables. Collapsing the continuum variables into composite scores yielded reliability coefficients ranging from .94 to .96.

Subsequent authors have also reported high levels of reliability as determined by inter-rater agreement. Van-Der Keshet (1988) in a study involving anorexic subjects reported Cronbach alpha coefficients ranging from 1.00 to .80, and Gacono (1988), in an investigation of several subgroups of psychopaths, obtained the following percentages of agreement between raters: projective identification, 100%; idealization, 100%; denial, 100%; and devaluation, 88%. Among the protocols selected for determining reliability, Gacono noted that there were no scoreable responses for splitting.

In summary, results from various studies indicate that the reliability of the scoring system for the Lerner Defense Scale, as judged by level of inter-rater agreement, is particularly high for an inkblot measure.

Validity and Findings

Kernberg (1975, 1977, 1979) has repeatedly asserted that the constellation of lower level primitive defenses distinguishes borderline and psychotic

---

response is spoiled by a perceptual oversight or distortion. In the F − response the percept is totally unacceptable.

patients on the one hand from neurotic patients on the other. Thus, to evaluate the construct validity of the scoring system, as well as the utility of Kernberg's proposals, the initial validating studies involved comparing the Rorschach records of borderline patients with the protocols of other clinical groups with respect to manifestations of primitive defenses.

Lerner and Lerner (1980) compared the Rorschach protocols of 15 outpatient borderline patients with 15 outpatient neurotics with regard to indices of primitive defense. The 30 Rorschach protocols were selected from the private files of one of the authors and scored using the proposed system. Because the testing had initially been conducted for research purposes, the test protocols had not been used in formulating the final diagnoses on which the selections were based. In this way the selection procedures were guaranteed to be unconfounded by psychological test data. The full assessments included independently obtained mental status examinations and social-developmental histories. As each of the patients subsequently entered either psychotherapy or psychoanalysis, the initial diagnosis was confirmed in discussions with the patient's therapist or analyst. The two original groups (of borderlines and neurotics) were matched on the variables of age, sex, and socioeconomic status. The Rorschach records obtained from the two groups did not differ significantly with regard to the total number of responses.

Several significant findings emerged from this study. The borderline patients used test indices of splitting, low-level devaluation, projective identification, and low-level denial significantly more often than did the neurotic patients. The measures of splitting and projective identification, which were observed exclusively in the borderline group, proved especially significant in discriminating the two groups. By contrast, indices of high-level devaluation and high-level denial were found more often in the protocols of the neurotic group. In general, and irrespective of level of severity, measures of idealization occurred more frequently in the records of the neurotic group. With devaluation the reverse was found. That is, borderline patients tended to depreciate their human figures more often than did the neurotic patients. A review of the individual Rorschach records highlighted the importance of high-level denial. When neurotic patients used low-level devaluation or low-level idealization, it was typically accompanied by manifestations of high-level denial. Such was not the case with the protocols of borderline patients. Their expressions of blatant depreciation and excessive idealization were not mitigated by forms of higher level denial.

The results of this study not only support theoretical propositions but they coincide with clinical experience as well. Those of us who work with borderline patients are familiar with these patients' intense rage, seeming imperviousness to their impact on others, and tendency to rapidly fluctuate between overvaluing their therapist and regarding their therapist with disdain and contempt. Indeed, with borderline patients, the therapist pays particular attention to how he or she is treated by the patient. The obtained findings shed light on these clinical occurrences. Specifically, it would appear that structures available to better-organized patients—in this instance, high-level denial and idealization—are not available to the borderline patient. Therapeutically, this suggests that because such controlling structures cannot be employed for containing affects and urges, control and regulation needs to be provided by the environment. This suggested stance is in accord with Winnicott who goes so far as to suggest that with certain patients the aggressive and destructive actions may be viewed as unconscious attempts to elicit specific responses from the environment.

In a companion study H. Lerner, Sugarman, and Gaughran (1981) compared the Rorschach records of a group of hospitalized borderline patients with those of a hospitalized schizophrenic group. In this study Rorschach protocols were obtained from patient files at a university teaching hospital. Patients at the facility received psychological testing as a standard procedure within the first several weeks of admission. The sample of borderline patients ($N = 21$) was selected according to criteria set out in DSM-III. The criteria were applied to information gleaned from a preadmission report that included a history of the present illness, past history, a mental-status examination, and a tentative diagnostic formulation. The sample of schizophrenic patients ($N = 19$) was selected using the Research Diagnostic Criteria (RDC) of Spitzer, Endicott, and Robbins, (1975). The RDC was applied to information obtained from the preadmission summaries in the same manner as DSM-III was used for the borderline sample. In this study, as in the Lerner and Lerner (1980) study, the Rorschach records for the two groups did not differ significantly with regard to the total number of responses.

Several significant findings emerged when the defense scores of the borderline and schizophrenic patients were compared. The borderline patients manifested indices of splitting significantly more often than did the schizophrenic patients, and four of the five scale measures of devaluation also were observed significantly more frequently in the borderline group. Indices of projective identification occurred exclusively in the borderline group. With regard to denial, the borderline patients gave significantly more responses at the middle and low levels, and when denial was treated as a composite score, it especially distinguished the two groups.

While the results of the Lerner and Lerner (1980) study supported Kernberg's (1975) formulation of two overall levels of defense organization that differentiate borderline and neurotic patients, the findings of Lerner,

Sugarman and Gaughran (1981) questioned his contention that borderline
and schizophrenic patients share a common primitive defensive constellation.

Lerner and Lerner (1982), in contrast with Kernberg, have suggested
that the results of this study indicate that the defensive organization of the
schizophrenic patient is different in kind along a number of developmental
and structural parameters from the defensive structure of the borderline
patient. Splitting, denial, projective identification, and various levels of
devaluation were found to discriminate significantly between the two
groups. Because the Rorschach measures of the defenses were based on an
appraisal of the full human response, it seemed to Lerner and Lerner (1982)
that "differences in the level of object representation underlying the
specific defenses" (p. 99) accounted for the group differences. Further
support for their inference came from the additional finding that the
schizophrenics offered far fewer human responses than did the borderline
patients.

While the Lerner, Sugarman, and Gaughran (1981) study was designed to
compare defensive structure between groups differing in severity of psychopathology, the study also yielded findings relevant to our understanding of the schizophrenic process. Of particular note were differences
between the groups in their capacity to internally represent objects.
Whereas the internal world of the borderline patient consists of highly
charged either totally depreciated or totally idealized representations, that
of the schizophrenic patient is devoid of internal representations. If inner
representations arise from the internalization of object relations that were
invested, then one might conjecture that schizophrenics never invested in
external relations and that this accounts for their empty and barren inner
object world.

Cross validation for several of the findings reported by Lerner and
Lerner (1980) and Lerner, Sugarman, and Gaughran (1981) is provided in a
study by Collins (1983). Employing Gunderson's Diagnostic Interview for
Borderlines and DSM- III criteria, Collins selected fifteen adult subjects
from each of three samples (borderline, neurotic and schizophrenic) from
several inpatient and outpatient facilities and administered the Rorschach
test. The 45 protocols were then scored using the Rorschach Defense
Scale. The differences among all three groups were highly significant,
supporting the general hypothesis that borderline patients exhibit a defensive structure significantly different from that of schizophrenics and neurotics. With respect to specific pairings, the borderline patients differed
from the schizophrenics on the defenses of splitting, projective identification, low-level idealization, and mid-level devaluation. Although not statistically significant because of the relatively low frequency of scores, the

records of the borderline group as compared with the neurotic group did offer more splitting scores and more projective identification scores.

Further Clinical Studies

More recent studies have used the Lerner Defense Scale scoring system to investigate the defensive structure of specific clinical populations assumed to have a borderline personality organization. The groups studied have included anorexic patients (Van-Der Keshet, 1988; Piran and Lerner, submitted; Brouillette, 1987), antisocial offenders (Gacono, 1988), and gender-disturbed children (Kolers, 1986).

Van-Der Keshet (1988) applied the defense scale to the Rorschach records of clinical anorexics, anorexic ballet students, nonanorexic ballet students, and a normal control group. The clinical anorexic group was further subdivided into those patients manifesting solely restrictive characteristics (i.e., restricting food intake) and those exhibiting bulimic symptoms (i.e., bingeing and purging). A comparison of the various groups on the defense scores revealed several interesting findings. As predicted, the two clinical anorexic groups and the anorexic ballet students used splitting and devaluation significantly more often than did the nonanorexic ballet students and the controls. The restricting anorexics were found to employ denial significantly more often than any of the other groups. The results related to idealization were especially informative. The normal control group employed idealization significantly more often than any of the other groups. While the anorexic ballet students did not differ from the nonanorexic ballet students with respect to idealization, both groups used the defense significantly more often than the bulimic anorexics.

Overall, Van-Der Keshet's (1988) study revealed similarities in defense patterning among the anorexic ballet students, restrictive anorexic patients, and bulimic anorexic patients and revealed differences between the foregoing groups and the nonanorexic ballet students and normal controls. Of particular interest to Van-Der Keshet were the findings related to idealization. Not only did idealization distinguish the normal controls from each of the other groups, but in addition, the score also differentiated the anorexic ballet students from the bulimic anorexics. Based on this finding Van-Der Keshet (1988) notes:

> . . . We can propose that although the anorexic ballet students share similarities with the more disturbed eating disordered groups in terms of level of defense organization, nevertheless they still differ from them in their capacity to build compensatory structures, as that capacity is manifest in using the idealizing defense more often. The anorexic ballet students have suc-

ceeded in building compensatory structures which enable them to function normally and to avoid the need for hospitalization, while the anorexic patients have actually failed in building those structures [p. 104].

Another important finding in Van-Der Keshet's study involves the differential use of denial between the two eating-disordered groups. Those treating restrictive anorexics have often employed more extreme types of intervention (e.g., forcing the patient to look in a mirror) as a way of confronting the patient's distorted body image. The obtained findings suggest that accompanying the distortion in body image is a strong reliance on denial and that such therapeutic interventions confront that denial.

In a series of studies (Piran and Lerner, 1987, Piran et al., 1988; submitted, using nonprojective instruments, Piran and Lerner found that although restrictive anorexic and bulimic anorexic patients both display a borderline level of personality organization, they differ with respect to impulse control. Whereas bulimics discharge impulses and conflicts directly through action, restrictive anorexics appear as overcontrolled, with massive inhibition and ego restriction. This consistent finding led Piran and Lerner to investigate the defensive structure of both groups more closely through the use of the Lerner Defense Scale. The sample consisted of 65 eating- disordered patients (bulimics, $n = 34$; restricters, $n = 31$) admitted or placed on a waiting list for admission to two large general hospitals specializing in the treatment of eating disorders. All subjects were female, aged 16 to 35, and fulfilled DSM-III criteria for anorexia nervosa. The authors found, in keeping with the respective nature of the symptomatology, that bulimic anorexics tended to use test indices of projective identification and low-level devaluation, whereas restrictive anorexics relied more often on denial and high-level idealization.

Thus, while restrictive and bulimic anorexics both use primitive defenses, the respective patterning of defenses differs. As indicated, the differing patterns are related to presenting symptoms and, indeed, might account for expression of symptoms; however, defenses have not explicitly been related to treatment planning. The obtained results suggest that in planning treatment defensive structure should be considered. For example, the role of denial in restrictive anorexics should be confronted whereas with bulimics one might choose to focus on their tendency to depreciate.

Brouillette (1987), in a most unique and important study, assessed the personality organization, including the defense structure, both of women suffering from eating disorders and of their mothers. The three groups of daughters, between 18 and 40 years of age, consisted of 11 women with anorexia nervosa, 10 women with bulimia, and 10 normal control women.

Rorschach records were obtained from all daughters and their mothers and assessed using scales devised to measure level of object representation, level of boundary disturbance, quality of reality testing, and nature of defenses. Impressive results were found in the comparison of mothers and daughters. First, no significant differences were found between daughters and mothers in all three groups on all measures of psychological functioning. Second, significant differences were found between the eating disorder groups and the normal control group for both the mothers and daughters on all of the same measures. Finally, neither the mothers nor the daughters in the anorexia nervosa group differed significantly on any measure from the mothers and daughters in the bulimic group. With respect to the defense scores, evidence of splitting, low-level devaluation, projective identification, and low-level denial occurred with significantly greater frequency in the protocols of anorexia nervosa patients and their mothers and bulimic patients and their mothers than in the records of the normal controls and their mothers. Although not statistically significant, there was a tendency within the bulimic pairing (daughter and mother) to use splitting more frequently than the anorexia nervosa pairing.

A second major clinical group that the Rorschach Defense Scale has been extended to is the antisocial personality. Based on Kernberg's (1975) contention that severe character disorders, including patients with an antisocial personality structure, are organized at a borderline level of personality organization, Gacono (1988) compared highly psychopathic males with low to moderately psychopathic males with respect to the proportion of borderline object relations and borderline defenses revealed on their Rorschach protocols. Thirty-three subjects who met the DSM-III-R criteria for Antisocial Personality Disorder participated in a semistructured interview and completed the Rorschach test. On the basis of a review of their records and information obtained in the interview, each subject was rated on the Hare Psychopathy Checklist. Using a score of 30 as a cutoff, 14 subjects were included in the high psychopathy group and 19 placed in the low to moderate psychopathy group.

A between-group comparison revealed that none of the individual defense scores significantly distinguished the two groups. Indeed, quite unexpectedly, the low to moderate psychopath group produced a total of 40 defense scores whereas the high psychopathy group produced only 24 such scores. A review of the individual categories revealed that the high psychopathy group as compared to the low to moderate group tended to use devaluation while the low to moderate group by comparison made more frequent use of projective identification and higher level denial. The Rorschach protocols of both groups showed a predominant use of lower levels of denial, and all levels of devaluation were found.

The results of Gacono's (1988) study are somewhat difficult to understand, especially in the light of the absence of a control group. Had a control group been included, one could first have determined if the psychopathy sample as a whole employed primitive defenses more than the controls did. One could then proceed as Gacono did and investigate differences within the psychopathy group. Further, Gacono did not account for the capacity of each of his subgroups to internally represent objects. It is possible that the low to moderate psychopathy group produced more defensive scores because they had more potentially scoreable responses, that is, responses with human content.

In accord with Hammond (1984), Gacono (1988) interpreted his findings in terms of limitations in the scoring system:

> First, borderline individuals often have difficulty experiencing objects as whole and may respond to the Rorschach by producing the kind of part human responses not scoreable by the system; secondly, human movement responses (M) symbolize an advanced human percept in motion. Children and some developmentally immature individuals may express movement responses in terms of animal content (FM), considered to be developmentally less mature. Lerner and Lerner's (1980) system prohibits the scoring of animal movement, thereby eliminating important data that reveal a subject's defensive functioning [pp. 120–121].

Collins (1983), also registered similar concerns.

Kolers (1986) extended the assessment of primitive defenses to gender disturbed children. Various ego functions, including defense, as manifested on the Rorschach records, of a group of feminine boys, their siblings, and a normal control group were evaluated and compared. The subjects, all age 5 to 12 years, consisted of 37 feminine boys diagnosed as having cross-gender disturbance, 19 siblings with no history of cross-gender behavior, and 23 normal controls. The investigator found that although the normal controls produced significantly more human figure responses, that is, more potentially scoreable responses, the gender-disturbed children and their siblings offered significantly more projective identification scores. Of the other defense scores, higher-level devaluation was found to occur significantly more often among the controls.

Of interest in Kolers' study was the finding that the projective identification score, while differentiating the normal controls from both the feminine boys and their siblings, failed to discriminate between the latter two groups. The meaning of this finding has been amplified by Ipp (1986). Ipp investigated the object relations and object representations of this same sample by applying to their Rorschach protocols the scale of Blatt and associates (1976) for assessing object representations, Blatt and Ritzler's (1974) instrument for evaluating boundary disturbances, and her own

Developmental Object Relations Scale (DORS) devised to measure developmental level of object relations. Using her own findings, especially those related to levels of boundary disturbance, and Lerner's (1985) notion of various levels of projective identification depending on the aim (i.e., defense, control, or communication) and the degree to which self boundaries are blurred and diffused, Ipp (1986) concluded that projective identification operates somewhat differently in the two groups.

Ipp (1986) found that the confabulation score on the Boundary Disturbance Scale occurred with significantly greater frequency in the protocols of the feminine boys than in the records of their siblings. Relating this finding to projective identification allowed her to conclude that in feminine boys projective identification is at a lower level, in which its aim is control and there is a severe blurring of self–other boundaries. By contrast, the siblings engage in a higher level projective identification in which self boundaries are not blurred and the defense is employed to empathize with potential sources of danger and to communicate through preverbal modalities.

In summary, because of the conceptual roots of the Lerner Defense Scale, initial studies using the scale were designed to evaluate the scoring system's efficacy in distinguishing groups of borderline patients from groups of other diagnostic entities. The combined findings of both initial studies (P. Lerner and Lerner, 1980; H. Lerner, Sugarman, and Gaughran, 1981) strongly support the contention that borderline patients present an identifiable constellation of defenses, different from that of neurotic and schizophrenic patients, and that the scoring system is a valid means of identifying these defenses. Subsequent studies extended the use of the scale to various clinical groups assumed to have an underlying borderline structure. In a series of studies (Brouillette, 1987; Piran and Lerner, 1988; Van-Der Keshet, 1988) scale scores distinguished eating-disordered patients from normal controls. Van-Der Keshet's (1988) investigation highlighted the role of idealization and added to its conceptual meaning. Brouillette's (1987) study was unique in that it dealt not only with anorexic patients but with their mothers as well. Results involving different defensive patterning between subtypes of eating disorder patients were equivocal and tended to be sample specific. Although the scale was effective in identifying specific defenses (devaluation and low-level denial) employed by a large sample of antisocial personalities, it was not useful in distinguishing between subgroups of such personalities. The scale has been extended to children. Kolers (1986) found that the projective identification score significantly discriminated gender-disturbed children and their siblings from a normal control group. Ipp (1986), in combining her own findings with those of Kolers, was able to add to our understanding of the concept of projective identification.

OTHER RORSCHACH MEASURES OF PRIMITIVE DEFENSE

Cooper and his colleagues (Cooper and Arnow, 1986; Cooper, Perry, and Arnow, 1988) have also developed a Rorschach scale designed, in part, to assess primitive defenses. Based on a somewhat different theoretical perspective and broader in scope than the Lerner and Lerner scale, Cooper's system was initially conceived as part of a complex approach to evaluating defenses in general, rather than specific borderline defenses in particular. Nonetheless, Cooper has identified the following five defenses, which he considers borderline defenses: splitting, devaluation, idealization, projective identification, and omnipotence (Lerner, Albert, and Walsh, 1987).

Drawn on the theoretical propositions of Winnicott (1953), Kohut (1977), and Stolorow and Lachmann (1980), Cooper's scale seeks to integrate object relations theory, Kohut's notions of narcissism, and Stolorow and Lachmann's concepts of developmental arrest and structural deficiency. In keeping with a position of developmental arrest, the scale takes into account Ames's (1966) empirical finding that with increased development there is an increased frequency of the human figure response on the Rorschach test and that this parallels and eventually supplants animal responses. This line of reasoning, begun by Ames and conceptually expanded in terms of defensive functioning by Stolorow and Lachmann (1980), leads to the formulation of "prestages" of defense, that is, stages that are considered predecessors of defenses proper: "Prestages are those initial precursors to a defense occurring prior to the consolidation of self and object representation, while a defense proper is the end point in a series of developmental achievements" (Lerner, Albert, and Walsh, 1987, p. 338).

In keeping with the notion of defense precursors, Cooper and Arnow (1986), in contrast to Lerner and Lerner (1980), did not limit their scores to the human figure response.

> Lerner and Lerner (1980) . . . restrict their analysis to percepts that include human figures, static or in motion. In agreement with Smith (1980), we find this circumscription unduly limiting for interpreting protocols in which there is a relative or absolute absence of human figures. More important, however, borderline defenses are more profitably examined with a broader data base regardless of the number of human responses [p. 144].

In addition to different theoretical starting points and varying definitions of what type of Rorschach content constitutes the primary object relations unit of analysis, the scoring systems differ in other ways as well. Scoring criteria for operationalizing certain defenses differ between systems.

Cooper's scale includes the scoring of omnipotence[5], and the Lerner and Lerner scale provides for the scoring of denial on a graded continuum.

Collins (1983), also concerned with the restrictive nature of the Lerner and Lerner (1980) scale, prior to Cooper, modified the Lerners' scale by extending the categories of percepts to be scored to include animal as well as human percepts. In comparison with the original scale, Collins found that his modified scale markedly increased the power of splitting and marginally increased the power of projective identification to discriminate borderline patients from schizophrenics.

In his study involving subgroups of antisocial offenders, Gacono (1988) also used Cooper's scale. Although not statistically significant, the high psychopathy group had more responses in the categories of prestage splitting, total splitting, omnipotence, and devaluation than the low to moderate psychopathy group. By contrast, the low to moderate psychopathy group had more responses in the categories of splitting, projective identification, and idealization.

The most comprehensive comparison of the two defense scales is represented in the work of Lerner, Albert, and Walsh (1987). Rorschach protocols used in two previous studies (Lerner and Lerner, 1980; Lerner, Sugarman, and Gaughran, 1981) and scored using the Lerners' system were recoded and scored according to the criteria set out by Cooper. Statistical analyses of differences between the four psychiatric groups (neurotics, outpatient borderlines, inpatient borderlines, schizophrenics) were completed separately in order to assess the power of each scale to discriminate between diagnostic groups and to evaluate the discriminatory capacity of specific defenses within each scale to differentiate among groups.

A profile analysis was conducted to assess the relative capacity of each scale to distinguish among groups. A parallelism of profiles test was run, and the results indicated that the two scales were not parallel. That is, subjects from the four clinical groups were responding somewhat differently to the two scales.

To assess statistical differences between scales in predicting group membership, a discriminant function was conducted. A review of this analysis revealed the following: (1) the Cooper Scale significantly differentiated neurotics from inpatient borderlines ($p < .01$), outpatient from inpatient borderlines ($p < .05$), and inpatient borderlines from schizo-

---

[5]Cooper defines omnipotence as an idealization of the self in which there is the conviction that one is entitled to admiration and privileged treatment. On the Rorschach test, omnipotence is seen in direct descriptions of self in blatantly positive and adulating terms; for example, "I think you are going to hear some exceptional responses. My vocabulary is incredible."

phrenics ($p < .002$); (2) the Cooper Scale failed to statistically discriminate neurotics from outpatient borderlines, neurotics from schizophrenics, and outpatient borderlines from schizophrenics; (3) the Lerner Defense Scale significantly differentiated neurotics from inpatient borderlines ($p < .001$), neurotics from schizophrenics ($p < .001$), outpatient borderlines from schizophrenics ($p < .001$), and inpatient borderlines from schizophrenics ($p < .001$); (4) the Lerner Defense Scale was unable to statistically distinguish between the two outpatient samples and the two borderline groups. While both scales validly discriminated between groups, in general these results suggest that the Cooper Scale is more effective in distinguishing between healthier outpatients whereas the Lerners' scale better discriminates more seriously disturbed inpatients.

To assess the discriminatory power of each defense, an analysis of differences among the four experimental groups was conducted separately for each scale. For Cooper's Scale, three specific defense scores distinguished among groups. Splitting distinguished inpatient borderlines from both neurotics and schizophrenics, devaluation differentiated both borderline groups from schizophrenics and neurotics from outpatient borderlines, and omnipotence separated the outpatient borderlines from neurotics and schizophrenics. Scale measures of idealization and projective identification failed to significantly differentiate among groups.

With respect to the Lerner Defense Scale, all five defenses distinguished among groups to a statistically significant degree. Splitting differentiated both borderline groups from neurotics and schizophrenics, as did devaluation and idealization. Projective identification occurred exclusively within the two borderline groups; thus, while it differentiated these groups from neurotics and schizophrenics, it did not separate the two borderline groups from each other. Finally, denial as well distinguished the borderline groups from the other two but not from each other.

One purpose of the study was to discern the relative discriminatory power of omnipotence, a score exclusive to Cooper's scale, and denial, a category exclusive to the Lerner Defense Scale. While both indices distinguished among groups, measures of omnipotence differentiated both outpatient groups from inpatient borderlines whereas denial distinguished neurotics from both inpatient groups and inpatient borderlines from schizophrenics. These findings are in accord with the overall pattern of results indicating the Cooper Scale's greater effectiveness distinguishing outpatient groups and the Lerner Defense Scale's greater effectiveness distinguishing inpatient groups.

To assess the overlap and distinctive features of each scoring system, the scales were intercorrelated. Significant correlations were obtained between subscale measures of splitting ($< .49$) and devaluation ($< .64$) but not between indices idealization (.13) and projective identification (.30). Within-scale correlations were derived and revealed differences in the structure of each test. For the Lerner Defense Scale measures of splitting, devaluation, denial, and projective identification were all intercorrelated, whereas for the Cooper Scale the defense measures correlated substantially less strongly. While the findings regarding the Lerner Defense Scale are consistent with theoretical formulations related to defense (Kernberg, 1975; Grotstein, 1981), the results also argue for the superior psychometric properties of the Cooper Scale.

In summary, a second approach to the assessment of primitive defenses is found in the work of Cooper (Cooper and Arnow, 1986). Broader in purpose and scope than the Lerner Defense Scale, the Cooper Scale includes five subscores developed to assess defenses associated with borderline functioning. Like the Lerners' system, Cooper's instrument relies heavily on the analysis of Rorschach content, but in contradistinction to it, the basic unit of analysis in the Cooper Scale extends beyond the human figure response to encompass a broad array of contents (animal responses, inanimate objects, etc.). In a comprehensive concurrent validity study both scales were found useful in distinguishing borderline patients from other diagnostic entities. At the same time, however, perhaps owing to their different conceptual starting points and their somewhat differing ways of operationally defining specific defenses, scores on the Cooper Scale seemed more effective in distinguishing among higher functioning outpatients whereas scores on the Lerner Defense Scale appeared more effective in differentiating poorer functioning inpatients.

A comparison of both scales highlights the issue of restricting the basic unit of analysis to the human figure response. Cooper has cogently argued that extending the unit of analysis to other contents broadens the data base. Collins (1983) and Gacono (1988) empirically found this to be the case, but at the same time, they also found that broadening the data base did not appreciably increase the predictive power of the defense scores. To this point Lerner, Albert, and Walsh (1987) have noted the following:

> While both scales validly discriminated between groups . . . the relative magnitude of group differences highlight the significance of borderline defensive functioning based upon operationalized criteria involving human responses or object representational capacity. It appears that primary process content is most pathogenically indicative of borderline defensive functioning when it effects relationships; that is, when it is embellished in human responses. This finding is important from the point of view of efficiency and theory. That an assessment of defenses only in terms of human responses can adequately predict to the borderline diagnostic group as effectively as the full gamut of responses is cost efficient [p. 352].

Beyond psychometric issues and the matter of cost efficiency, the differing stances of Cooper and the Lerners on the question of restricting the analysis to full human figures reflect genuine attempts to remain as close to their respective theoretical underpinnings as possible. Broadening the unit of analysis permitted Cooper to better operationalize such cornerstone concepts as prestages of defense, part-object relations, and levels of integrative failure. Central for the Lerners is the theoretical proposition that defenses and object relations are inextricably related. Thus, restricting the unit of analysis permits them to infer not only defensive structure but level of object representational capacity as well.

CONCLUSION

In this chapter I have reviewed the current status of a scale devised by Lerner and Lerner to assess primitive defenses. Early studies employing the scale demonstrated its efficacy in accord with theoretical formulations, in distinguishing borderline patients from other diagnostic entities. Later studies used the scale to evaluate the defensive structure among other types of clinical groups assumed to have a borderline personality structure.

Despite the consistency of results obtained, the reviewed studies should be regarded as simply a first step in our attempts to investigate and understand the complexities involved in the borderline concept. Much controversy surrounds the borderline diagnosis—and what constitutes the borders of the borderline entity. Thus, comparing groups of diagnosed borderline patients with other types of patients is necessary but insufficient.

Focusing on defense is important in that defense represents a structural variable (Kernberg, 1975), and therefore this permits us to move beyond descriptive considerations. However, defense has typically been studied in isolation and has not been studied in terms of its relationship with other structural variables (e.g., reality testing, internalized object relations). An exception is represented in the work of Lerner and Lerner (1982), who attempted to relate defense to level of object representation. With the development of various Rorschach scales designed to assess other structural variables, such as developmental object relations (Kwawer, 1980; Coonerty, 1986; Ipp, 1986), boundary disturbances (Blatt and Ritzler, 1974), and object representation (Blatt et al., 1976), we are now in a position to examine the dynamic interplay among structural factors and approximate more closely the richness of Kernberg's theory and the clinical complexity represented in the individual borderline patient.

14

Developmental Object
Relations

As recently as 1975, I observed that although Pruitt and Spilka (1964) had developed a promising scale for assessing object relations, investigators still regarded the human movement response (M) and the human figure response (H) as the most appropriate indices for assessing object relations.

With a shift in emphasis in psychoanalytic theory toward a view of object relations from a developmental perspective, the past 13 years have witnessed the emergence of a host of psychoanalytically informed Rorschach scales devised to assess quality of object relations along a developmental continuum.

To varying degrees these scales have been conceptually rooted in Mahler's (Mahler, Pine, and Bergmann, 1975) theory of separation–individuation. Mahler observed and described the steps in the separation–individuation process, which begins with the earliest signs of the infant's differentiation or hatching from a symbiotic fusion with the mother; proceeds through the period of the infant's absorption in its own autonomous functioning to the near exclusion of the mother; continues through the all-important period of rapprochement in which the child, precisely because of a more clearly perceived state of separateness from mother, is prompted to redirect attention back to mother; and finally culminates in a feeling of an early sense of self, of individual identity, and of constancy of the object.

In this chapter I review several of these newer, conceptually based scales, including the work of Urist (1977), Kwawer (1980), Coonerty (1986), and Ipp (1986). Representative research employing the scales will be discussed; however, because these scales are so recent, they have not as yet generated a great deal of usage. Each scale will be presented in full in appendices at the end of this chapter. Also included in this chapter is a discussion of Lerner and Lerner's (1986) efforts to apply an object relations perspective to the psychoanalytic theory of thinking.

RESEARCH SCALES

Mutuality of Autonomy

The first scale to be reviewed is Urist's (1977) Mutuality of Autonomy Scale. Urist developed a measure based solely on Rorschach imagery to assess stages in the child's shifting sense of self in relation to the mother. The series of scale points are not seen as discrete categories but, rather, as differentiations along a continuous and coherent line of development. At the lower, more primitive end of the scale one finds Rorschach imagery that reflects themes of an undifferentiated, symbiotic fusion of body parts. At the next higher stage themes relate to the child's experience of self and mother as each having physical proprietorship over their respective bodies; however, the body of one can be sensed as under the control of the other. Themes of mirroring represent the third stage, herein, the child's relatedness involves the other being regarded as an extension of the child's own need state. In the fourth stage there are signs of differentiation, but the prevailing anaclitic imagery reflects object relations on a predominantly need satisfying basis. Higher scale points reflect an approach to object constancy in which others are viewed as separate and valued in their own right. The most advanced stage involves the capacity for empathy, the ability to invest in the subjective world of another while maintaining mutual autonomy.

Based on the foregoing, the scale consists of the following seven ascending points: envelopment–incorporation, magical control–coercion, reflection–mirroring, anaclitic–dependent, simple interaction, collaboration–cooperation, reciprocity–mutuality. The scale is applied to all relationships manifested in Rorschach content, that is, relationships between humans, animals, natural forces, and so forth. For a fuller description of the scale, consult Appendix B.

In the original study, the scale was applied to the Rorschach records of 60 patients representing a broad spectrum of levels of psychopathology. Using therapist ratings and clinical ratings as independent measures of object relations, Urist (1977) found the scale to correlate significantly with these ratings.

Whereas in the first study the scale was applied to the entire Rorschach protocol, in a second study (Urist and Shill, 1982) the scale was applied exclusively to excerpted Rorschach responses, including responses in which a relationship was implied (e.g., "squashed bug"). In this study involving 60 adolescent inpatients and outpatients with various diagnoses, independent ratings of object relations were obtained by applying a clinical version of the Mutuality of Autonomy Scale to the patients' confidential records. Here again, significant correlations were found between the Rorschach scale scores and independent clinical ratings.

Tuber (1983) extended the Mutuality of Autonomy Scale to the Rorschach records of children. He found a statistically significant relationship between scale ratings based on Rorschach protocols administered at time of admission to a residential treatment center and the incidence of rehospitalization upon follow-up 5 to 20 years later.

In a nonclinical child population Ryan, Avery, and Grolnick (1985) obtained significant correlations between Mutuality of Autonomy Rorschach scores and teacher ratings of interpersonal functioning, academic grades, and the child's perceived sense of control (internal versus external).

Borderline Interpersonal Relations Scale

As part of an attempt to study early disturbances in the object relations of borderline patients, Kwawer (1980) devised a Rorschach scale consisting of various points that represent stages of level of relatedness in the unfolding of selfhood through differentiation from a primary mothering figure. Underlying the scale is the notion that borderline pathology recapitulates stages of symbiotic relatedness and other primitive modes of unity and disunity. Narrower in scope than the Mutuality of Autonomy Scale because of its emphasis on more primitive modes of object relating, Kwawer's scale also relies exclusively on Rorschach content (see Appendix C).

An initial stage, referred to as Narcissistic Mirroring, includes responses in which mirrors or reflections play a prominent role. Responses at this level are understood as indicating a heightened state of self-absorption in which the other is experienced solely as an extension of the self and used for the exclusive purpose of mirroring or enhancing the self. A second stage, entitled Symbiotic Merger, consists of responses that reflect a pow- erful push toward merger, fusion, and reuniting. A third stage of interpersonal differentiation is found in separation and division responses. The Rorschach imagery here is reminiscent of the biology of cell division reflected in the following response: "These two things appear to have been once connected but broke apart." The fourth and final stage, Metamorphosis and Transformation, is reflective of the experience of a very early and rudimentary sense of self. Here, incipient selfhood is manifest in themes of one-celled organisms, fetuses, and embryos.

In pilot work Kwawer, (1980) found that Rorschach records of border-line patients could be significantly distinguished from those of a matched control group on the basis of the scoring categories. More specifically, each of the borderline patients offered at least one scoreable response, and this was not the case with the controls.

To determine whether highly psychopathic males are organized at a borderline level, Gacono (1988) compared a group of highly psychopathic males with a group of low to moderately psychopathic males on several Rorschach measures, including Kwawer's scale. Thirty-three subjects, se-lected on the basis of Hare Psychopathy Checklist who met the DSM-III-R criteria for Antisocial Personality Disorder were subdivided into a high psychopathic group ($n = 14$) and a low to moderate psychopathic group ($n = 19$). On Kwawer's scale the high psychopathy group, as predicted, produced a significantly greater number of borderline responses than did the moderate group. Whereas every subject in the high psychopathy group produced at least one borderline response, five subjects in the low to moderate group did not produce any borderline responses. Overall, the abundance of borderline responses, as judged by Kwawer's criteria, pro-duced by the total sample (n = 33) prompted Gacono (1988) to consider Kernberg's (1976) contention that the majority of individuals meeting the criteria for antisocial personality, regardless of level of psychopathy, are organized at a borderline level of functioning.

Gacono's (1988) findings are interesting in that while differences were found between the psychopathic groups on the Borderline Interpersonal Scale, the groups did not differ significantly with respect to their use of primitive defenses (note Chapter 13). As such, these findings are seemingly inconsistent with Kernberg's contention regarding the intimate relation-ship between defense and the internalization of object relations. Yet a detailed review of Kwawer's scale, especially the Narcissistic Mirroring category, indicates a strong emphasis on narcissism. Therefore, Gacono's contention that the antisocial personality is organized at a borderline level, may be premature. Based on the results using Kwawer's scale, it may be more accurate to say that such people tend to relate themselves to others in a narcissistic manner. Both conceptually and empirically, the relation-ship between narcissism and borderline disturbances remains unclear. This issue, and studies bearing on the question, are discussed in Chapters 15 and 17.

Coonerty's Scale of Separation-Individuation

The most direct application of Mahler's theory to the Rorschach test is represented in the work of Coonerty (1986). Using the descriptions of Mahler, Pine, and Bergman (1975) as a guideline, Coonerty developed a scale for identifying and categorizing Rorschach responses reflective of concerns and issues associated with the preseparation stage and each of the phases of the separation-individuation process. Referable to the preseparation phase are internal responses (blood, heart, lungs, etc.) and responses lacking boundaries (fabulized combination, etcetera). Rorschach imagery reflective of merging, engulfment, and hatching is taken as indicative of concerns arising from the early differentiation subphase of separation-individuation. Themes related to the practicing subphase involve narcissistic issues; thus, reflective Rorschach content includes mirroring responses, pairing responses, omnipotent responses, and insignificant creative responses. Responses indicative of rapprochement issues include figures separating or coming together with resulting damage to one or both, figures engaged in a push–pull struggle, figures whose form changes, figures whose affect changes, and figures enmeshed and unable to separate. The scale can be found in Appendix D.

Coonerty (1986) applied the scale to the Rorschach protocols of 50 borderline patients and 50 schizophrenic patients drawn from the testing files of a large teaching hospital. Subjects were all adult patients, 18 to 65 years of age, who met DSM-III criteria based upon initial screening evaluations, including a detailed psychological, medical, developmental, social, and psychiatric history. Reliability of the scale was found to be 96% agreement between two raters. As predicted, the borderline group verbalized more separation-individuation themes than did the schizophrenic group, whereas the schizophrenics showed more pre–separation-individuation themes.

Van-Der Keshet (1988), in a study referred to in the previous chapter, applied the separation-individuation scale as well to the Rorschach records of clinical anorexics, anorexic ballet students, nonanorexic ballet students, and a normal control group. As described, the clinical anorexic group was further subdivided into those patients manifesting restrictive characteristics and those exhibiting bulimic symptoms. A comparison of the various groups on the scale revealed several interesting findings. While no main effect was found among the groups on the preseparation scale, several significant findings were obtained on the separation-individuation scores. Bulimic anorexics produced significantly more engulfment responses than did any of the other groups. Mirroring responses distinguished the anorexic ballet students from each of the other groups. Finally, the controls had significantly fewer rapprochement responses than the other four groups. The overall pattern of results not only lent construct validity to Coonerty's scale but also revealed the scale's usefulness in highlighting significant dynamic configurations associated with specific clinical groups.

The combined findings from Van-Der Keshet's (1988) study regarding both the separation-individuation scale and the measure of primitive defenses lend strong support to the notion of eating-disordered patients being organized at a borderline level. This will be discussed further in Chapter 16. In addition, the convergence of results also supports the construct validity of each of the individual scales. Studies, such as Van-Der Keshet's, in which several conceptually linked measures are employed, are especially important; however, it is now necessary to take the additional step of interrelating the scales.

Developmental Object Relations Scale

Based on the earlier work of Urist (1977) and Tuber (1983), Ipp (1986) also attempted to translate Mahler's formulations into Rorschach-related terms. Limited to the assessment of animate (human and animal) movement responses; like Urist's scale, underlying this scale is the assumption that the manner in which an individual portrays relationships between animate figures on the Rorschach test reflects his or her experience and representation of human relationships.

The scale consists of five basic categories and two subcategories, with each category conceptualized as representing a developmentally significant gradient in the individual's emerging sense of self and sense of the other. At the lower end of the scale is the category Catastrophic Disintegration. Included here are responses in which there is a sense of annihilation by external forces greater than the self. Inanimate movement and strong agitation typically accompany these percepts. The category Symbiosis includes percepts that are either undifferentiated or merge with each other. These responses are often vague and amorphous and are accompanied by a strong positive or negative affective component. The category separation-individuation is subdivided into the subcategories Rapprochement and Differentiating/Practicing. Included under rapprochement are responses that reflect active efforts toward separation and autonomy. These efforts are often accompanied by separation anxiety, as expressed in implicit threats to the self or to the individual's independence.

Somewhat lower than rapprochement is the subcategory Differentiation/Practicing. Here, percepts reflect an awareness of separateness but at a more primitive level. Failures in separating are anticipated or stated. False Autonomy refers to a pseudo form of individuation. Beneath superficial, higher level functioning are feelings of emptiness and low self-esteem, and this is reflected in the Rorschach imagery. Mirroring responses are included here. The highest category, Toward Object Constancy, includes responses in which fully differentiated figures are interacting with each other. A distinction is drawn between figures engaged in a more dependent relationship and figures engaged in activity in which there is no compromise of each other's autonomy. Cutting across all categories is a benevolent/malevolent dimension with neutral responses considered as benevolent. The scale can be found in Appendix E.

As part of her attempt to study the personality structure of a group of gender-disturbed children (see Chapter 13), Ipp (1986) applied the scale to the Rorschach protocols of 37 feminine boys diagnosed as having cross-gender disturbance, 19 siblings with no history of cross-gender behavior, and 23 normal controls. A comparison of scale scores for the three groups revealed the following: the subcategory Autonomy significantly distinguished the controls from both the feminine boys and their siblings, with the normal controls achieving the higher scores. The feminine boys and their siblings scored significantly more responses at the Differentiation/ Practicing substage than the normal controls. None of the categories significantly distinguished the feminine boys from their siblings. And both the feminine boys and their siblings offered significantly more malevolent responses than the normal controls.

In summary, the scale revealed similarities between the feminine boys and their siblings and differences between both groups and the normal controls. As predicted, the Rorschach responses of both the feminine boys and the siblings fell mainly within the Differentiating/Practicing category whereas the responses of the controls were at a higher level.

OBJECT RELATIONS AND THINKING

Basic psychoanalytic concepts that had been understood in exclusively structural and economic terms are increasingly being reformulated in light of the growing realization of the decisive impact of early object relations on personality development. The application of these relatively new formulations to the concept of defense was reviewed in Chapter 13.

As part of this overall conceptual thrust, Lerner and Lerner (1982, 1986), in a series of papers, applied an object relations perspective to the psychoanalytic theory of thinking. Specifically, they attempted to integrate Piaget's theory of cognitive structure formation with Mahler's observations and theory of separation/individuation. Within that integrative effort they outlined the role of the care-giving object in facilitating the unfolding and subsequent development of cognitive structures as well as in contributing to specified difficulties in cognition that might ensue when the object fails to fulfill its necessary functions.

A summary of that integration is presented in Table I. Included in the

Table I

Integration of Piaget and Mahler

Interdigitated Stages	Piaget's Stages of Cognitive Development	Mahler's Periods of Separation and Individuation	Major Cognitive Tasks	Role of the Object	Potential Cognitive Impairments
Stage I (Early Sensorimotor)	Sensorimotor Period (Stages 1 & 2)	Normal autism and symbiosis	Beginning awareness of external objects	Holding behavior	Lack of affective relatedness to the environment
Stage II (Mid-Sensorimotor)	Sensorimotor Period (Stages 3 & 4)	Differentiation and practicing	Differentiating objects from their contextual surroundings	Supporting strivings toward separation and mirroring autonomous functioning	Overdependence on the environment and stimulus-boundness
Stage III (Early Preoperational)	Preoperational Period	Rapprochement subphase and consolidation of individuality and the beginnings of object constancy	Internalization and representation	Maintenance of emotional availability in the wake of the child's fluctuations between closeness and distance	Impairment in evocative object constancy and failures in the interiorization of learning skills

table is a schematic review of Piaget's early stages of cognitive development and of Mahler's phases of separation-individuation, a brief statement of the major cognitive task for each of the interdigitated developmental periods, a note of the necessary role and function of the object, and a listing of cognitive impairments that result from the object's failing to fulfill its function.

In what follows I attempt to extend this object relations model of thinking and cognitive impairment to the Rorschach test. This extension should be regarded as simply a beginning effort to integrate several existing Rorschach scores and indices into a new conceptual framework, which, when refined, could serve as a broad theoretical basis for research. For example, I hope that, in time, this type of conceptual model will be used to explore the broad area of learning disabilities more systematically. Then too, presenting this model now—despite its relative incompleteness—may alert diagnosticians, especially those who work with children, to a different way of thinking about traditional Rorschach indices.

Interdigitated Stage I: Early Sensorimotor

The first interdigitated stage is referred to as "early sensorimotor" since it includes the first two phases ("exercising the ready-made sensorimotor schema" and "primary circular responses") of Piaget's sensorimotor period. According to Piaget, a major shift occurs during these stages that involves the infant's incipient awareness of external objects. This shift noted by Piaget coincides with the infant's entrance into the phase of normal symbiosis in Mahler's theory.

In the second month the beginning awareness of the need-satisfying object marks the onset of the symbiotic phase. Herein, the infant behaves and functions as though infant and mother were an omnipotent system—a dual unity encircled by one common boundary. The inborn stimulus barrier begins to crack, and with a cathectic shift toward the sensori-perceptive periphery, a protective shield begins to form around and to envelop the symbiotic orbit of the mother–child dual unity. The infant begins to perceive need satisfaction as coming from some part-object and begins turning toward that source.

Within the symbiotic orbit, the two partners or poles are regarded by Mahler as "polarizing the organizational and structuring processes. The structures that derive from this double frame of reference represent a framework to which all experiences have to be related before they are clear whole representations in the ego of the self and the object world" (Mahler, Pine, and Bergman, 1975, p. 57). Whereas the capacity of the infant to invest the mother serves as a precursor to all subsequent relationships, the "holding behavior" of the mother functions as a "symbiotic organizer—the midwife of separation and individuation" (p. 57).

Evidence from various sources (Ribble, 1943; Graham, 1978; Wright, 1981), including case studies by Klein (1930) and Mahler (1960), suggests that the depth and quality of the infant's interest in external objects is a function of the nature of the mother's holding behavior. The combined findings indicate that failures in maternal holding during this early sensorimotor-symbiotic stage result in a lack of affective relatedness to the environment with subsequent cognitive deficits, including a limited amount of information about and interest in the environment, a restricted vocabulary and an inability to conceptualize and interpret the world in human terms.

According to this model, patients whose symbiotic phase has been disrupted by failures in maternal holding would present as severely impaired in their capacity to relate to others and as unable to genuinely experience and express affects. Such behavior, especially the inability to conceive of the world in human terms, should be readily discernible in the testing behavior and Rorschach performance of such patients. One would expect that such individuals would approach testing in a detached, insulated, essentially unavailable way. Attempts by the examiner to establish an emotional relatedness would not only be unwelcome but would be experienced as intrusive, with the patient responding with irritation and further withdrawal. The Rorschach protocol would be strikingly devoid of human content and reflective of a lack of investment in reality. Fantastic creations would populate the records of those whose investment in reality was regressively replaced by an investment in fantasy. Such creations might be elaborate and vivid but woefully lacking in human forms. The Rorschach records of others, whose capacity to fantasize was also impaired, might feature percepts that were lifeless, vague, and amorphous.

Interdigitated Stage II: Mid-Sensorimotor

Whereas in the early sensorimotor period the major cognitive achievement involves the infant's progressive interest in his environment, in the mid-sensorimotor period—Piaget's stages three, four, and five—the main cognitive task is differentiating objects from their environmental surround. According to Piaget, as objects are differentiated, they begin to be represented by internal symbols. Differentiation, then, is a precursor of representation, as well as intimately and reciprocally related to it.

This mid-sensorimotor period corresponds in Mahler's theory with the first two phases of the separation-individuation process proper: differentiation and practicing.

According to Mahler, at about six months of age tentative experimentation begins. Manually, tactilely, and visually, the infant begins to explore the mother—her face, body, and attire. The infant literally pulls back from her so as to see her. For Mahler, this visual pattern of checking mother is the most significant indicator of the beginning of somatopsychic differentiation.

The second subphase of separation-individuation, practicing, has two parts: an early phase marked by the infant's attempts to move physically away from mother, by means of crawling, climbing, and so on, and the practicing subphase proper, characterized by free locomotion. These early explorations enable the infant to establish familiarity with a broader segment of the world and also permit the recognition of mother from a distance. Despite the increased investment in autonomous activity, mother continues to be needed as a "home base," a center for "refueling."

By juxtaposing Piaget with Mahler one can see that the advances in cognition associated with the mid-sensorimotor period occur within the context of the infant's hatching from the symbiotic relationship with the mother and progressing to the point of taking distance from the mother by means of various forms of locomotion. What appears crucial here is the mother's capacity to recognize, tolerate, and permit optimal distance.

It is hypothesized that if the mother does not permit differentiation, fails to mirror the infant's efforts at autonomous behavior, or does not serve as a predictable and continuously available "home base," then cognitive difficulties involving an overdependence on the environment with attendant failures in representation will ensue. Evidence supporting this proposal comes from the sizable literature on field dependence, the seminal findings of Blatt and his colleagues regarding disturbances in object representations, and my own clinical findings from the assessment of troubled children.

Rorschach indices of overdependence on the environment, and hence of disturbances referable to this developmental period, are the FCarb score and the fabulized combination. As discussed in Chapter 7, implied in both types of responses is a tendency to comply with external demands and cognitive passivity marked by an inability to take distance from the inkblots and respond to them with perspective. Implicit in each response is a relinquishment of a more objective, critical attitude and a surrender to the stimulus properties of the inkblot.

Patients who are overdependent on their external milieu often provide responses that are strikingly stimulus bound. For example, to Card I one patient responded, "In the middle it looks like a woman with a dress on. Her hands are up and there is no head." With detachment and a sense of perspective, one would recognize that a figure cannot have its hands up if it is missing a head.

Interdigitated Stage III: Early Preoperational

Piaget's sixth, and final, stage, "invention of new means through mental combinations," is a transitional stage to the next period—the preoperational period. Whereas the child in the sensorimotor period is relatively restricted to direct interactions with his environment, in the preoperational period internalization and the representation of external experiences by means of internal symbols become significantly more important. The emerging ability for evocative recall and the greater capability for manipulating symbols that represent the environment permit a mental life relatively autonomous from the environment.

These advances in cognition coincide with Mahler's rapprochement subphase and with her final subphase, in which the child moves toward emotional object constancy. Herein, the child's increased awareness of being separate from mother leads him to attempt to reestablish contact with her, but in a new and different way.

Because the child is caught between competing currents of both desiring closeness yet wanting to preserve a precarious autonomy, his behavior is marked by vexing oscillations between pulls toward closeness and pushes toward distance. Mahler's observations confirm the critical importance of the mother's capacity to maintain continual libidinal availability while recognizing and accepting the child's fluctuating behavior.

Findings from both the testing and the broader clinical literature, especially from those studies related to borderline pathology (Kernberg, 1975; Kwawer et al., 1980), suggest that when the mother is unable to maintain her emotional availability, impairments in internalization and representation ensue (see Table 1). Specifically, there is an arrest at a sensorimotor level of object representation, with an impairment in evocative object constancy and a consequent vulnerability to separation and loss. The rent in the internalized object world between good and bad part-objects is not mended. There are massive inhibitions in learning based on failures in the interiorization of learning skills, and emotional and gestural behavior, not language, remain as the basic mode of communication.

Several of the Rorschach scales already reviewed in this chapter and the previous chapter are applicable here in that they were designed to assess these very processes and their impairments. For example, the Concept of the Object Scale of Blatt's and associates (1976) is useful for assessing level of object representation, while the scales of Coonerty (1986) and Ipp (1986) may be employed to assess vulnerability to loss. The failure to integrate good and bad object representations (a manifestation of splitting, as noted previously) has been operationalized by Lerner and Lerner (1980) and Cooper (1981). Finally, as outlined in chapter 7, the Fc score is an especially sensitive indicator of the tendency to rely on emotional and gestural behavior as a means of communicating.

SUMMARY

In this chapter I have reviewed several more recent Rorschach Scales that were developed to assess level of object relations from a developmental perspective. Based in varying degrees on Mahler's theory of separation-individuation, each scale has tended to rely on thematic content. Satisfactory levels of reliability, as determined by degree of interrater agreement, have been reported for each scale. Owing to their relative recency these scales, with the exception of Urist's scale, have not received wide currency in the Rorschach literature. Indeed, one of the purposes of this book is to acquaint readers with their availability. In preliminary work, each scale has been found useful in elucidating the patient's level of object relations and the developmental stage-related difficulty present in specific clinical populations.

Also presented in this chapter was an object relations model of thinking, together with preliminary attempts to extend the model to the Rorschach test. This book is replete with the notion that psychoanalytic theory is a complex composite of several submodels, each of which furnishes a different yet helpful perspective for exploring and understanding some facet of personality development and functioning. Accordingly, any one piece of behavior may be viewed from various angles. For example, the destructive acting-out behavior of an adolescent may be understood in a variety of different ways: as an expression of poorly modulated aggression, as a result of failures in defense, as an action statement of an implicit sense of self, and as an interpersonal demand upon the environment for a particular type of response. While these possible explanations represent different perspectives and, if treatment were an issue, might imply differing forms of intervention, they nonetheless are not mutually exclusive or inconsistent. In an analogous way, Rorschach responses too may be viewed through various conceptual lenses. For instance, whereas Coonerty (1986) would regard a mirroring response (e.g., a girl gazing at herself in a mirror) as indicating a failure in separation-individuation referable to the practicing subphase, Kwawer (1980) would consider this response indicative of a tendency to relate oneself to others in a narcissistic manner. In this context, then, the object relations model of thinking represents another conceptual lens for viewing the Rorschach responses.

As noted in the preface, Rapaport et al. (1945–1946) considered the Rorschach test a potential means for operationalizing psychoanalytic concepts whose operational definitions could then be used for testing basic formulations. Creative investigators have done just this; that is, they have devised innovative scales for operationalizing concepts that heretofore were hazy and elusive. I believe we have reached a point where what is called for is an interrelating of these scales across various clinical and normal populations. In this way, the Rorschach test can truly add to the evolving scope of psychoanalytic theory.

APPENDIX B
RESEARCH SCALES
MUTUALITY OF AUTONOMY SCALE

The Rorschach scale developed by Urist (1977) consists of various points, which are presented below.

1. Figures are seen as engaged in some relationship or activity where they are together and involved with each other in such a way that conveys a reciprocal acknowledgment of their respective individuality. The response contains explicit or implicit reference to the fact that the figures are separate and autonomous but involved with each other in a way that recognizes or expresses a sense of mutuality in the relationship (e.g., on Card II: "two bears toasting each other, clicking glasses").

2. Figures are seen as engaged in some relationship or parallel activity. There is no stated emphasis or highlighting of mutuality, nor is there any sense that the dimension is compromised in any way within the relationship (e.g., on Card III: "two women doing their laundry").

3. Figures are seen as leaning on each other, or one figure is seen as leaning or hanging on another. The sense here is that objects do not "stand on their own two feet" or that in some way they require some external source of support or direction.

4. One figure is seen as the reflection, or imprint, of another. The relationship between objects here conveys a sense that the definition or stability of an object exists only insofar as it is an extension or reflection of another. Shadows, footprints, and so forth, would be included here.

5. The nature of the relationship between figures is characterized by a theme of malevolent control of one figure by another. Themes of influencing, controlling, and casting spells are present. One figure may literally or figuratively be in the clutches of another. Such themes portray a severe imbalance in the mutuality of relations between figures. On one hand, figures may be seen as powerful or helpless, while at the same time others are omnipotent and controlling.

6. Not only is there a severe imbalance in the mutuality of relations between figures but the imbalance is cast in decidedly destructive terms. The relation between two figures simply fighting is not considered destructive in

terms of the individuality of the figures whereas one figure being tortured or strangled by another is considered to reflect a serious attack on the autonomy of the object. Also included here are relationships that are portrayed as parasitic, where a gain by one figure results, by definition, in the diminution or destruction of the other.

7. Relationships here are characterized by an overpowering, enveloping force. Figures are seen as swallowed up, devoured, or generally overwhelmed by forces completely beyond their control.

APPENDIX C
RESEARCH SCALES
BORDERLINE INTERPERSONAL RELATIONS
(Kwawer, 1980)

The diagnostic criteria for borderline object relations as defined by Kwawer (1980) are described below.

Engulfment. This criterion includes responses that depict the prototypical object world as overwhelming and engulfing. Often form level is scored "vague" or "+/-". Conceptions of evil and malevolence add to the experience of being unwelcome in one's own world. For example:

> Two enormous pink globs that are appetizing, but once you become engulfed. They've already ensnared two blue birds and it looks like two bats are about to suffer the same fate [to Card X].

Symbiotic merging. This criterion includes responses that symbolize processes of attachment, merger, and fusion in which symbiotic attachments are attempted or resisted. Responses of joined Siamese twins are numerous in this group, although they do not characterize this group exclusively. For example:

> Two women, like Siamese twins attached to each other . . . you can see their body, their thigh and their legs under the dress [to Card I].

Violent symbiosis, separation, and reunion. In this criterion, responses indicate unconscious assumptions equating either attachment or separation, or both, with murder or violent destruction. For example:

> Two forces meeting. I see an explosion when they meet [to Card II].
> Two ugly women fighting over the contents of a box [to Card VIII].

Malignant internal processes, including primitive incorporation. This criterion includes responses in which early experiences of a parasitic, destructive tone are represented. Views of internal organs, transparencies affording views of bodily contents, and perspectives highlighting the experience of the body's interior as a container for one's self are included. For example:

> Two pink rats climbing up the entrails of the human being . . . They could have devoured the bowels or kidneys at the base [to Card VIII].

It's part of the body . . . reminds me of something organic–tripe? The inner lining of the stomach is called tripe [to Card VI].

Birth and Rebirth. This criterion includes responses that directly state the individual's psychic involvement with early stages of self-development. For example:

This part looks like the early stages of an embryo . . . the face . . . ordinarily starts out with the division . . . could be the beginning of the form of the body [to Card VI]. Two female embryos, in a womb, ready to split . . . Almost identical . . . Nourishment coming up to the twins . . . starting to become individuals [to Card III].

Metamorphosis and transformation. This criterion includes responses that can be interpreted as indicating enmeshment in early stages of incipient selfhood in the development from biological to human, or interpersonal, life. Often these responses are symbolized through themes of one-celled organisms, fetuses, and embryos. For example:

Two ants dressed up in men's clothes . . . It almost seems like their bodies were transformed into human bodies, but their heads remained ants. They were acting like human beings [to Card III]. It's a woman metamorphosizing into an animal [to Card V].

Narcissistic mirroring. This criterion includes responses that convey the idea of self-absorption and self-involvement, in which the other exists solely to mirror the self or is experienced as an extension of self. For example:

These are two men mirroring each other, two little mimes [to Card II]. A man fixing himself up in front of a mirror . . . It was a double image [to Card III].

Separation-division. This criterion includes responses portraying conflict and ambivalence about separation and reunion. Responses are often cast in terms of biological cell division, as though the individual were struggling with developmental difficulties in the separation-individuation phase. For example:

These two things appear to have been at one point connected and broken apart . . . It's as if on the inside there was some continuity between the two [to Card IX]. Looks like a cell in separation . . . One has divided and two haven't quite joined together [to Card X].

Boundary disturbance. This criterion includes responses reflecting themes of fluidity, weakness, permeability of ego boundaries, and often internal–external confusion. For example:

Some sort of protection so something can't get in here . . . To just protect enough so that nothing comes in. It doesn't seem to be terribly firm; it just protects from water or something . . . it's very vague [to Card IX]. Jellyfish ... kind of clear and you can see through to the blood vessels [to Card IV].

Womb Imagery. This criterion includes responses in which the content or affective tone reflects private fantasies of early uterine experience. For example:

An impression of fossils. It's from a cave ... Remind me of bone impressions like fossils are pressed in rock [to Card VIII]. A place ... when you are going to go someplace peaceful for the rest of your life ... It's soft, mysterious, peaceful, and quiet [to Card IX].

APPENDIX D
SEPARATION-INDIVIDUATION THEME SCALE

Identifying Theme Categories
A.   Preseparation-Individuation Phase
    1.   Internal Response (e.g., "blood," "heart," "lung" "tissues," "liver"). Such responses involve internal body parts completely isolated from a larger response involving a whole being.
    2.   Boundaryless Response (e.g., "A man's spine and rib cage are x-rayed here with the raccoons climbing up the spine to the ribs"). Such responses show two percepts normally seen as separate seen as one instead, with no recognition of the incongruence involved and no ambivalence.
B.   Separation-Individuation Phase
    1.   Early Differentiation
        a.   Merging Response (e.g., "These are two girls, maybe not, they seem to be together with the same head"). Such responses involve merging or fusion without any degree of negatively charged engulfment or enmeshment.
        b.   Engulfment Response (e.g., "There seems to be someone in there, but I can barely see her, she's being swallowed by this monster here"). Such responses include all instances where the object is overwhelmed or smothered.
        c.   Hatching Response (e.g., "I was going to say caterpillar, but not really a caterpillar, it's turning into something else, maybe a butterfly, maybe some kind of magic thing"). This response, similar to Kwawer's metamorphosis, reflects birth, rebirth, or transformation.
    2.   Practicing Phase: Narcissism
        a.   Narcissistic Mirroring (e.g., "Girl gazing at herself in a mirror, kind of mesmerized"). This response includes mention of a mirror or the phenomenon of reflecting.
        b.   Pairing Responses (e.g., "Two women, exactly alike, one here

and one right next to her, looking at each other"). This category is only for pairs not at all differentiated and engaged in a mirroring-like task.

c. Omnipotence Responses (e.g., "This is a tall, gorgeous queen, so powerful, gold glittering on her gown").

d. Insignificant Creature Responses (e.g., "He's so little, almost like a worm compared to the others"). Also includes responses showing perspective (e.g., "Like a giant's perspective looking at a little worm he could tramp on while it is crawling; he is so powerful, the worm is helpless").

3. Rapprochement

a. Figures Separating/Coming Together With Resulting Damage to One or Both (e.g., "They're touching hands but it's as if one of them is trying to save the other from electrical shock and they both get fried").

b. Figures Separating/Coming Together Engaged in Indecision or a Push–Pull Struggle (e.g., "It's a girl helping an old lady down the steps but the old lady seems to be yanking her hand away, she is screaming but the girl is pulling away").

c. Figures Whose Form (e.g., Human–Animal or Human–Insect) Changes (e.g., "Two girls eating out of the same bowl, no, that's ridiculous, they look like some kind of weird creature, maybe it's some new gigantic rats").

d. Figures Whose Affect Changes (e.g., "It's a mean look, no it's an angel smiling").

e. Figures Enmeshed, Stuck, Unable to Separate (e.g., "I don't know, this seems like some people doing something but they seem stuck together somehow, all struggling in every direction but whatever is doing it, they can't get free").

APPENDIX E
SCORING MANUAL FOR THE RORSCHACH DEVELOPMENTAL OBJECT RELATIONS SCALE (DORS) (IPP, 1986)

The scale consists of five basic categories posited along a developmental continuum. Two of these categories are further divided into two subcategories. The categories are as follows:

1. Toward object constancy: autonomy   dependency
2. False autonomy
3. Separation-Individuation: rapprochement
   differentiation/practicing
4. Symbiosis
5. Catastrophic disintegration

In addition to being scored according to the above categories, the Rorschach responses are also evaluated along a benevolent/malevolent dimension, with neutral responses achieving a benevolent rating. Previous research (Blatt, 1974) has demonstrated that the quantity and quality of malevolent responses significantly differentiate between various psychopathologies.

GENERAL SCORING CONSIDERATIONS

1. The form level of the response is determined according to Mayman's (1970) system.

2. Any response in which a relationship is stated or implied qualifies for a score. Since this scale is intended for application with a child population, there is greater latitude in terms of the range of acceptable responses. Therefore, scoreable responses include humans, quasi-humans, animals and inanimate objects in implied activity. A scoreable response also includes a perception of only *one* figure animate or inanimate being or having been acted upon.

> Examples: "squashed blueberries" (scoreable since someone or something has squashed the blueberries)
>
> "frustrated man" (something or someone is causing the frustration)
>
> "planets exploding" (occurs as a result of the forces of the environment)

3. Careful attention must be given to the language usage and elaborations offered in any given response (including reactions/responses to the inquiry), as these factors serve to further delineate the response and highlight its idiosyncratic nature.

Example: "people sitting" as opposed to "people sitting on a broken chair" (The latter would qualify for a lower order score, for example, rapprochement.

SPECIFIC SCALE POINTS AND THEIR SCORING

1. *Toward Object Constancy*

(a) *Autonomy*

Included here are fully differentiated figures interacting with each other or engaged in parallel activity in which there is no compromise of either figure's individuality or autonomy. The figures must be of accurate form quality and may include humans, quasi-humans or animals. Insects are not scoreable in this category, since they are not regarded as a higher order representation even in the responses of a child population.

> Examples: Card I: "two people dancing"
>
> Card III: "two women doing their laundry"
>
> Card VII: "two girls talking to each other"
>
> Card IX: "two witches laughing"

(b) *Dependency*

Included here are fully differentiated figures involved in a more dependent relationship with another. Implicit here is the individual's need for external support or direction. An important criterion for this

score is that the individual's dependency does not blur his identity;
when it does, the response qualifies for a lower order score.

Examples: Card I: "sick old lady lying on her bed"
           Card III: "two dogs trying to stand up
           Card IV: "a monster sitting on a chair . . . waiting for
                      somebody to give him food . . . like a mon-
                      ster father"
           Card VIII: "some tigers . . . on some hands . . . holding
                      some hands"

2. *False Autonomy*

This category refers to a pseudo form of individuation (corresponding to Winnicott's "false self") that renders a superficial sense of
functioning higher than is really operant. This level masks a sense of
emptiness and renders an "as if" quality to the percept. Included here
are mirroring responses (for example, reflections in water), shadows,
footprints, masks, skeletons, and responses that suggest an almost
exclusively external locus of control (for example, puppets).

Examples: Card I: "a ghost . . . and its reflection"
           Card V: "a lady that looks like a butterfly . . . was
                      probably dressed like one for show"
           Card VI: "two sleepwalkers"
           Card X: "a candle . . . it had a little thing at the end
                      holding it up and it *didn't have a fuse.* (This
                      response extends beyond a dependency re-
                      sponse [category lb]; the candle does not have
                      a fuse—the essence is missing.)

3. *Separation-Individuation*

This category is divided into 2 subcategories.

(a) *Rapprochement*

Included here are responses in which the percepts reflect active
efforts toward separation-individuation. These efforts may or
may not reflect ambivalence and are often accompanied by some
degree of separation anxiety. The latter is generally expressed in
the form of an implicit threat to the self or to the individual's
autonomy. Responses that are suggestive of metamorphosis or
transformation also qualify for this score (e.g., a butterfly turning
into a lady).

Percepts should be whole figures or at least clearly differentiated body parts such as a face or a head (bones are unacceptable).
Accurate form level is important although F spoil responses
would also qualify since the attendant anxiety often reduces what
would be Fo or F + to F spoil.

Examples: Card III: "two people *trying* to pull a rope . . . their
                      feet are *slipping* in some black paint"
                      (represents an unsuccessful attempt at
                      independence attended by anxiety)
           Card VII: "a submarine . . . comes right off the

water to see where you're going" (emergence of self)

Card VI: "a big cat . . . *looking* really big, he was *acting* big, and he was showing his muscles, showing how strong he was . . . you know how cats' hair sticks out when they're *not brushed*" (attempt to separate and be independent, but shows off and needs to be brushed)

Card VII: "two girls with *mad* faces . . . trying to go away"

Card X: "rocket going up in the air . . . because it was *halfway off the ground*"

(b) *Differentiating/Practicing*

This subcategory represents lower order separation-individuation responses. Included here are percepts that reflect some awareness of separateness and differentiation but at a more primitive level than in the previous subcategory. Beyond the anxiety, there is clear anticipation or statement of failure of the separation. Percepts may reflect attempts at mastery of basic motoric skills but without a differentiated sense of self. Explicit threat to the self is common and the threat often extends from the card to the self, that is, there is a loss of boundaries as reflected by the self and references used (e.g., "The monster is coming to get me"). In this subcategory, there are more part-objects, more weak form level responses as well as poor form responses.

Examples: Card II: "plane . . . looks like it's crashing because of holes in the wings"

Card II: "two clowns without heads . . . stepping in a bucket of paint"

Card VI: "King Kong . . . he was dead . . . and they split him in half and opened him wide"

Card VII: "wrecked-up teeth"

Card X: "chihuahua, *almost*"

4. *Symbiosis*

The dominant themes in this category are undifferentiated percepts and the merging of percepts with each other. The response may or may not have malevolent content. The responses are often vague and amorphous in form but are attended by a strong positive or negative affective component. Specific content relevant to this category includes womb and, birth imagery (e.g., umbilical cord). The essential difference between this category and the dependency category (1b) is the loss of identity and blurring or destruction of boundaries that is operant in the symbiotic stage. Similarly, the imagery characteristic of symbiosis is to be differentiated from the *emerging and metamorphosis* imagery characteristic of the rapprochement category (for example, "a caterpillar turning into a butterfly" [rapprochement] vs. "candle turning into a pool of wax" [symbiosis]).

Examples: Card VIII: "the monster was eating food and then he
died, the cheetahs got killed and the food
came out . . . got killed and he ate the same
color of food that matched him."

Card X: "Blob is squished blueberries and the pits are
coming out of them. All the juice comes out."

5. *Catastrophic Disintegration*

Included here are percepts in which there is a sense of annihilation
by external forces greater than the self (e.g., cosmic disasters). Inanimate movement and strong agitation generally accompany these
percepts.

Examples: Card X: "planets exploding"

Card IX: "a fire raging through everything . . . nothing
is left"

Card X: "the end of the world"

15

The Borderline Concept
and the Rorschach Test

The borderline concept, as Sugarman and Lerner (1980) have noted, "has a long, uneven and particularly controversial history in both psychiatry and psychoanalysis" (p. 11). The term *borderline*, as these authors point out, "has been referred to as a 'wastebasket' diagnosis for patients who could not be classified as neurotic or psychotic (Knight, 1953), as an 'unwanted category' traceable to Bleuler's (1924) attempts to classify patients whose conventional behavior masked an underlying schizophrenia (Gunderson and Singer, 1975), and more recently as a 'star work'— seeming to illuminate a great deal" (Pruyser, 1975, p. 11).

The concept of borderline, as well as its designation as a pathological entity, has arisen from the convergence of two streams of conceptual development within psychiatry—descriptive psychiatry, with its emphasis on discrete and observable phenomena and exclusive nosological categories, and psychoanalysis, with its focus on attempting to establish structural, dynamic, and developmental roots of the disorder.

Contemporary contributions to the descriptive stream come from three major areas: empirical research and reviews (Grinker, Werble, and Drye, 1968; Gunderson and Singer, 1975; Carpenter, Gunderson, and Strauss, 1977; Perry and Klerman, 1978), genetic and adoption studies (Kety et al., 1968; Rosenthal, 1975; Wender, 1977), and psychopharmacological studies (D. Klein, 1973, 1975). The combined findings indicate that borderline disorders are (1) psychologically similar to but distinguishable from the neuroses and schizophrenia, (2) linked genetically to schizophrenia, and (3) related psychopharmacologically to affect disorders.

The second stream, the psychoanalytic, originated in early explorations of character development and character pathology. Beginning with

Reich's pioneering work on character analysis, particularly, in *The Impulsive Character* (1933), this stream extends through Alexander's (1930) description of the "neurotic character," Stern's (1938) extension of the "neurotic character" to the "ambulatory schizophrenic," Deutsch's (1942) important contributions regarding the "as if" personality, and Schmideberg's (1947, 1959) writings regarding a group of patients who were "stable in their instability."

The movement within psychoanalysis from a more descriptive and dynamic perspective to a more structural one is represented in the work of Knight (1953) and his emphasis on the severe ego weaknesses underlying the borderline patient's superficial object relations and seeming adaption to environmental demands. For Knight, these patients were more disturbed than they appeared, and he outlined three basic aspects of the syndrome to be considered in establishing a differential diagnosis: (1) the use of compensatory defenses and symptoms to cover over the underlying defects, (2) the patient's lack of awareness of his or her psychotic-like manifestations, and (3) an inability to maintain anchoring in reality in unstructured situations, such as projective tests.

Beginning in 1966 with a reexamination of the borderline concept and the range of disorders of character from the perspective of structural derivatives, the work of Kernberg (1975, 1976) has had an enormous impact on the field. In integrating contributions from the British school of object relations with more classical formulations from structural theory, he has been able to develop a unitary-process conceptualization of psychopathology and to demonstrate that a descriptive classification of borderline disturbances is insufficient in that it includes only "presumptive diagnostic elements" (Kernberg, 1975, p. 8).

Kernberg (1970) conceptualized a hierarchical organization of levels of character pathology based on instinctual, ego, superego, defense, and object relations considerations. For Kernberg, from a structural perspective, patients organized at a borderline level exhibit the following: (1) nonspecific manifestations of ego weaknesses (deficits in anxiety tolerance, impulse control, and subliminatory potential), (2) shifts toward primary process modes of thinking, (3) a reliance on specific primitive defensive operations, (4) disruptions in superego development, (5) a disturbance of internalized object relations, and (6) identity diffusion.

Based on the conceptual groundwork laid by Kernberg and the increasing number of empirical studies emerging from descriptive psychiatry, and beginning with the publication in 1980 of *Borderline Phenomena and the Rorschach Test* (Kwawer et al., 1980), a host of empirical investigations that have sought to bring greater clarity and precision to the borderline concept have appeared in the Rorschach literature in the past decade. In general, these studies have focused on the quality of reality testing, the nature of thought disorder, the type of boundary disturbance, the level of defensive operation, and the quality of object relations of the borderline patient. In virtually every study, the experimental design has involved comparing, with respect to a specified variable, a group of borderline patients with a group of assumably more or less disturbed patients. Collectively, these studies have provided informative and clarifying findings; at the same time, however, they have highlighted conceptual ambiguities in the field. In the remainder of this chapter I review these investigations and then discuss one especially contentious issue—that of diagnosis, or what exactly constitutes the borders of the borderline concept.

REALITY TESTING

Of the three major structural variables associated with borderline pathology (identity diffusion, level of defensive operation, and reality testing), Kernberg (1975) considered reality testing the crucial structural variable in that it distinguishes borderline from psychotic personality organization, with some capacity for reality testing being maintained among borderlines while more severe impairments are found among psychotics.

To assess this proposition, Hymowitz and associates (1983) compared the Rorschach test and Weschler Adult Intelligence Scale (WAIS) records of two groups of psychiatric inpatients diagnosed as having either a borderline or a psychotic personality organization on the combined basis of Kernberg's (1981) structured interview and the Diagnostic Interview for Borderlines (Kolb and Gunderson, 1980). Reality testing was operationally defined in terms of the form quality of Rorschach responses, and Mayman's (1970) system for rating form perception was used. As predicted, the borderline subjects achieved higher scores than the psychotic subjects with the differences in F+ percentage attaining statistical significance. A closer inspection of the data revealed that only the borderline patients could produce the more original (Fo) and better-conceived form responses (F+). The attempts of the psychotic subjects to go beyond the ordinary form response faltered and resulted in reality departures from the inkblots.

On the basis of DSM-III criteria, Exner (1986) distinguished a group of borderline personality disorders from a group of schizotypal personality disorders and then compared the Rorschach records of each group with the other, as well as with two sets of Rorschach protocols obtained from first-admission schizophrenic patients. The first set of records were collected soon after admission and the second obtained shortly before discharge. Using the F+ percentage as an index of reality testing, Exner found that there was little difference in reality testing between the schizophrenic and schizotypal patients but that both groups scored significantly lower (indicating greater impairment) than the borderline patients.

THOUGHT DISORDER

Beginning with Rapaport, Gill, and Schafer's (1945–46) formulations regarding overideational and coarctated preschizophrenics, it has long been held that borderline patients require external structure to compensate for defects in internal structure. Singer (1977) extended this notion into a near-axiomatic rule for the diagnosis of borderline pathology: individuals with such pathology exhibit thought disorder on unstructured tests, such as the Rorschach test, yet manifest relatively normal performance on more structured tests, such as the WAIS.

To examine the role of structure on the thinking of borderline patients, Edell (1987) compared Rorschach protocols and scores with a more structured test of cognitive slippage in patients with borderline personality disorders and schizophrenic disorders and in normal controls. The borderline group included patients diagnosed as schizotypal personality disorder and mixed borderline–schizotypal disorder. All Rorschach records were scored for thought disorder on the basis of a measure developed by Johnston and Holtzman (1979), The Thought Disorder Index (TDI). The TDI is a revision of Watkins and Stauffacher's (1952) Delta Index, which quantifies categories of deviant verbalizations initially described by Rapaport, Gill, and Schafer (1945–1946). The TDI includes 21 categories of thought disorder, with each instance in each category weighted for severity at one of four levels (.25, .50, .75, and 1.0). To assess milder forms of thought disorder or cognitive slippage, a structured multiple-choice vocabulary test developed by Chapman and Chapman (1982) was employed. This measure includes two subtests, one requiring discrimination between subtle nuances of meaning and the other involving a knowledge of more obscure words. Edell's findings supported his hypothesis that borderline patients do manifest thought disorder but that such manifestations are limited to more unstructured tasks. More specifically, he found that the borderline and schizophrenic groups did not differ from one another on total TDI score but that each differed significantly from the control group. He also found that the borderlines were indistinguishable from the normal controls on the more structured test of cognitive slippage and that each group differed significantly from the schizophrenic patients. Edell reported two other findings that are of importance. First, he noted that the borderlines, schizotypals and mixed borderline–schizotypals were indistinguishable from one another in both quantity and quality of thought disorder. Second, he noted that although the borderline and schizophrenic groups did not differ on total TDI, there was a significant tendency among the schizophrenics to offer responses at the more severe levels of thought disorder.

Findings at variance with Edell (1987) have been reported by Hymowitz, and associates (1983) and Exner (1986). Hymowitz and associates (1983) also used the Thought Disorder Index; however, they applied it to both the Rorschach and the WAIS records of their sample of borderline and psychotic patients. They found that the TDI scores on each of the tests distinguished the two groups. They reported that minor disruptions in the WAIS were equally frequent in both groups, but that more severe disruptions were twice as prevalent among the psychotics, and that only the psychotic patients offered impaired responses at the .75 and 1.0 levels.

Exner (1986) found marked differences in the presence of thought disorder between a group of patients with borderline personality disorders and a group with schizotypal personality disorders. Whereas the borderline patients showed comparatively little evidence of thought disorder on the Rorschach test, the schizotypals, much like the schizophrenics, offered responses that were strange and distorted and revealed considerable slippage.

H. Lerner, Sugarman, and Barbour (1985) have questioned the assertions that borderlines do not differ from schizophrenics in the amount of thought disorder shown on the Rorschach test and that only their differential performance on a more structured test discriminates the groups. Speaking from an object relations perspective rather than from the earlier egopsychology model, they argue that differences in thought disorder between borderlines and schizophrenics are qualitative and not a matter of quantity or of the degree of structure. Groups of outpatient neurotics, outpatient borderlines, inpatient borderlines, and inpatient schizophrenics were compared with respect to classic Rorschach expressions of thought disorder as originally developed by Rapaport, Gill, and Schafer (1945–46). Although Lerner and associates (1985) had reconceptualized the scores in terms of the concept of boundary disturbances, nonetheless they found that the inpatient borderline group offered significantly more confabulatory responses than the other groups and that the inpatient schizophrenics were distinguishable by their offering of contaminations.

The findings of Lerner and associates (1985) are important in that they help to explain the seemingly disparate findings reported by Edell (1987) and Hymowitz and associates (1983) and to account for the observation reported by these investigators that schizophrenics offer the most severe instances of thought disorder. Clearly, viewing thought disorder as a unitary dimension and investigating it purely quantitatively is insufficient.

Following Watkins and Stauffacher (1952) and their attempts to arrange thought disorders along a single continuum of severity, subsequent investigators have continued these efforts and in the process have obscured possible qualitative differences among various types of thought disorders. It should be remembered that Rapaport's indices of deviant verbalizations represented an attempt to find Rorschach counterparts to what Freud (1900) had initially described as the mechanisms of dream work. Thus, contaminations of a Rorschach response were considered equivalent to Freud's mechanism of condensation, and the Rorschach confabulatory response was thought to parallel the mechanism of displacement. Therefore, while Rapaport's indices may vary in level of severity and may be collectively grouped under the broad umbrella of "primary process," at the same time they may possibly be tapping quite different processes. If this be the case, then differences in thought disorder between borderline patients and schizophrenic patients is not one of amount, but rather one of kind. This issue, together with the question of the relationship between thinking and other aspects of personality functioning (i.e., object relations, defense, etc.), is examined in subsequent sections in this chapter.

The questions raised by Exner's (1986) findings are diagnostic in nature and relate to the relationship between the diagnoses of borderline personality disorder and schizotypal personality disorder. Exner viewed the two as quite distinct and considered the schizotypal disorder closer to the schizophrenic disorder than to the borderline disorder. Where to place and how to conceptualize the schizotypal disorder is important, and this issue too is discussed later in this chapter.

BOUNDARY DISTURBANCES

Ego boundaries are hypothetical constructs that refer to the capacity to create particular cognitive and affective distinctions along some bipolar coordinate of experience where previously no distinction was possible. The establishment of boundaries between self and nonself and between fantasy and reality (inside and outside) is considered the earliest and most fundamental stage in the development of object representations.

Using three of Rapaport's indices of thought disorder (contamination, confabulation, fabulized combination) as measures of various levels of severity of boundary disturbances, Blatt and Ritzler (1974) found such indices to be related to disturbances in a variety of ego functions (capacity for reality testing, quality of interpersonal relations, nature of object representations) in a mixed schizophrenic and borderline sample. The authors further found that poorly articulated boundaries occurred most frequently in the more disturbed, chronic patients, who had impoverished object relations, impaired ego functions, and a lifelong pattern of isolation and estrangement.

Because different forms of psychopathology can be understood in terms of an impairment of the capacity to sustain specific boundaries, several authors have attempted to identify the boundary disturbance particular to the borderline patient.

H. Lerner, Sugarman, and Barbour (1985) found that independently diagnosed borderline patients could be distinguished from both schizophrenics and neurotics on the basis of level of boundary disturbance. Borderline patients were found to experience difficulty maintaining the inner–outer boundary as assessed through the confabulation response of the Rorschach; that is, these patients had difficulty discriminating between an external object and their own affective reaction to that object. By contrast, the schizophrenic patients experienced difficulty in maintaining the developmentally earlier boundary between self and other, as reflected in the contamination response.

In a study involving boundary disturbances in depressive, borderline, and schizophrenic hospitalized inpatients, Wilson (1985) obtained findings strikingly similar to those of Lerner and associates (1985). He too found that the borderline group scored significantly higher on the Rorschach indices of laxness and (moderately severe) inner–outer boundary disturbance. The schizophrenic group, in comparison, scored significantly higher on measures of self–other boundary disturbance.

Thus, findings from the studies of both Wilson (1985) and Lerner and associates (1985) are consistent in indicating that whereas the developmental structural impairment of the borderline patient is at the point of the inner–outer boundary, for the schizophrenic patient it is at the earlier point of self–other boundary formation.

DEFENSE

Kernberg has identified two overall levels of defense organization, one associated with neurotic pathology and the other with borderline and psychotic pathology. At the lower level of organization (borderline and psychotic) splitting, or primitive dissociation, is the basic defense, which is augmented through the related mechanisms of low-level denial, primitive idealization, primitive devaluation, and projective identification. At the higher developmental level, repression replaces splitting as the major defense and is bolstered by the related operations of intellectualization, rationalization, undoing, and higher-level forms of denial and projection.

Two comprehensive Rorschach scoring systems (P. Lerner and Lerner, 1980; Cooper, Perry, and Arnow, 1988) were developed to assess the more primitive defenses. These scales, together with the research each has generated, are discussed in Chapter 13. Here I briefly review those findings directly related to the defensive structure of the borderline patient.

In an initial study, Lerner and Lerner (1980) applied their defense scale to the Rorschach protocols of 15 outpatient borderlines and 15 outpatient neurotics. As predicted, the borderline subjects used test indices of splitting, low- level devaluation, projective identification, and low-level denial significantly more often than did the neurotic subjects. The measures of splitting and projective identification appeared exclusively in the borderline group. Indices of high-level devaluation and high- level denial were found more frequently in the records of the neurotic group.

H. Lerner, Sugarman, and Gaughran (1981) extended the defense scale to a comparison of the Rorschach records of a group of hospitalized borderline patients with those of a hospitalized schizophrenic group. Here too the borderline patients were found to have a unique and distinctive defensive structure. Indices of splitting and four of the five scale measures of devaluation were observed significantly more often in the borderline group, and scores reflective of projective identification occurred exclusively in the borderline group. Denial, when treated as a composite score also distinguished the two groups, with borderlines scoring higher.

Collins (1983), in a cross-validating study, obtained findings supportive of those reported by Lerner and Lerner (1980) and Lerner, Sugarman, and Gaughran (1981). Rorschach protocols were collected from a sample of 15 borderline patients, 15 neurotic patients, and 15 schizophrenic patients and scored using the Lerner Defense Scale. Overall differences among the three groups were highly significant, supporting the general hypothesis that borderline patients reveal a defensive structure significantly different from that of neurotics and schizophrenics. Major differences were found between the borderline and schizophrenic patients. The borderlines offered significantly more responses reflective of splitting, projective identification, low-level idealization, and mid-level devaluation. Although not statistically significant, the borderline patients, as compared with the neurotic group, used indices of splitting and projective identification more frequently.

Using the hypothesis that borderline personality disorders would manifest greater disturbance in defensive organization than narcissistic personality disorders, Farris (1988) applied the Lerner Defense Scale to the Rorschach records of nine matched pairs of borderline and narcissistic patients. A comparison of the two groups revealed that the borderline patients produced a significantly greater number of responses reflecting the use of primitive defenses than did narcissistic subjects. Each of the defense categories was submitted to a chi-square analysis. Significant differences were found regarding the defenses of splitting and projective identification. In both categories the borderline subjects produced a significantly greater number of primitive defense responses than did the narcissistic subjects.

Rooted in the theoretical contributions of Kernberg (1975) and Stolorow and Lachmann (1980) and in the test work of Schafer (1954), Holt (1970), and Lerner and Lerner (1980), Cooper, Perry, and Arnow (1988) devised a content-based scoring system for assessing 15 defenses, including the designated borderline defenses of devaluation, omnipotence, primitive idealization, projection, projective identification, and splitting. Rorschach protocols were obtained from 68 subjects, including 21 diagnosed as borderline personality disorder, 14 diagnosed as having borderline traits, 17 diagnosed as antisocial personality disorder, and 16 diagnosed as bipolar II affective disorder. All borderline personality disorders met DSM-III criteria and scored above 150 on the Borderline Personality Scale. Those diagnosed as having borderline traits met four (rather than five) of the eight DSM-III criteria and obtained a lower cutoff score on the Borderline Personality Scale. The antisocial personalities were diagnosed according to DSM-III criteria, and the affective disorders were diagnosed on the basis of the Research Diagnostic Criteria. These diagnostic variables, together with two continuous measures (a subset of 36 items of the Borderline Personality Scale and the weighted Antisocial Personality Scale), were used for data analysis.

To examine the discriminant validity of the defense scale, correlations were obtained between subject diagnostic variables and the individual defense scores. The Borderline Personality Disorder Scale was found to correlate positively with the defense scores of devaluation, projection, splitting, and hypomanic denial, and negatively with intellectualization. The number of positive DSM-III borderline criteria correlated positively with each of the same defenses except for projection. The dichotomous and continuous antisocial personality variables and the affective disorder variable did not correlate with any of the borderline defenses. The relationship between defense mechanisms and specific aspects of borderline pathology was examined by calculating correlations between the defenses and each of the nine subscales of the Borderline Personality Disorder Scale. As predicted, splitting correlated positively with Subscale VI (splitting of other images) and Subscale VII (unstable identity, including splitting of self-images) as well as with a greater number of the BPD subscales than did the other defenses.

In a study reviewed in Chapter 13, Lerner, Albert, and Walsh (1987) applied the borderline defense measures of the scale of Cooper, Perry, and Arnow (1988) scale to the Rorschach protocols collected in two previous studies (Lerner and Lerner, 1980; Lerner, Sugarman, and Gaughran, 1981). In a discriminant function analysis the borderline defense scores significantly distinguished inpatient borderlines from neurotics, outpatient borderlines from inpatient borderlines, and inpatient borderlines from schizophrenics. Three defense scores—splitting, devaluation, and omnipotence—were found especially effective in discriminating among groups.

In summary, in a variety of studies it has been demonstrated that patients organized at a borderline level manifest a discernible defensive structure different in kind from those of neurotic patients, schizophrenic patients, and patients with narcissistic personality disorders. Characterizing this defensive structure are the operations of splitting, projective identification, omnipotence, primitive devaluation, primitive idealization, and low-level denial.

OBJECT RELATIONS

A concept basic to Kernberg's work that has received considerable examination is that of "internalized object relation." Attempts to assess this concept have involved the study of impairments in object representations found in patients with various forms of pathology, including those with borderline levels of personality organization. While several authors (Modell, 1963; Krohn, 1974; Kernberg, 1975) have described the borderline patient's object hunger, desperate search for direct contact, and intense fear of object loss, only recently have investigators been able to relate these observations to such underlying factors as level of internal object representation.

Using the scoring system of Blatt and associates (1976), Blatt and Lerner (1983) applied the scale to the Rorschach records of several patients each of whom was independently selected as a prototypic example of a specific clinical disorder. In reviewing the protocol of a borderline patient the authors found that the object representations progressively deteriorated both over time and with stress. Initially, the representations were accurate, well-differentiated, and appropriately articulated; however, this gave way to representations that were inaccurately perceived, inappropriately articulated, and seen as part, rather than whole, figures. The latter finding, the shift from whole to part figures, is consistent with Kernberg's proposition that under the pressure of intense anxiety the borderline patient defensively attempts to manage the anxiety by splitting the object into more tolerable good- and bad-part units.

Farris (1988) in his comparative study of borderline and narcissistic patients also applied the scale of Blatt and associates (1976) to the subjects' Rorschach protocols. Using a summary score, he found, as predicted, that the narcissistic subjects showed a significantly higher level of object differentiation, articulation, and integration than did borderline subjects.

Spear (1980) differentiated two subtypes of borderline personalities and then compared their Rorschach records with one another and with the records of a group of schizophrenic patients on the basis of both the structural measure of Blatt and associates (1976) and Krohn and Mayman's (1974) thematic measure of object representations. One subgroup of borderline patients included more infantile personalities characterized by emotional lability, intense dependency, concerns regarding object loss, and proclivity for anaclitic depression. The other group consisted of obsessive/paranoid personalities characterized by intellectualization, isolation of affect, and a proneness for introjective depression. Two major findings were obtained. First, while the structural measure significantly distinguished the combined borderline group from the schizophrenic group, it did not differentiate the two borderline groups. Second, the thematic measure distinguished the two borderline groups and differentiated the infantile borderlines from the schizophrenics; however, it failed to differentiate the obsessive/paranoid borderlines from the schizophrenic group.

Although the scale of Blatt and associates (1976) consists of six developmental dimensions, in his initial study Spear (1980) used one summary developmental score. Further, the thematic scale was originally devised to assess object representations as manifested in dream material. To rectify these methodological shortcomings, Spear and Sugarman (1984) replicated the earlier study; in their study the six developmental dimensions of Blatt's scale were treated separately, and the thematic aspect was evaluated using a modified version of Urist's (1977) Mutuality of Autonomy Scale. An examination of the Rorschach protocols of a sample consisting of 22 obsessive/paranoid borderline patients, 17 infantile/hysterical borderline patients, and 15 schizophrenic patients yielded the following results: (1) four of the six developmental dimensions distinguished the combined borderline group from the schizophrenic group; (2) only the differentiation subscale differentiated each of the three groups; (3) the differentiation subscale also differentiated the infantile/hysterical borderline group from the combined obsessive/paranoid borderline group and schizophrenic group; (4) three scores on the thematic measure distinguished the two borderline groups; (5) none of the thematic measures distinguished the obsessive/paranoid borderlines from the schizophrenics; and (6) the infantile/hysterical borderlines were significantly more developmentally advanced than the schizophrenics on two of the thematic scores. From these findings the authors concluded that from a structural perspective the borderline groups were relatively homogeneous, but from a thematic perspective the infantile/hysterical borderline patients functioned at a higher object relations level and the obsessive/paranoid borderline patients functioned at a lower level, closer to that of the schizophrenic patients.

The most comprehensive study of impairments in level of object representation among groups differing in severity of psychopathology is the work of H. Lerner and St. Peter (1984). These authors applied the Blatt scale to a sample of four groups, including outpatient neurotic patients, outpatient borderline patients, hospitalized borderline patients, and hospitalized schizophrenic patients. Overall, strong support was found for the general proposition that impairments in level of object representation, as indicated by the assessment of the developmental–structural properties of human responses given to the Rorschach test, show distinct patterns in groups differing in type and severity of psychopathology. Several other informative and unexpected findings were also obtained. Subdividing the responses into those accurately perceived and those inaccurately perceived, the investigators found an inverse relationship between developmental level of the concept of the object and degree of psychopathology. That is, the less severe the psychopathology the higher the developmental level of the patient's object concept. This inverse relationship, however, did not hold for the inaccurately perceived responses. Here, quite surprisingly, the hospitalized borderline group achieved the highest levels of human differentiation, articulation, and integration (i.e., for inaccurately perceived responses). Because response accuracy is taken as an indicator of quality of reality testing, this finding prompted H. Lerner and St. Peter to question the relationship between reality testing and object relations and led them to compare the protocols of the two borderline groups.

It was found that although the outpatient borderlines produced more accurate and less inaccurate human responses than did their hospitalized counterparts, their responses tended to involve quasi-human rather than whole human figures. In other words, although the outpatient borderlines were able to perceive objects accurately (intact reality testing), the perception was accompanied by a distancing and dehumanizing of the object. The hospitalized borderlines, by contrast, were unable to distance their objects, and as a consequence, their reality testing suffered. If one conceptualizes the ability to distance and devalue objects as reflective of the defenses of splitting and primitive devaluation and the inability to distance and devalue objects as indicative of the absence or failure of these defenses, then the findings may be interpreted as supporting Kernberg's (1975) contention regarding the intimate relationship between quality of reality testing, nature of the defensive structure, and the organization of internalized object relations.

Finally, in reviewing the thematic content of the human responses, the investigators found that the hospitalized borderline patients, in comparison with the three other groups, offered the most malevolent content and were the only group to produce inaccurately perceived malevolent responses. Conceptually, these patients may be understood in terms of their inability to defend against or escape from internal malevolent objects.

A review of the above findings leads to several interesting conclusions:

(1) there is consistent evidence to suggest that the object representations of borderline patients are significantly more impaired and less developmentally advanced than are those of neurotic and narcissistic patients; (2) when a sample of borderline patients is subdivided on the basis of character types and the object representation concept is viewed in terms of its constituent components, the borderline subgroups differ significantly on select components; (3) from a structural perspective the object representations of various borderline patients are relatively homogenous and different from and more advanced than those of schizophrenic patients; (4) from a thematic perspective the object representations of infantile/hysterical borderline patients are significantly more advanced than those of schizophrenic patients, and the representations of obsessive/paranoid borderline patients are indistinguishable from those of schizophrenics; and (5) object representations, and hence object relations, are intimately related to reality testing and defense organization and are most profitably investigated and understood in that context.

DEVELOPMENT

This section includes a heterogenous group of studies that have all approached the investigation of the borderline patient from a developmental perspective. The studies differ in the targeted area of investigation (i.e., cognitive–perceptual, object relations, etc.) as well as in their conceptual roots.

Farris (1988), in a study that has been referred to often in this work, also investigated differences in cognitive–perceptual functioning between borderline and narcissistic patients. Applying Friedman's (1953) developmental level scoring system to the subjects' Rorschach protocols, Farris found that the narcissistic subjects achieved significantly higher scores than did the borderline subjects. He interpreted the finding as indicating that borderline patients, as compared with narcissistic patients, are fixated or arrested at an earlier developmental point, are more prone to transient disruptions in reality testing, and have stronger regressive tendencies.

Farris's finding that the borderline subjects tended to produce more poorly structured, amorphous, and more fabulized combinations was consistent with findings obtained by Singer and Larson (1981) in an earlier study. These investigators had used a scoring system derived from Becker's (1956) modification of Friedman's (1953) developmental scoring system to investigate ego functioning and had applied it to the Rorschach protocols of a sample of 114 subjects, including borderline patients. In addition to finding that borderline patients produce developmentally poorer responses, Singer and Larson found that a discriminant function analysis involving 11 variables correctly classified 20 of the 25 borderline subjects.

Coonerty (1986), as discussed in Chapter 14, using Mahler's theory of separation and individuation, devised a developmental object relations scale for identifying and scoring Rorschach responses reflective of concerns and issues associated with the preseparation stage and with each of the subphases of the separation-individuation process. The scale was applied to the Rorschach records of 50 borderline subjects and 50 schizophrenic subjects. Coonerty found that while the borderline group produced significantly more responses indicative of separation-individuation concerns, the schizophrenic group, by contrast, offered significantly more responses indicative of preseparation concerns.

Despite different methodologies and different conceptual underpinnings, there is a consistent thread that runs through these studies. The combined findings of Farris (1988) and Singer and Larson (1981) suggests that the level of cognitive–perceptual functioning of borderline patients is higher than that of schizophrenic patients but lower than that of narcissistic patients. In both investigations the authors used measures scoring developmental level. P. Lerner (1975) in his review of developmental level scoring systems noted that implicit in the underlying theory is the assumption that "level of maturation is a unitary dimension underlying several diverse aspects of human functioning and that a study of any one aspect has predictive import for other aspects." (p. 27) He further suggested that "if this assumption is tenable, then one should be able to predict from Rorschach indices other areas of psychological functioning which lend themselves to developmental ordering" (pp. 27–28). Because Mahler's theory lends itself to developmental ordering (i.e., development of an autonomous sense of self and of constancy of the object), Coonerty's (1986) finding that borderline patients expressed themes referable to a later developmental stage than did schizophrenic patients is consistent with developmental theory and, hence, with the other findings.

Beyond this, Coonerty's results are especially important in that they lend support to those writers (Masterson and Rinsley, 1975; Settlage, 1977) who locate the occurrence of developmental arrest in borderline patients during the separation-individuation phases.

SUBTYPES OF BORDERLINE PATIENTS

Controversy abounds in the theoretical (Gunderson and Singer, 1975; Edell, 1984) and the testing (Exner, 1986; Carr, 1987; and Edell, 1987) literatures regarding the nosological placement of the schizotypal personality disorder. Several authors (Serban, Conte, and Plutchic, 1987; Edell,

1987) view the schizotypal personality as a subvariant of and indistinguishable from the borderline personality, whereas others (Exner, 1986; Carr, 1987) conceive of the schizotypal disorder and the borderline disorder as separate and distinct entities, with the schizotypal patient more closely approximating the schizophrenic disorder. This specific issue is important because in a broader sense it raises the question of the outer boundaries of the borderline diagnosis and prompts one to consider from what perspective the borderline patient can most profitably be viewed.

Edell (1987), as noted previously, found that borderline patients, schizotypal patients, and patients with a mixed diagnosis of the two were indistinguishable from each other on a measure of thought disorder but were significantly different from a group of schizophrenics and a group of normal controls.

In contrast, Exner (1986) found marked and pervasive differences between the Rorschach records of a group of borderline patients and those of a group of schizotypal patients. He reported significant differences in quality of thinking, intactness of reality testing, degree of self-absorption, and effectiveness of affect control. Specifically, whereas the schizotypal patients revealed more disturbed thinking, greater disruptions in reality testing, and higher levels of self-absorption than the borderlines, the borderline patients showed greater disturbance with regard to affect control. Furthermore, when both groups were compared with a group of schizophrenic patients, three distinct patterns of psychological organization and functioning emerged. While there was much overlap between the schizotypal group and the schizophrenic group regarding their organizational characteristics, the groups differed significantly with respect to their level of functioning. The borderline group differed from the others both in organization and in functioning. According to Exner, both the schizotypals and schizophrenics presented as introversive, detached, somewhat affectless, and highly ideational. Not surprisingly, their disruptions and symptoms appeared in the realm of ideation. By contrast, the borderline patients appeared as affect oriented and their impairments centered around affect oriented modulation and regulation. Because of the similarities noted in organization and style between the schizotypals and schizophrenics, Exner suggested that one might refer to the schizotypals more accurately by the older term "borderline schizophrenics."

The distinction Exner (1986) drew between the borderlines and schizotypals is very similar to the distinction between two subtypes of borderline patients made by Spear (1980) and Spear and Sugarman (1984). Like Exner's borderline group, Spear's infantile/hysterical borderlines were characterized by emotional lability, heightened dependency, and vulnerability to object loss. Similarly, the obsessive/paranoid borderlines, like Exner's schizotypals, were depicted as hyper-ideational and as manifesting an isolation of affects. Spear and Sugarman (1984) found that although both subgroups achieved the same level of object representation on a structural measure, on a thematic measure they differed significantly; these researchers also found that the obsessive/paranoid subgroup more closely resembled the schizophrenic patients. Like Exner, yet quite independently, these authors suggested that one might judiciously reserve the term "borderline schizophrenic" for the obsessive/paranoid borderline patient.

Despite the consistency and impressiveness of their findings, the conclusions reached by Exner (1986) and Spear and Sugarman (1984) may be interpreted differently, especially in light of the work of H. Lerner and St. Peter (1984). Both in conception and in design Exner's study was pitched at a descriptive level. The variables studied and the Rorschach measures used were stylistic in nature, and the conclusions reached related to characterological features. That descriptive or characterological differences appear among borderline patients is not unexpected; indeed, it was this observation that led Kernberg (1975) to argue that an exclusive emphasis on descriptive features was necessary but insufficient and that one should also consider underlying structural factors. Spear and Sugarman (1984) focused on a structural variable, level of object representation, but they studied this factor in isolation, and conceptually they stopped short of considering the interrelationship among various structural variables.

Lerner and St. Peter (1984) also investigated level of object representation, but in recognizing differences that appeared between outpatient and hospitalized borderline groups, they also considered defense and reality testing. This permitted them to interpret their findings in terms of the dynamic interplay between various structural variables and thereby remain closer to the richness of Kernberg's theory and the clinical complexity of the individual borderline patient.

The results of the Lerner and St. Peter (1984) study—in particular, the observed differences between the borderline groups on the structural variables of level of object representations, quality of reality testing, and effectiveness of defenses—lend themselves to the notion of a psychopathological continuum with a spectrum of borderline disorders. From a developmental perspective, Rinsley (1979) and Stone (1980) have both advanced the concept of a "spectrum" for understanding the pathogenesis of the various borderline disorders. These authors proposed a "diathesis-stress" model, with the role of genetic loading and constitutional factors assuming increased weight toward the more severe, psychotic-like end of the continuum and intrafamilial, interpersonal, and experiential factors assuming greater importance with the less severe borderline disorders. Placing issues of etiology aside and assuming a structural perspective, Lerner and St. Peter (1984) conclude that "points on this . . . continuum appear to be a function of levels of internalization and concomitant cognitive and affective development, all within an interpersonal matrix involving the progressive differentiation, articulation, and integration of the representational world" (p. 18).

SUMMARY

The past decade has witnessed an increasing number of empirical Rorschach-based studies focused on the borderline patient and specific borderline processes. Rooted in either descriptive psychiatry or psychoanalytic theory, these investigations have sought to clarify and define more rigorously the borderline patient's type of thought disturbance, level of reality testing, level of boundary disturbance, defensive structure, and quality of object relation.

The borderline concept has been beset by various conceptual ambiguities, including whether an exclusively descriptive diagnostic schema, such as represented in DSM-III, is sufficient, whether the borderline patient reveals a stable personality disturbance or a form of less severe psychosis, and whether the borderline disturbance is primarily a disorder of ego functioning or of object relations. Collectively, the foregoing studies have provided findings that help to clarify these issues. For example, from a purely descriptive perspective the schizotypal and borderline patient are distinctly different, yet when looked at from a structural perspective in terms of underlying personality variables (e.g., defensive structure, level of internalized object relations), one sees similarities. This would suggest that a purely descriptive approach is necessary but not sufficient; a dynamic--structural approach is needed as well.

With respect to the issue of personality disturbance versus a less severe type of psychosis, various lines of evidence indicate that borderline patients are qualitatively different from psychotic patients and, hence, should be viewed as manifesting a type of personality disturbance. Specifically, the level of boundary disturbance is of a different nature in the two groups; boundary disturbances are less severe in borderline patients, while, at the same time, psychotic patients, unlike borderlines, are especially impaired in representing objects.

Given the current status of research and the measures now available, the question of primary disorder—whether the impairment is in ego functioning or in object relations— requires reformulation. I believe we are at a point in our understanding of borderline patients where we can instead ask in what ways the disturbances in ego functioning are related to the disturbance in object relations and how we might understand these impairments from a developmental perspective.

16

Variants of the Borderline Concept and the Rorschach Test

Paralleling the increased interest in and investigation of the borderline patient has been the greater research attention accorded specific groups of patients whom clinicians and researchers have come to associate with what they call "primitive mental states." Despite presenting various symptoms, these patients appear to share archaic personality elements that become evident in profound regressions, especially in treatment. Their disturbances reflect a variety of etiologies whose common denominator would appear to be a history of frustrating, rather than satisfying, early object relations. Based on the assumption that underlying the clinical presentation and the expression of symptoms there is a commonly shared borderline personality organization, many of the Rorschach scoring systems devised to assess borderline patients have been extended to the protocols of these patients as well. In this chapter I review those studies that have applied these Rorschach scales to the following clinical populations: eating disorder patients, patients manifesting gender identity disturbances, and antisocial personalities. Several of these studies have been described and discussed previously (in general, from the point of view of the measures employed). Here, I emphasize the obtained findings, in part to demonstrate the contribution of Rorschach studies to our understanding of specific forms of psychopathology.

EATING DISORDER PATIENTS

Many of the early Rorschach studies involved clinical, impressionistic appraisals of the protocols of anorexic patients; despite limitations inherent in this methodology, the findings reported have often been substantiated in more rigorous and systematic investigations.

Roland (1970) studied the Rorschach protocols of 23 anorexic patients. On the basis of content analysis, he reported strong depressive trends, feelings of rejection, suicidal ideation, body image distortions, difficulties in reality testing, and tenuous controls.

From a review of the Rorschach records of 40 anorexic patients, Selvini-Palazzoli (1974) concluded that no specific test pattern characterized these patients. She did find, however, that her sample could be subdivided into two groups on the basis of the presence or absence of thought disorder.

Wagner and Wagner (1978) presented and reviewed the Rorschach records of three cases of anorexia (two females and one male). Based on the patterning of scores, they suggested that each case could be diagnosed as conversion hysteria with repressed orality. Although their diagnosis is questionable, a review of the actual protocols reveals the subjects' attunement to oral imagery (i.e., food, eating, etc.) and the prevalence of responses reflective of a somatic preoccupation (i.e., body parts and organs, etc.).

Small, and associates (1982) compared the Wechsler records and Rorschach protocols of a group of 27 hospitalized anorexics with those of a group of schizophrenic females. On the basis of a combination of findings related to the differential use of conventional Rorschach scores (i.e., location, determinants, form level) and varying responses to structure (that is, quality of test performance on the more structured WAIS versus the less structured Rorschach test), the authors concluded that the anorexic patients were organized at a higher level than the schizophrenic patients but that they shared features in common with borderline personalities. These similarities included a proclivity toward disturbed thinking on unstructured tests and a sensitivity to depression and affective needs. The authors also compared the Rorschach protocols on the Delta index, a measure of thought disorder devised by Watkins and Stauffacher (1952); these results are reported under the section on thought disorder.

Weisberg, Norman, and Herzog (1987) compared the Rorschach protocols of 57 normal-weight bulimic women, a group of outpatient depressed women, and a group of nonpatient controls. With a variety of scores developed by Exner (1974), the groups were compared with respect to the following areas of personality functioning: depression, suicidal ideation, emotional lability and impulsivity, egocentricity and narcissism, thought disorder, anger and negativity, and coping and organizational style. The authors found that in contrast to the nonpatient controls, the bulimic and depressed groups were similar in their overall high level of dysphoric affect, emotional lability and impulsivity, avoidance of affective stimulation, state of emotional overload, relatively poor perceptual accuracy, lower interest in other people, and lack of a set coping style. Compared with both other groups, however, the bulimic patients displayed greater egocentricity and anger and negativity. In contrast to the depressives, who appeared more introspective, the bulimics presented as "underincorporators," meaning that they often failed to attend to important information in their environment.

In contrast with the above studies, which have either been impressionistic and anecdotal or associated with conventional Rorschach scores, the group of studies reviewed in the following paragraphs all employed conceptually based scoring systems. As in the previous chapter, these studies are discussed under the general headings of reality testing, thought disorder, boundary disturbances, defense and object relations.

Reality Testing

To assess level of reality testing, each of the studies reviewed here employed the form level scoring manual developed by Mayman (1970). Based on the earlier work of Rapaport, Mayman's (1970) system consists of seven distinct and graded scores that range from "reality adherence" at one extreme to "reality abrogation" at the other extreme. Numerical values have been assigned to each of the form level ratings by Holt (1977).

Van-Der Keshet (1988) applied the scoring system to the Rorschach records of groups of anorexic ballet students, nonanorexic ballet students, restricting anorexics, bulimic anorexics, and normal controls. In accord with her predictions, the author found that the nonanorexic ballet students and the controls attained a significantly higher level of reality testing than the anorexic ballet students. No differences were found between the restrictive anorexics, the bulimic anorexics, and the anorexic ballet students. The nonanorexic ballet students and the controls demonstrated a significantly higher level of reality testing than the restrictive anorexics and the bulimic anorexics. The author noted that although the three eating disorder groups manifested a lower level of reality testing, their perception of reality was still accurate.

In a study involving not only patients with eating disorders but their mothers as well, Brouillette (1987) compared form level ratings of groups of restricting anorexics, bulimic anorexics, normal controls, and, for all three groups, their mothers. The author reported several interesting findings. First, in all three groups, no significant differences were found between the daughters and mothers (generation factor) regarding level of reality testing. Second, the normal controls and their mothers, both separately and paired together, achieved significantly higher levels of reality testing than did either group of eating disorder patients and their mothers. Third, no significant differences were reported between the restricting anorexics and the bulimic anorexics, nor between their mothers. As with Van-Der Keshet's (1988) findings, a closer review of Brouillette's results indicates that although the eating disorder patients and their mothers attained lower reality testing ratings, their perception of reality could be characterized as accurate.

Finally, Piran (1988) compared the form level ratings of a group of restricting anorexic patients with those of a group of bulimic patients. Although no significant differences between the groups was reported, there was a tendency for the bulimic patients to display a lower level of reality testing.

In summary, when compared with normal controls, eating disorder patients have been found to present a lower level of reality testing, yet in each instance their reality testing overall has been judged as adequate. Nonetheless, it should be noted that in each of these studies numerical values have been assigned to each of the form level ratings, means have been calculated, and then the means have been compared. Theory and clinical experience suggest that the reality testing of eating disorder patients, especially bulimics, is highly variable. Therefore, in future research it would be important to focus on the range of form level ratings.

Thought Disorder

In a study referred to earlier Small and associates (1982) compared the Rorschach protocols of a group of anorexics with those of a comparable group of schizophrenics on an index of thought disorder (Delta Index) developed by Watkins and Stauffacher (1952). Interestingly, no significant differences were found between the two groups, and the mean scores for both groups fell into what Watkins and Stauffacher refer to as the "pathological range."

Piran (1988) reported comparable results: restricting and bulimic anorexics did not differ from each other regarding the degree of thought disorder, but both groups scored within the pathological range. Analyzing specific measures, Piran also reported that whereas bulimics offered a greater number of fabulized combinations, the restricting anorexics produced more over-elaborate symbolism responses.

Although both studies reported Delta Indexes that fall within the pathological range of thought disorder, the results are difficult to interpret because of the nature of the Delta Index. In the previous chapter it was noted that Watkins and Stauffacher (1952) assigned weights to various types of disordered thinking on the assumption that thought disorder was a unitary dimension. But, as noted, that assumption may be in error. What is called for are studies, like Piran's (1988), that examine qualitative aspects of disturbed thinking in separate samples of restrictive and bulimic anorexics and that also include a control group in the experimental design.

Boundary Disturbance

Strober and Goldenberg (1981) examined boundary disturbances in a group of anorexic patients and in a group of depressed patients. To assess the concept of boundary disturbance five indices were used, including affect elaboration, overspecificity, incongruous-fabulized combinations, barrier, and penetration. As predicted, the researchers reported that the anorexic group experienced a greater loss of internal–external boundaries and more difficulties with conceptual boundaries than did the depressed group.

Kaufer and Katz (1983) also found evidence of serious self–other and reality–fantasy boundary disturbances in a group of anorexic women as compared to a matched control group of normal women. The breakthrough of primary process material was taken as an indication of severe disruption in the boundary between reality and unconscious processes (i.e., the repressive barrier).

Other studies employed a scale for assessing boundary disturbances devised by Blatt and Ritzler (1974). As discussed in the previous chapter, these authors selected three of Rapaport's indices of thought disorder (contamination, confabulation, fabulized combination) and reconceptualized the scores as indicating various levels of severity of boundary disturbances.

Sugarman, Quinlan, and Devenis (1982) applied the Boundary Disturbance Scale to the Rorschach protocols of 12 anorexic patients and 12 normal controls. The anorexic patients produced significantly more contamination responses, which the authors interpreted as indicating disturbances in maintaining the boundary between self and other.

Van-Der Keshet (1988) also found significant boundary disturbances among eating disorder patients and anorexic ballet students, though the level of disturbance noted was less severe than that previously reported by Sugarman and associates (1982). Van-Der Keshet reported no main effect for the contamination test index. By contrast, major effects were obtained for both the confabulatory and fabulized combination responses. With respect to the confabulation response she found the following: anorexic ballet students produced significantly more confabulatory responses than the nonanorexic ballet students and the controls; no differences were found between the anorexic ballet students, the restricting anorexics, and the bulimic anorexics; and bulimic anorexics offered significantly more confabulations than the restricting anorexics. With regard to the fabulized combination score, the bulimic anorexics produced more of these responses than any of the other groups. Finally, using an overall summary boundary disturbance score, Van-Der Keshet found that the anorexic ballet students and the bulimic anorexics demonstrated a significantly higher level of impairment in maintaining boundaries compared to the other groups but did not differ from each other. In summary, Van-Der Keshet's results indicate that there are important differences in level of boundary disturbance between restricting and bulimic anorexics and that with bulimic anorexics and anorexic ballet students the boundary implicated is that between inner and outer (fantasy and reality).

Boundary disturbances in eating disorder patients and their mothers have been studied by Brouillette (1987). No significant differences were found between restricting anorexics and bulimic anorexics nor between their mothers; however, when both patient groups were combined and both mother groups were combined, these joint groups revealed significantly greater boundary impairment than did a group of normal controls and their mothers. Further, no significant differences were noted between daughters and mothers in any of the three groups. Because Brouillette used a summary score, the specific level of boundary disturbance was not determined.

In summary, consistent findings from several studies indicate that individuals with eating disorders manifest significant boundary disturbances. Although the particular level of boundary disturbance involved appears to be sample specific, in general the findings suggest that the impairment includes the developmentally earlier and more fundamental boundaries of self–other and reality–fantasy. It is unclear whether there are differences in severity in boundary disturbances between subtypes of eating disorder patients though there is some suggestion that bulimic patients exhibit more severe impairments.

Defense

Because applications of the Lerner Defense Scale for assessing primitive defenses were reviewed in Chapter 13, the following paragraphs are only a summary of those findings related to eating disorder subjects. Van-Der Keshet (1988), in general, found similarities in defensive patterning among restricting anorexic patients, bulimic anorexic patients, and anorexic ballet students and found differences from normal controls and nonanorexic ballet students. Both clinical anorexic groups and the anorexic ballet students used splitting and devaluation significantly more often than the control group, and the restricting anorexics were further distinguishable by their frequent use of denial.

Brouillette (1987) found that splitting, low-level devaluation, projective identification, and low-level denial occurred with significantly greater frequency in the protocols of restricting anorexic patients and their mothers and of bulimic patients and their mothers than in the records of normal controls and their mothers.

Piran and Lerner (1988) compared the defensive structure of restricting anorexics with that of bulimic anorexics. Consistent with the respective nature of their presenting symptoms, the bulimic anorexics tended to use projective identification and low-level devaluation while restricting anorexics, by contrast, relied on denial and high-level idealization.

The overall findings from these studies indicate that eating disorder patients tend to use more primitive defenses. Test measures of splitting, low-level devaluation, and projective identification consistently distinguish these patients from controls. There is also evidence to suggest that while both restricting anorexics and bulimic anorexics utilize primitive defenses, the specific defenses they use are somewhat different and are consistent with their symptomatology.

Object Relations

Attempts to study the object relations of eating disorder patients have typically involved an application of Blatt and associates' (1976) scale for assessing the concept of the object to the subjects' Rorschach records.

On the basis of a comparison of the Rorschach protocols of a group of 12 anorexic patients and 12 controls, Sugarman, Quinlan, and Devenis (1982) reported that the anorexic patients did not differ significantly from the controls in level of object representation.

Brouillette (1987), in contrast, found that the level of object representation in a group of restricting anorexics and their mothers and in a group of bulimics and their mothers was significantly lower than that of a control group consisting of nonpatients and their mothers. No significant differences were found between mothers and daughters in any of the three groups, between restricting anorexics and bulimic anorexics, or between mothers.

Piran (1988) investigated and found significant differences in object representations between restricting and bulimic anorexic patients. Whereas the two groups did not differ on the scale dimensions of differentiation and articulation, significant differences were obtained on the frequency of action responses and the content of the action. The bulimics not only incorporated action in their responses significantly more often than did the restrictors, but in addition, the action incorporated was of a malevolent nature. Intrigued by this finding, Piran looked at the quality of malevolent action more closely. Subdividing the malevolent content into sadistic ("attack"), masochistic ("victim"), and sadistic–masochistic catego ries, she found that sadistic responses appeared exclusively among the bulimics.

In general, findings regarding impairment in level of object representation among eating disorder patients are inconclusive and somewhat inconsistent; however, it should be noted that there is a paucity of research in this area and that the studies that are available have all used the same scale (Blatt et al.'s, 1976, Concept of the Object Scale). Of particular interest is Piran's finding that malevolence is more characteristic of the interaction of bulimic patients than of restricting anorexic patients. This specific result is consistent with findings from the studies of defense in which several investigators noted that the bulimic patients employed primitive devaluation significantly more often than did the restrictive anorexics. The combined findings suggest that bulimic patients, as compared with the restricting anorexics, are actively involved in a struggle with internal "bad objects." From the perspective of internal object relations, the bulimics are quite similar to the inpatient borderlines described by Lerner and St. Peter (1984), whereas the restrictive anorexics are closer to the outpatient borderlines (refer to pp. 233–234).

Development

Two developmental object relations scales have been applied to the Rorschach records of eating disorder patients. Van-Der Keshet (1988), in her often-mentioned study, used Coonerty's (1986) scale (refer to Chapter 14) to assess separation–individuation themes in eating disorder patients and anorexic ballet students. Piran (1988), using Kwawer's (1980) measure (see Chapter 14), compared bulimics with restrictive anorexics with respect to primitiveness of interpersonal relations.

Van-Der Keshet (1988) reported several important findings regarding the prevalence of separation–individuation themes in the five groups studied. First, the bulimic patients produced significantly more responses involving the theme of engulfment than did any of the other groups. Second, the mirror response, regarded as an index of narcissism, was observed significantly more often in the records of the anorexic ballet students than in any of the other groups. Finally, the normal controls obtained a significantly lower mean score than any of the other four groups on the rapprochement measure, indicating that they alone had achieved a level of nonconflicted autonomy.

In keeping with Van-Der Keshet's (1988) finding that themes of engulfment are particularly prominent in the responses of bulimic patients, Piran's (1988) study found more primitive interpersonal themes in the Rorschach records of bulimic anorexics as compared to restricting anorexics. More specifically, Piran noted that the percentage of protocols with responses displaying primitive themes was significantly higher in the bulimic group.

In summary, in an attempt to determine if eating disorder patients are organized at a borderline level, several investigators have extended scales initially developed to assess borderline phenomena to the Rorschach records of these patients. In general, the findings do indicate that eating disorder patients are organized at a borderline level, if one uses Kernberg's (1975) concept and criteria of borderline; this conclusion, however, should be regarded cautiously. It is important to recognize that the term *border-line* constitutes a diagnosis and that the various studies reported here involve levels of personality functioning and development that are defined by different criteria. To be sure, eating disorder patients have been found to manifest low reality testing, impaired thinking, serious boundary disturbances, primitive defenses, and unresolved conflicts regarding separation –individuation; but, as with the borderline concept generally, it is quite possible that eating disorder patients too may be viewed from the perspective of a spectrum. Finally, whereas earlier studies regarded anorexia as a homogeneous entity, more recent investigations have subdivided anorexic patients according to presenting symptoms (restrictive versus bulimic) and have found important differences between these subgroups.

GENDER IDENTITY DISTURBANCES

A second group of patients assumed to have a borderline personality organization who have been studied with the Rorschach test includes are those individuals who present gender identity disturbances. The specific groups investigated have included extremely feminine boys and male transsexuals.

Having observed the chaotic regressions in psychotherapy and the caricatured feminine behavior and mannerisms of extremely feminine boys, Tuber and Coates (1985) examined the self and object representations of a group of 14 such subjects. All were between the ages of 5 and 12 years, were of at least average intelligence, and had met the DSM-III criteria for gender identity disorder of childhood. Normative Rorschach data published by Ames, Metraux, Rodell, and Walker (1974) were used for comparative purposes. Results of the investigation revealed several significant findings, especially those related to the representation of human figures. While the percentage of whole human responses given by the gender disorder boys was approximately equal to that of the normative sample of Ames et al. (1974), their records contained eight times as many quasi-human responses (H). The quasi-human responses often took the form of monstrous, aggressive creatures. Moreover, the content of the fully human responses was significantly different from the content of the quasi-human responses. Subdividing the content of all responses into the categories benevolent, neutral, and malevolent, the authors found that fully human responses were equally represented in the benevolent and malevolent categories. By contrast, more than 80% of the quasi-human responses involved malevolent content, such as creatures and monsters imbued with menacing or threatening intent or action.

Impairment in self and object representations was further manifested in the fluidity and fusion that characterized many of these youngsters' responses. On the basis of Blatt and Ritzler's (1974) concept of a hierarchy of "boundary disturbances" to categorize and conceptualize the fluid and fused percepts, 18 instances of contamination and fabulized combination responses were found. Responses in which the over-elaboration of affect signaled a disturbance in the boundary between reality and fantasy were also observed with significant frequency. Quite startling and significant was the finding that each of the 14 subjects produced at least one response of either the fused or overelaborated type.

Paralleling the behavioral phenomenology of these boys, the study also revealed overt gender confusion and stereotypical feminine responses. Caricatured female representations, elaborate depiction of stereotypical female objects (e.g., jewelry), and female clothing were the types of responses frequently found in the records of this group. Gender confusion was evident in responses in which the gender of a percept was changed during the response from one sex to another and in responses in which male and female body parts were arbitrarily combined into a single response.

Mindful of the core role of separation anxiety in the dynamic life of these children, Coates and Tuber (1988) examined the concept of autonomy of self in a second study. They applied a modified version of Urist's (1977) Mutuality of Autonomy Scale to the Rorschach records of the original sample of 14 feminine boys. Like Urist's original scale, the modified version consists of seven points along a progressive continuum including mutual, reciprocal, empathic, malevolent, overwhelming, engulfing, and destructive relatedness.

Strong evidence of the disturbed quality of these youngsters' object relations and object representations was obtained. Of the 14 subjects, 12 had at least one response in the seriously disturbed range—that is, a range characterized by an experience of the object as controlling or dominating at best, and parasitic–attacking or engulfing at worst. Seven of the boys' records had at least one response in which one figure was actively destroying another. The remaining five included at least one response in which domination or control of one figure by the other was paramount.

The nature of the data also permitted the investigators to examine the notion of the idealization of the maternal figure, a dynamic frequently associated with gender dysphoric males. To do this, responses indicative of benign, reciprocal relatedness were reviewed. Eleven such responses were identified. Of the eleven, nine involved women while the other two involved animals of an unspecified sex. Thus, interactive depictions of benign relatedness were associated virtually exclusively with female representations. By contrast, an inspection of the responses involving malevolent content or parasitic interaction was noteworthy for the glaring absence of female representations. The authors (Coates and Tuber, 1988) concluded from this analysis:

> This haven of positive female reciprocity is further safeguarded by their ability to avoid seeing women in responses characterized by malevolence or destruction. Instead, malevolence is ascribed to more regressed quasi-human male figures, thereby preserving the maternal figure [p. 654].

Ipp (1986) also studied the quality of object relations and object representations of extremely feminine boys and of their siblings as well. Using somewhat more rigorous methodology, she reported findings strikingly similar to those of Tuber and Coates (1985). Ipp's subjects, all age 5 to 12 years, included 37 feminine boys diagnosed as having cross-gender disturbance, 19 siblings with no history of cross-gender behavior, and 23 normal controls. Rorschach records were obtained from all subjects and scored for level of object representation (Blatt et al., 1976), severity of boundary disturbance (Blatt and Ritzler, 1974), and developmental level of object relations (Ipp, 1986). Results from the Scale of Blatt and associates (1976) indicated that the feminine boys and their siblings, as compared with the normal controls, achieved less differentiated, articulated, and integrated responses and produced significantly more inaccurately perceived fully human responses and significantly more both accurate and inaccurate quasi-human responses. Furthermore, while the controls had significantly more benevolent interaction in their human responses than did the feminine boys, the siblings displayed greater malevolence in their responses than did the feminine boys.

In further support of the findings of Tuber and Coates (1985), Ipp (1986) also found serious boundary disturbances in the records of the feminine boys. While the feminine boys differed from the controls on all three levels of boundary disturbances, the differences were especially prominent on the more severe levels of self–other and fantasy–reality. At these more severe levels, the feminine boys also produced significantly more responses than did their siblings.

Ipp's (1986) Developmental Object Relations Scale differs in emphasis from Urist's (1977) Mutuality of Autonomy Scale. Although both focus on more primitive modes of relating, Urist's (1977) scale highlights the nature of interaction whereas Ipp's (1986) scale categorizes responses into developmental stages based on Mahler's theory of separation-individuation. Two points on Ipp's scale significantly distinguished the groups. The controls offered significantly more responses referable to the autonomy stage than did either the feminine boys or the siblings. By contrast, both the feminine boys and their siblings had significantly more responses scored at the differentiation/practicing stage than did the controls. Cutting across all categories in the Ipp scale is a benevolence–malevolence dimension. On this measure the feminine boys offered significantly more malevolent content than the controls.

Using several conceptually based scales and several scores devised by Exner (1974), Murray (1985) investigated borderline manifestations in the Rorschach records of male transsexuals. The sample consisted of a group of 25 male transsexuals, a group of 25 male borderlines, and a control group of 25 male college students. Rorschach protocols were obtained from all subjects and scored for intensity of aggression (Holt's defense demand score), quality of object relations (Mutuality of Autonomy Scale), level of reality testing (Exner's X + percentage) and degree of self–object differentiation (Exner's special scores). Highly significant results were reported. Compared to the normal controls, both the transsexuals and the borderlines displayed significantly more intense levels of aggression, highly impaired object relations, poorer reality testing, and greater boundary disturbances. Further, the transsexuals and the borderlines did not differ significantly on any of these variables. A measure of egocentricity failed to distinguish the three groups.

Collectively, the results of all four studies strongly suggest that males, both adults and children, manifesting gender dysphoric behavior and attitudes present a borderline personality organization. Their self and object representations are impaired; they present severe boundary disturbances; their object relations are on a more primitive level; they have not successfully negotiated all the phases of separation-individuation; and they struggle with aggression and malevolent objects. The studies of Coates and Tuber (1988) and Ipp (1986) indicate that conceptually based Rorschach scales designed for adults, either directly or with modifications, can be extended to the protocols of children. Further, the work of Coates and Tuber (1988) illustrates how clinical observations can be translated into Rorschach-related terms and then evaluated using quantifiable measures.

ANTISOCIAL PERSONALITY

More recently, investigators have been extending conceptually based scales to the Rorschach records of a third group of individuals assumed to have a borderline personality organization: the antisocial personality. The antisocial personality has typically been described as manifesting little tolerance for boredom, anxiety, or frustration, lacking in empathy, having chronically impaired object relations, lacking in subliminatory channels, and having a specific manner for regulating self-esteem. These characteristics have led several theorists to view the antisocial personality as a more pathological variant of narcissistic disorder organized at a borderline level of personality functioning (Kernberg, 1977; Rinsley, 1979; Gacono and Meloy, 1988).

Gacono (1988), in a study referred to in Chapters 13 and 14, compared a group of highly psychopathic males on the following variables: borderline object relations, borderline defenses, and level of narcissism. As previously described, 33 antisocial offenders were subdivided into high and low groups on the basis of the Hare Psychopathy Checklist, and their Rorschach records were compared.

Using Kwawer's (1980) scale to assess borderline object relations, Gacono found that the high psychopathy group produced more total responses than the low to moderate group in the following categories: symbiotic merging, violent symbiosis, birth-rebirth, narcissistic mirroring, separation division, boundary disturbance, womb imagery, and total object relations. The low to moderate psychopathic group had more responses than the high group in the following categories: malignant internal processes and metamorphosis and transformation.

Borderline defenses were operationalized in terms of the Lerner Defense Scale for assessing primitive defenses. Although none of the individual defense scores significantly distinguished the two groups, certain patterns were noted. Whereas the high psychopathic group tended to make greater use of devaluation, the low to moderate group made more frequent use of projective identification and higher level denial. When the scores of the two groups were combined, a predominant use of lower levels of denial and all levels of devaluation was reported.

When the two groups were compared on the Cooper and Arnow (1986) scale, a similar patterning of defenses was found. That is, whereas the high psychopathic group used devaluation more frequently, the low to moderate group offered more responses reflective of projective identification. On this scale the high group gave more splitting responses and more instances of omnipotence.

A Self-Focus Sentence Completion Test developed by Exner (1974) was employed to evaluate level of narcissism. No significant differences between the groups was noted; indeed, the mean score for the low to moderate psychopathic group was higher indicating a tendency toward greater self-focusing.

SUMMARY

In this chapter I have reviewed a host of studies that have applied conceptually based Rorschach scoring systems to the protocols of clinical populations assumed to have a borderline personality organization. The groups investigated have included eating disorder patients, gender dysphoric children and adults, and antisocial offenders. In several studies eating disorder patients were found to manifest poor reality testing, impaired thinking, serious boundary disturbances, lower level defenses, and a failure to separate and attain full autonomy. Differences have been reported between eating disorder patients subdivided into restricting and bulimic groups. The differences noted in defensive patterning, quality of object relations, and dealing with malevolent objects roughly parallel those observed between hospitalized and outpatient borderline patients (Lerner and St. Peter, 1984). As such, the eating disorder patient, like borderline patient, may be most profitably viewed as being represented on a spectrum or continuum.

Evidence regarding borderline-level processes in gender dysphoric adults and children is compelling. Both groups across several studies manifested impaired self and object representations, severe boundary disturbances, lower level object relations, and significant difficulties in separating and individuating. Gender disturbances have provided an especially useful arena for displaying the Rorschach test's efficacy in highlighting the interplay between aberrant behavior and underlying dynamics.

Findings regarding the antisocial personality have been inconclusive. One major study reviewed here compared subgroups of psychopathic males. From a design point of view, what is called for are studies employing various comparison populations and including a normal control group. From a theoretical perspective, much controversy surrounds the relationship between narcissism and borderline processes and both appear to interface with the antisocial personality.

17

Rorschach Measures of Narcissism and the Narcissistic Patient

With the emergence of new models of personality development in psychoanalysis have come new formulations regarding the nature and genesis of psychopathology. Whereas earlier formulations emphasized the role of conflict between relatively well-developed structures in giving rise to symptom formation, more recent formulations stress the pathology of the structures themselves, interpreting them as a consequence of incomplete or arrested development.

A foremost example of psychopathology based on impaired structure formation is the narcissistic disturbances. Although much has been written in the theoretical and clinical literatures regarding narcissistic disturbances, in contrast with borderline disorders, little has appeared in the research literature. In this chapter I review the concept of narcissism, detail descriptions of the narcissistic patient advanced by Kernberg (1975) and Kohut (1971, 1977), report on attempts to use the Rorschach test to assess the narcissistic patient for clinical purposes, and, finally, discuss the limited research involving the Rorschach test.

CONCEPT OF NARCISSISM

With his publication in 1914 of the paper "On Narcissism," Freud laid the conceptual groundwork from which all subsequent theoretical developments of the concept have arisen. In that paper he defined secondary narcissism as a withdrawal of libido from the external world with a redirection of the libido onto the ego, designated the ego ideal as the "heir" or adult version of infantile narcissism, recognized the intimate relation-

255

ship between self-esteem and narcissistic libido, and observed that a particular type of object choice and object relation was referred to as "narcissistic" on the basis of the quality of need for the object and the psychic function served by the object.

Authors subsequent to Freud have replaced the term "ego" with that of "self," have redefined narcissism as the "libidinal investment of the self" (Hartmann, 1950), and have extended the concept of self along several lines by: (1) redefining it as part of the structure ego, understood to mean the conscious, preconscious, and unconscious representations of the total person; (2) elaborating the role of internalization in the structuring of self-representations; (3) elaborating the processes by which self and object representations become differentiated and then internalized as stable, enduring, internal structures; and (4) distinguishing between self as structure and self as experience (Teicholtz, 1978).

THE NARCISSISTIC PATIENT

Despite major advances in our understanding of and capacity to treat narcissistic patients, the field, historically and presently, has been beset by a lack of agreement as to what constitutes a "narcissistic patient." Two major, but quite different, clinical descriptions have emerged.

Kernberg (1975), from a more structural perspective, reserves the designation for those patients "in whom the main problem appears to be the disturbance of their self-regard in connection with specific disturbances in their object relations . . ." (p. 227). Maintaining that most narcissistic patients are a subvariant of the borderline level of personality organization, he describes these patients as manifesting a heightened degree of self-absorption, an inordinate need to be loved and admired, and an overinflated sense of themselves amid a desperate desire for adoration. He further suggests that their emotional life is shallow, they exhibit little genuine empathy for the motives and feelings of others, and they feel restless and bored unless their self-regard is being nourished. Potential providers of narcissistic supplies are idealized whereas those from whom these patients expect little are depreciated and treated with contempt. Beneath a veneer of warmth and charm, in Kernberg's view, such persons are cold, arrogant, ruthless, and exploitive. From this perspective, the psychopath or sociopath would be considered a subtype of narcissistic disorder.

Kohut (1971) too provided a comprehensive clinical description of the narcissistic patient, but he viewed these disturbances from a different perspective (self psychology) and characterized the narcissistic patient quite differently from Kernberg. He did not conceive of the narcissistic

patient as organized at a borderline level but, rather, places the disturbance closer to the neurotic end of the psychopathological continuum.

Kohut identified a specific symptom complex (i.e., lack of enthusiasm and zest, perverse activity, subjective feelings of deadness) as characteristic of the narcissistic patient; however, he saw such a cluster of
symptoms as diagnostically insufficient. Instead, he evoked the concept of
the "cohesive self" and suggested that it is the instability or propensity for
regression of this structure that constitutes the critical diagnostic sign of a
narcissistic personality. Kohut also identified and described a set of atypical transference patterns that characterize the narcissistic patient and
unfold in treatment. Referred to overall as selfobject transferences, specific subtypes include the mirroring transference and the idealizing transference. Although Kohut was less definitive in his description of the
narcissistic patient than Kernberg is, from his case descriptions one distills
a picture of a group of people who are excessively self-conscious and
self-preoccupied, who experience continuous feelings of vulnerability,
who defend against lowered feelings of self-esteem with grandiosity, and
who experience a particular type of depressive affect involving feelings of
depletion, emptiness, and nonexistence.

THE NARCISSISTIC PATIENT AND THE RORSCHACH TEST:
CLINICAL CONTRIBUTIONS

The conceptual and clinical contributions of Kernberg (1975) and Kohut
(1971) have been extended to the Rorschach by H. Lerner (1988) and
Arnow and Cooper (1988). Both applications are extensive and comprehensive, and although each is geared toward clinical assessment, rich
formulations are provided in each and could conceivably furnish a basis for
more empirical study.

Based on Kernberg's (1975) structural analysis, H. Lerner (1988) inten-
sively reviewed the test records of ten patients all of whom met DSM-III
criteria for narcissistic personality disorder. The five females and five
males composing the sample were all single, from middle-class or upper-
middle-class families, and ranged in age from 16 to 26 years.

Lerner suggests that in assessing narcissistic patients the test features to
be looked for include

" . . . a social facade characterized by egocentricity and self-references; an
extreme personalizing of experience and discourse coupled with an almost
rigid tendency to avoid anxiety and anxiety-arousing situations; and a
solicitation of the examiner's affection, assistance, and admiration, often
juxtaposed with subtle and not so subtle devaluations of the test and the

examiner. Representations of the grandiose self, of its constituent elements
(a "shadowy" real self, an ideal self, and an ideal other), and of what this
structure masks—intense narcissistic rage and a deep conviction of unwor-
thiness and frightening images of barrenness, emptiness, and void—can be
discerned on the Rorschach. Further, test representations of borderline
defenses, boundary disturbances, and a preponderance of malevolent objects are frequently exhibited by these patients" [p. 264].

Using formal scores, thematic content, and test behavior, Lerner outlines
Rorschach indices of these features under the broad headings of specific
and nonspecific manifestations of ego weakness, affect organization, pathology of internal object relations, defensive structure, and treatment
considerations.

Kohut's (1971, 1977) formulations have been applied to the Rorschach
testing situation by Arnow and Cooper (1988). Viewing the testing experience as a context for the expression of primary needs for selfobjects as well
as for the arousal of feelings when such needs are not met, these authors
suggest that test responses can be thought of as containing three referents
or interpretive dimensions—the state of the self, the role of archaic selfobjects, and anticipations regarding new objects.

Arnow and Cooper also describe Rorschach indices associated with
certain syndromes of self-pathology initially identified by Kohut and Wolf
(1978). The specific syndromes include the understimulated self, the overstimulated self, the fragmented self, and the overburdened self.

The person with an understimulated self craves stimulation in order to
ward off feelings of inner deadness associated with an unresponsive
selfobject. One sees in such persons either massive attempts to seek
stimulation or the empty depression that lies beneath the frantic search.
According to Arnow and Cooper (1988), either the search or the underlying depression may be expressed on the Rorschach test. The sought-for
stimulation becomes manifest in imagery depicting a high level of sensory
input, such as "the Mardi Gras," "colorful sea scene," and "a brilliantly
colored galaxy." By contrast, the empty depression that appears when the
search fails is evident in themes of barrenness, deadness, and desolation.

The overstimulated self arises from repeated experiences in which the
self is required to serve as a selfobject for others. The self, in these
instances, feels drawn into the role of maintaining the delicate and precarious narcissistic balance of its selfobjects. Such people typically feel that
their selfobjects have selectively responded to their own self's exhibitionistic behavior, emphasizing accomplishments and achievements in isolation from the broader self. Accordingly, Arnow and Cooper suggest that
those with an overstimulated self provide Rorschach records in which
themes of performance and accomplishment pervade. Not only are themes

of performance expressed directly in responses (e.g., "dancing bears"); in addition, ordinary percepts are elevated to special productions through elaborate embellishments. The fantastic creations, for these individuals, are not in the service of self-enhancement; rather, they derive from a need to comply with the imagined expectations of the other.

The fragmented or fragmenting self represents a form of narcissistic disequilibrium consequent to the failure of selfobjects to provide integrating responses. Historically, the selfobject has not responded to the whole self but rather to selected parts of the self that satisfy the needs of the selfobject. For Arnow and Cooper, patients with fears of fragmenting offer Rorschach percepts in which there is concern about the integrity of objects or preoccupations reflecting hypochondriacal worries. These authors further suggest that the experience of a fragmented self may also be expressed in images that are broken or falling apart, such as "a broken glass" or "an exploding bug with parts all scattered."

The overburdened self results from a failure to merge with an omnipotent, soothing selfobject. The early experience of turning to a selfobject for calming typically failed and resulted instead in the intensification of dysphoric affect. As a consequence of the empathic failure, the self does not develop the capacity to soothe itself or protect itself from being traumatized by the spreading of emotions, especially the spreading of anxiety. The object relations of these persons vividly reflect the danger of exposing the self to interactions that threaten its capacity to modulate affects. The ever- present fear of losing emotional control colors the overburdened self's perception of involvement and underlies the characteristic aloofness and preoccupation with control. Rorschach percepts offered by these individuals directly express their apprehension regarding emotional control. For example, on Card IX a patient offered the following response: "A volcano but it's covered with snow so the lava never erupts."

In addition to the broad overviews provided by H. Lerner (1988) and Arnow and Cooper (1988), other authors too (refer to Lerner and Lerner, 1988) have identified Rorschach indices for assessing specific aspects of narcissistic pathology. These more specific features include the narcissistic patient's excessive self-absorption, the role of omnipotence, the particular quality of depressive affect, and the mode of object relating.

Self-absorption

Exner (1974) developed an index for assessing egocentricity. Consisting of the proportion of reflection and pair responses to the total number of Rorschach responses, the index was found to relate to intense self-focusing and disturbances in self-esteem (Exner, Wylie, and Bryant, 1974).

H. Lerner (1988) and Arnow and Cooper (1988) also considered mirror and reflection responses as indicative of excessive self-involvement, but they placed this observation in a broader and more object relational context. Accordingly, while such responses convey self-absorption, they also indicate a need to be mirrored and confirmed. In describing a patient H. Lerner (1988) put it this way: "Her frequent perception of mirror images on the Rorschach speak quite graphically to . . . her reliance upon the reflection of herself in others in order to know herself . . ." (p. 288).

Omnipotence

A second major feature characteristic of the narcissistic patient involves feelings of omnipotence. These patients not only present an overinflated view of themselves (grandiose self) but also cling to omnipotence for defensive purposes, including the maintenance of ego integration. Rorschach expressions of omnipotence have been developed by H. Lerner (1988), P. Lerner (1988), and Arnow and Cooper (1988). Each has noted narcissistic patients' compelling need to be treated as special, their craving for admiration, and their irritating sense of entitlement, as well as how these factors eventuate in the patients' ongoing assaults on the structure of the testing procedure. For such patients test responses have a particular purpose. They are not offered with the intent of conveying meaning or of sharing an experience but rather are given with the desire to impress the examiner and to create a product that they believe will bring confirmation of their overinflated sense of self. Finally, populating the protocols of patients with omnipotence are an abundance of self-aggrandizing percepts, such as kings, goddesses, temples, insignias, crests, and crowns.

Depression

Despite questions regarding the capacity of narcissistic patients to experience genuine feelings of loss for others, there is agreement that the depressive affect they do experience has a distinctive and distinguishing quality. Referred to by Kohut (1977) as "depletion depression," this affect is characterized by unbearable feelings of emptiness, deadness, and nonexistence and reflects a self-perception of weakness, helplessness, and vulnerability.

H. Lerner (1988) has pointed to the role of narcissistic injury as a major source of depressive affect for these patients and has suggested that Rorschach imagery reflective of damage or flaw may be taken as an expression of such injury. For example, such content as "a butterfly with damaged wings," "an alligator coming out of the mud," and a "tired, wet moth" can be interpreted as reflective of a sense of self as damaged, exploited, or victimized.

P. Lerner (1988) developed Rorschach indices reflective of emptiness. Defining emptiness as a sense of deadness together with an inner impoverishment of feelings, fantasies, and wishes, he found that patients experiencing emptiness provide enfeebled records in which there is a sparseness of responses and in which few dimensions other than form are used. Their responses, in general, tend to be muted and drab, lack in vitality, and make little impact upon the examiner. Their attunement to white areas is thought to reflect a sensitivity to themes of hollowness. The empty patient, according to Lerner, is reality bound, yet the contents perceived typically convey themes of emptiness and deadness. Thus, abundant through their records are such percepts as skeletons, deserts, faceless creatures, and dead trees.

Mode of Object Relating

A fourth dimension involves Rorschach manifestations of the narcissistic patient's mode of object relating. As noted previously, Freud (1914) distinguished between a true object relation and a narcissistic object relation, suggesting that in the latter the object is not regarded as separate and distinct but is seen rather as an extension of the self and is needed to fulfill functions that should, but cannot, be managed intrapsychically.

In Chapter 14 several Rorschach developmental object relations scales are reviewed. Each scale includes reflection and mirror responses and conceptualizes such content as indicating a relatively early phase of relatedness in which the object whose sole purpose is to mirror the self, is regarded as an extension of the self.

Mayman (1977) identified aspects of the human movement response that distinguish and typify individuals who tend to relate on a more narcissistic basis. He suggested that such individuals offer M responses in which (1) the response is offered with undue conviction; (2) the action ascribed and the attributes provided are more fabulized than inherent in the percept itself; (3) there is intense absorption and involvement in the behavior of the perceived figures; and (4) the testee infuses himself or herself into the figure as if vicariously sharing in the other's experience. Implicit in Mayman's indices is the notion that the nature of the relationship between the testee and his or her M responses reflects and parallels the quality of relationship the testee establishes with his or her objects.

Finally, H. Lerner (1988) has identified test behavior and test responses reflective of narcissistic withdrawal. He suggests that one can observe a withholding or letdown in the patient in responsse to an empathic failure in the test situation. Because this reaction often has an intimidating quality, it may nudge "the examiner out of a position of neutrality into a more superego-like position of apologizing, being nice to the patient, and, in the process, away from a position of intellectual curiosity and active inquiry" (p. 293). This tendency of the patient to withdraw may also be inferred from Rorschach responses involving quasi-human figures (clowns, witches, caricatures, etc.) or human figures distanced in time and space. Here, such figures are taken as self-representations and convey the patient's sense of "a lack of authentic affective relatedness to the environment" (p. 294).

THE NARCISSISTIC PATIENT AND THE RORSCHACH TEST: RESEARCH CONTRIBUTIONS

Despite the many conceptual articles and the increasing number of rich clinical reports, systematic research related to the concept of narcissism and to the narcissistic patient is glaringly absent. Similarly, while the concept of object representation has been well investigated, the concept of self representation has received remarkably little attention from researchers.

Two noteworthy exceptions are represented by the work of Farris (1988) and Van-Der Keshet (1988). Although both studies were discussed in previous chapters, they are reviewed here because of their relevance to the topic of narcissism.

On the basis of the premise that patients with a narcissistic personality disorder, compared with patients with a borderline personality disorder, are better organized, are developmentally more advanced, and function more effectively, Farris (1988) compared the Rorschach protocols of nine matched pairs of narcissistic and borderline patients on several well-established Rorschach scales. The obtained findings supported his hypothesis. He found that the narcissistic patients scored significantly higher on a cognitive–perceptual measure of developmental maturity, achieved a significantly higher level of object representation, produced significantly fewer responses reflective of the use of primitive defenses, and offered more responses indicative of phallic-oedipal concerns.

Van-Der Keshet (1988) compared the Rorschach records of groups of restrictive anorexics, bulimic anorexics, anorexic ballet students, nonanorexic ballet students, and normal controls with respect to their defensive structure. Using the Lerner Defense Scale for assessing primitive defenses, she found that the measure of idealization distinguished the normal controls from each of the other groups but also differentiated the anorexic ballet students from the bulimic anorexics. In keeping with Kohut's (1977) formulations, Van-Der Keshet (1988) conceptualized the idealization score as reflecting a narcissistic "compensatory structure" rather than a defense.

Kohut (1977) noted that failures by the "mirroring" selfobject can be compensated for by successes with an "idealized" selfobject. He put it this way: "A failure experienced at the first way station can be remedied by a success at the second one" (Kohut, 1977, p. 180). The resultant psychological structures that develop under these circumstances are referred to as "compensatory structures."

Two Rorschach scales have been developed to assess aspects of the narcissistic personality structure; each, however, has important limitations. Relying upon Reich's (1933) description of the phallic-narcissistic character, Harder (1979) devised a scoring system to assess the ambitious-narcissistic character style. Unfortunately while the scale closely parallels Reich's depiction of the phallic-narcissistic character, it differs in significant ways from the narcissistic patients described in the current literature. P. Lerner (1988) is in the process of developing a scale to operationalize Winnicott's (1961) concept of the "false self." He has identified and described Rorschach indices reflective of components of the false self; however, his work has not reached the stage of a refined quantitative system. Despite their respective limitations, both scales are presented here, since they represent potentially useful starting points for more systematically investigating the narcissistic personality.

Ambitious-Narcissistic Character Style

In keeping with Reich's (1933) characterization of the phallic-narcissistic character and Shapiro's (1965) notion of character style, Harder's (1979) scale consists of the following five component headings: intrusive/thrusting, exhibitionism/voyeurism, urethral excitation, mastery/competence/power, and self-potency. The categories are applied to Rorschach content, particularly those percepts that involve activity being channeled through specific interpersonal modes. For example, responses reflective of the intrusive/thrusting component include figures exploring new territory, vigorous physical activity, objects propelled through space, and so forth. In addition, cutting across all component categories is an intensity dimension.

In an initial study (Harder, 1979) the scale was applied to the Rorschach records of 40 relatively well-functioning male college students all of whom intended to pursue a professional program or graduate school. Satisfactory levels of reliability based on percent of inter-rater agreement were reported. Parallel forms of the scale were developed for the Thematic Apperception Test (TAT) and the Early Memories Test; therefore, validity could be determined by the level of relationship between the Rorschach scale and these other measures, as well as by its relationship with an independent criterion measure. The scales were found to intercorrelate, thus indicating that they were measuring a common dimension. With regard to the criterion measure, the Rorschach scale, more so than the other scales, significantly differentiated subjects rated by clinically trained judges as ambitious/narcissistic in style from subjects rated as not ambitious/narcissistic.

In an attempt to identify personality correlates of the concept of defensively high self-esteem (a conscious, exaggerated satisfaction with the self used defensively to ward off feelings of low self-regard), Harder (1979) extended the scale to the Rorschach protocols of 40 male college students subdivided into four groups based upon clinicians' ratings of defensiveness of self-esteem and level of self-regard. As predicted, subjects rated as defensively high on self-esteem scored significantly higher on the Rorschach measure of Ambitious-Narcissistic Character Style than did subjects in the other three groups.

Farris (1988) found that although his narcissistic and borderline subjects did not differ on a summary composite score from Harder's scale, they did differ with respect to two specific categories. For the category Phallic Organ, the narcissistic patients produced a number of ambitious-narcissistic responses reflecting a greater departure from the expected frequency than did the borderline patients. Similarly, narcissistic subjects produced a greater number of Body Narcissism responses than did borderline subjects.

False Self Scale

Based on the theoretical formulations of Winnicott (1961), the test writings of Schachtel (1966), and his own clinical experience, P. Lerner (1988) is in the process of developing a scale to assess the concept of the false self.

Winnicott (1961) conceived of the false self as an elaborate defensive structure that served to hide and protect the true self from the dangers of control, ridicule, and exploitation. The origins of the false self are found in the infant's seduction into a compliant relationship with a nonempathic mother. Accordingly, when the mother substitutes part of herself for the infant's spontaneous gestures, the infant experiences traumatic disruptions of his or her developing sense of self. When these impingements become a core feature of the mother–child relationship, the infant will attempt to defend himself or herself by developing a second, reactive personality organization—the false self. The false self sensitively monitors and adapts to the conscious and unconscious needs of the mother and in so doing provides a protective exterior behind which the true self is afforded the privacy it requires to maintain its integrity. The false self, then, becomes a key feature of the personality organization and functions rather as a caretaker, managing life so that an inner self might not experience the threat of annihilation resulting from excessive pressure on it to develop according to another's needs.

A review of the concept indicates that basic to the false self are hyperalertness and heightened sensitivity to the expectations and anticipations of others, with a concomitant tendency to mold one's own feelings, behaviors, and attitudes accordingly. P. Lerner (1988) found a specific test-taking attitude, two formal Rorschach scores, and specific contents especially sensitive to these aspects of the false self.

Test-Taking Attitude

Patients who present with a false self often begin testing under a cloak of vigilance and with a readiness to be distrustful. They are there but with one foot out the door, as it were. Quickly, various aspects of the examiner, including office furnishings, tone of voice, and testing directions, come under careful scrutiny. For example, if on the Rorschach test the examiner inquires after each card, after the first such series of inquiries these patients often attune at once to what is being asked for and thereafter supply such information during free association, thereby rendering the examiner's role unnecessary. In other words, these patients move toward a compliant self-sufficiency and virtually begin testing themselves. The examiner's experience, paradoxically, is that of being the one examined. Not only is every movement closely monitored but all comments are carefully scrutinized and regarded as evidence to be weighed and judged before the relationship is allowed to deepen and possibly move toward mutuality. The patient's attitude quite understandably evokes a marked countervigilance and hypercautiousness on the part of the examiner. Recognizing that certain comments meant to be helpful may be taken as an attack, the examiner becomes more careful and inhibited.

Formal Scores

Two formal scores are considered especially sensitive to false self features. The first, the Fc score, as noted in Chapter 7, is applied to responses that are delineated and determined by variations in shading. The variations in shading are subtle; therefore, to achieve such a response one must seek out, discover, and attune to finer nuances, as well as feel one's way into something that is not readily apparent. To do this requires perceptual sensitivity in addition to a searching, articulating, and penetrating type of activity. Individuals with this type of sensitivity— who have their antennae out, if you will—tend to present as hypervigilant, thin-skinned, and excessively vulnerable, and each of these characteristics is consistent with aspects of the false self.

A second formal score reflective of the false self is the color arbitrary score, Carb. This score is accorded to responses in which the use of color is clearly incompatible with the content (blue monkeys, pink dogs); yet the subject clings to its inclusion and makes minimal effort to account for the blend. Schachtel (1966) has noted the role of compliance in this response: the subject relinquishes a more objective, critical, and judging attitude and provides a percept he or she knows is not realistic. In this respect, the score conveys a sense of unreality.

Content

One would expect that individuals who are constantly alert to danger, who are concerned with protection and privacy, who relate themselves to others in a compliant way, and who experience only fleeting feelings of inauthenticity would offer Rorschach imagery reflective of these experiential themes. Indeed, such themes do appear in the Rorschach records of patients who present with a false self: one finds content reflective of hiding and accommodation, such as masks, costumes, camouflage and chameleons. Further, human or animal figures are often seen as performing or serving (e.g., waiters, clowns, magicians, trained seals, circus bears).

As part of an attempt to assess vulnerability to victimization, Nifakis (1989) has applied these concepts to the Rorschach records of 17 adult women who experienced sexual abuse as children and 16 normal controls. To operationalize the test-taking attitude, Nifakis developed a three point rating scale in which both the examiner and independent judges rated the subject's "attunement and sensitivity" to the examiner. Although the study is not yet complete, preliminary results indicate the following: (1) the test-taking attitude index significantly distinguished the two groups in the predicted direction, (2) there was a strong but not statistically significant tendency for the sexually abused subjects to use the Fc score more frequently than the controls, and (3) the Carb score and the content did not differentiate the two groups.

SUMMARY

In this chapter I have briefly reviewed the concept of narcissism and discussed the assessment of the narcissistic patient by means of the Rorschach. On the basis of the clinical contributions of Kernberg and Kohut, two highly comprehensive Rorschach systems have been developed to assist the clinical examiner in evaluating various aspects of narcissistic pathology. Each system describes such pathology in several areas of personality functioning and provides Rorschach manifestations and other clinical illustrations. In contrast with the increasing clinical literature, research applications of the Rorschach test to the study of the narcissistic patient and narcissistic phenomena have appeared sparingly. Typically, researchers have considered mirror, reflection, and pair responses indicative of a tendency to relate to others on a narcissistic basis. This work was reviewed in Chapter 14. Two other research scales to assess aspects of the narcissistic patient have been developed; however, each has limitations. While Harder's (1979) scale, designed to assess the Ambitious-Narcissistic Character Style, parallels descriptions provided by Reich, it does not capture several essential features of the narcissistic patient as described by Kernberg or Kohut. P. Lerner has devised several indices reflective of aspects of the false self concept; however, at this point his work represents a loose-fitting collection of indices rather than an integrated scale.

Epilogue

As noted in the preface, the 1980s witnessed a significant increase in the use of the Rorschach Inkblot Test for the study and understanding of people. This movement contrasts with the 1960s, when both personality assessment and personality theory had fallen into disrepute. Throughout that earlier period, coming under severest attack were projective techniques, including the Rorschach test, and psychoanalytic theory. The veritable explosion of new treatment modalities onto the psychotherapeutic marketplace, many of which stressed brevity and cost efficiency, together with the expanding roles being filled by psychologists, seemed to render traditional personality assessment obsolete, if not anachronistic.

With respect to the Rorschach test, the drought is clearly over. Propelling the renewed interest in the Rorschach has been the empirical work of John Exner (1974) and major shifts in psychoanalytic theory. In this book, I have combined an introduction to the psychoanalytic approach to the Rorschach with an attempt to update that approach by integrating recent theoretical and research advances.

References

Abraham, K. (1921–25), Psycho-analytic studies on character-formation. In: *Selected Papers on Psycho-Analysis.* London: Hogarth Press, 1927, pp. 370–417.

Alexander, F. (1930), The neurotic character. *Internat. J. Psycho-Anal.,* 11:292–311.

Allison, J. (1967), Adaptive regression and intense religious experiences. *J. Nerv. Ment. Dis.,* 145:452–463.

Allison, J., Blatt, S. & Zimet, C. (1968), *The Interpretation of Psychological Tests.* New York: Harper & Row.

Ames, L. (1966), Longitudinal survey of child Rorschach responses: Older subjects aged 10 to 16 years. *Genetic Psychol. Monogr.,* 62:185–229.

Ames, L., Metraux, R., Rodell, J. & Walker, R. (1974), *Child Rorschach Responses.* New York: Brunner/Mazel.

Appelbaum, S. (1963), The masochistic character as a self-sabateur. *J. Proj. Tech.,* 27:35–45.

Appelbaum, S. (1959), The effect of altered psychological atmosphere on Rorschach responses. *Bull. Menn. Clin.,* 23:179–189.

Appelbaum, S. & Colson, D. (1968), A re-examination of the color-shading Rorschach test response and suicide attempts. *J. Proj. Tech. & Pers. Assess.,* 32:160–164.

Appelbaum, S. & Holtzman, P. (1962), The color-shading response and suicide. *J. Pers. Assess.,* 26:155–161.

Arnow, D., & Cooper, S. (1988), Toward a Rorschach psychology of the self. In: *Primitive Mental States and the Rorschach,* ed. H. Lerner & P. Lerner. New York: International Universities Press, pp. 53–70.

Bachrach, H. (1968), Adaptive regression, empathy and psychotherapy: Theory and research study. *Psychother.,* 5:203–209.

Beck, S. (1944–45), *Rorschach's Test.* New York: Grune & Stratton.

Becker, W. (1956), A genetic approach to the interpretation and evaluation of the process-reactive distinction in schizophrenia. *J. Abnorm. & Soc. Psychol.,* 53:229–336.

Benfari, R. & Calogeras, R. (1968), Levels of cognition and conscience typologies. *J. Proj. Tech. & Pers. Assess.,* 32:466–474.

Binder, H. (1932–33), Die Helldunkeldeutungen im psychodiagnostischen Experiment von Rorschach. *Schweiz. Arch. Neurol. Psychiat.,* 30:1–67.

Bion, W. (1967), *Second Thoughts: Selected Papers on Psychoanalysis.* London: Heinemann.

271

Blatt, S. (1974), Levels of object representation in anaclitic and introjective depression. *The Psychoanalytic Study of the Child,* 29:107–157. New Haven, CT: Yale University Press.

Blatt, S., Allison, J., & Feirstein, A. (1969), The capacity to cope with cognitive complexity. *J. Pers.,* 37:269–288.

Blatt, S., Berman, W., Bloom-Feshbach, S., Sugarman, A., Wilber, C. & Kleber, H. (1984), Psychological assessment in opiate addicts. *Nerv. Ment. Dis.,* 172:156–165.

Blatt, S., Brenneis, C., Schimek, J. & Glick, M. (1976). A developmental analysis of the concept of the object on the Rorschach. Unpublished manuscript, Dept. Psychology, Yale University.

Blatt, S. & Lerner, H. (1982), Investigations in the psychoanalytic theory of object relations and object representations. *Empirical Studies Psychoanal. Theory,* Vol. 1, ed. S. Masling. Hillsdale, NJ: The Analytic Press, pp. 189–249.

Blatt, S. & Lerner, H. (1983), The psychological assessment of object representation. *J. Pers. Assess.,* 47:7–28.

Blatt, S. & Ritzler, B. (1974), Thought disorder and boundary disturbances in psychosis. *J. Consult. Clin. Psychol.,* 42:370–381.

Blatt, S., Schimek, J. & Brenneis, C. (1980), The nature of the psychotic experience & its implications for the therapeutic process. In: *The Psychotherapy of Schizophrenia,* ed. J. Strauss et al. New York: Plenum.

Bleuler, E. (1924), *Textbook of Psychiatry.* New York: Dover.

Blum, H. (1981), Object inconstancy and paranoid conspiracy. *J. Amer. Psychoanal. Assn.,* 29:789–814.

Brouillette, C. (1987), A Rorschach assessment of the character structure of anorexia nervosa and bulimia patients and of their mothers. Unpublished doctoral dissertation, Dept. of Applied Psychology, University of Toronto.

Carpenter, W., Gunderson, J. & Strauss, J. (1977), Considerations of the borderline syndrome: A longitudinal comparative study of borderline and schizophrenic patients. In: *Borderline Personality Disorders,* ed. P. Hartocollis. New York: International Universities Press, pp. 231–253.

Carr, A. (1987), Borderline defenses and Rorschach responses: A critique of Lerner, Albert and Walsh. *J. Pers. Assess.,* 51:349–351.

Chapman, L. & Chapman, J. (1982), Subtle cognitive slippage scale. Unpublished manuscript.

Coates, S. & Tuber, S. (1988), The representation of object relations in the Rorschachs of extremely feminine boys. In: *Primitive Mental States and the Rorschach,* ed. H. Lerner & P. Lerner. New York: International Universities Press, pp. 647–664.

Cohen, I. (1960), An investigation of the relationship between adaptive regression, dogmatism and creativity using the Rorschach and dogmatism scale. Unpublished doctoral dissertation, Dept. of Psychology, Michigan State University.

Collins, R. (1983), Rorschach correlates of borderline personality. Unpublished doctoral disseration, Department of Applied Psychology, University of Toronto.

Coonerty, S. (1986), An exploration of separation–individuation themes in the borderline personality disorder. *J. Pers. Assess.,* 50:501–511.

Cooper, S. (1981), An object relations view of the borderline defenses: A Rorschach analysis. Unpublished manuscript.

Cooper, S. & Arnow, D. (1986), An object relations view of the borderline defenses: A review. In: *Assessing Object Relations Phenomena,* ed. M. Kissen. New York: International Universities Press, pp. 143–171.

Cooper, S., Perry, J. & Arnow, D. (1988), An empirical approach to the study of defense mechanisms: I. Reliability and preliminary validity of the Rorschach defense scale. *J. Pers. Assess.,* 52:187–203.

Dana, R. (1968), Six constructs to define Rorschach M. *J. Proj. Tech. & Pers. Assess.,* 32:138–145.

Deutsch, H. (1942), Some forms of emotional disturbance and their relationship to schizo-phrenia. *Psychoanal. Quart.,* 11:301–321.

Dudek, S. & Chamberland-Bouhadana, G. (1982), Primary process in creative persons. *J. Pers. Assess.,* 46:239–247.

Easser, R. (1974), Empathic inhibition and psychoanalytic technique. *Psychoanal. Quart.,* 43:557–580.

Easser, R. & Lesser, S. (1965), Hysterical personality: A re-evaluation. *Psychoanal. Quart.,* 34:390–405.

Easser, R. & Lesser, S. (1966), Transference resistance in hysterical character neurosis–technical considerations. *Developments in Psychoanalysis at Columbia University.* New York: Columbia University Press, pp. 69–80.

Edell, W. (1984), The Borderline-Syndrome Index: Clinical validity and utility. *J. Nerv. Ment. Dis.,* 172:254–263.

Edell, W. (1987), Role of structure in disordered thinking in borderline and schizophrenic disorders. *J. Pers. Assess.,* 51:23–41.

Exner, J. (1974), *The Rorschach: A Comprehensive System,* Vol. 1. New York: Wiley.

Exner, J. (1986), Some Rorschach data comparing schizophrenics with borderline and schizotypal personality disorders. *J. Pers. Assess.,* 50:455–471.

Exner, J., Wylie, J. & Bryant, E. (1974), Peer preference nominations among outpatients in four psychotherapy groups. Unpublished manuscript, Rorschach Workshops, Bayville, NY.

Fairbairn, W. (1952), *Psychoanalytic Studies of the Personality.* London: Tavistock.

Farris, M. (1988), Differential diagnosis of borderline and narcissistic personality disorders. In: *Primitive Mental States and the Rorschach,* ed. H. Lerner & P. Lerner. New York: International Universities Press, pp. 299–338.

Feirstein, A. (1967), Personality correlates for unrealistic experiences. *J. Consult. Psychol.,* 31:387–395.

Fenichel, O. (1945), *Psychoanalytic Theory of Neurosis.* New York: Norton.

Fibel, B. (1979), Toward a developmental model of depression: Object representation and object loss in adolescent & adult psychiatric patients. Doctoral dissertation, Department of Psychology, University of Massachusetts, Amherst.

Freud, A. (1936), *The Ego and The Mechanisms of Defense.* New York: International Universities Press.

Freud, S. (1900), The interpretation of dreams. *Standard Edition,* 4 & 5. London: Hogarth Press, 1953.

Freud, S. (1908), Character and anal erotism. *Standard Edition,* 9:167–175. London: Hogarth Press, 1959.

Freud, S. (1914), On narcissism: An introduction. *Standard Edition,* 14:73–102. London: Hogarth Press, 1957.

Freud, S. (1915), The unconscious, *Standard Edition,* 14:159–216. London: Hogarth Press.

Freud, S. (1923), The ego and the id. *Standard Edition,* 19:12–59. London: Hogarth Press, 1961.

Freud, S. (1926), Inhibitions, symptoms and anxiety. *Standard Edition,* 20:87–172. London: Hogarth Press, 1959.

Freud, S. (1931), Libidinal types. *Standard Edition,* 21:215–220. London: Hogarth Press, 1961.

Friedman, H. (1953), Perceptual regression in schizophrenia. An hypothesis suggested by use of the Rorschach test. *J. Proj. Tech.,* 17:171–185.

Gabbard, G. (1989), Two subtypes of narcissistic personality disorder. *Bull. Menn. Clin.,* 53:527–532.

Gacono, C. (1988), A Rorschach analysis of object relations and defensive structure and their relationship to narcissism and psychopathy in a group of antisocial offenders. Unpublished doctoral dissertation, United States International University.

Gacono, C. & Meloy, J. R. (1988), Comments on the relationship between cognitive style and defensive process in the psychopath. *E.D.I.T. Newsletter.* Minnetonka, MN.

Gardiner, M. (1971), *The Wolf-Man.* New York: Basic Books.

Gedo, J. & Goldberg, A. (1973), *Models of the Mind: A Psychoanalytic Theory.* Chicago: University of Chicago Press.

Goldberger, L. (1961), Reactions to perceptual isolation and Rorschach manifestations of the primary process. *J. Proj. Tech.,* 25:287–302.

Graham, I. (1978), Representational and cognitive aspects of a depressive personality. Presented to the Toronto Psychoanalytic Society, Toronto, Ontario.

Grala, C. (1980), The concept of splitting and its manifestations on the Rorschach. *Bull. Menn. Clin.,* 44:253–271.

Greenberg, N., Ramsay, M., Rakoff, V. & Weiss, A. (1969), Primary process thinking in myxedema psychosis: A case study. *Can. J. Behav. Sci.,* 1:60–67.

Grinker, R., Werble, B. & Drye, R. (1968), *The Borderline Syndrome: A Behavioral Study of Ego Functions.* New York: Basic Books.

Grotstein, J. (1981), *Splitting and Projective Identification.* New York: Aronson.

Gunderson, J. & Singer, M. (1975), Defining borderline patients: An overview. *Amer. J. Psychiat.,* 132:1–10.

Guntrip, H. (1952), A study of Fairbairn's theory of schizoid reactions. *Br. J. Med. Psychol.,* 25:86–103.

Guntrip, H. (1961), *Personality Structure and Human Interaction.* New York: International Universities Press.

Hammond, J. (1984), Object relations and defensive operations in gender identity disordered males. Unpublished doctoral dissertation, United States International University.

Harder, D. (1979), The assessment of ambitious-narcissistic character style with three projective tests: The Early Memories, T.A.T., & Rorschach. *J. Pers. Assess.,* 43:23–32.

Hartmann, H. (1950), Comments on the psychoanalytic theory of the ego. In: *Essays on Ego Psychology.* New York: International Universities Press, pp. 115–141, 1965.

Hatcher, R. & Krohn, A. (1980), Level of object representation and capacity for intensive psychotherapy in neurotics & borderlines. In: *Borderline Phenomena & the Rorschach Test,* ed. J. Kwawer et al. New York: International Universities Press, pp. 299–320.

Hoffer, W. (1968), Notes on the theory of defense. *The Psychoanalytic Study of the Child,* 23:178–188. New York: International Universities Press.

Holt, R. (1968), D. Rapaport, M. Gill & R. Schafer, *Diagnostic Psychological Testing,* revised ed. New York: International Universities Press.

Holt, R. (1970), *Manual for the Scoring of Primary Process Manifestations and Their Controls in Rorschach Responses.* New York: Research Center for Mental Health.

Holt, R. (1977), A method for assessing primary process manifestations and their controls in Rorschach responses. In: *Rorschach Psychology,* ed. M. Rickers-Ovsiankina. Huntington, NY: Krieger, pp. 375–420.

Holtzman, P. & Gardner, R. (1959), Leveling and repression. *J. Abnorm.& Soc. Psychol.,* 59:151–155.

Horowitz, M. (1972), Modes of representation of thought. *J. Amer. Psychoanal. Assn.,* 20:793–819.

Hymowitz, P., Hunt, H., Carr, A., Hurt, S. & Spear, W. (1983), The W.A.I.S. and the Rorschach in diagnosing borderline personality. *J. Pers. Assess.,* 47:588–596.

Ipp, H. (1986), Object relations of feminine boys: A Rorschach assessment. Unpublished doctoral dissertation, York University.

Jacobson, E. (1971), *Depression-Comparative Studies of Normal, Neurotic and Psychotic Conditions.* New York: International Universities Press.

Johnson, D. (1980), Cognitive organization in paranoid & nonparanoid schizophrenia. Unpublished doctoral dissertation, Department of Psychology, Yale University.

Johnston, M. & Holtzman, P. (1979), *The Nature and Measurement of Thought Disorder.* San Francisco: Jossey-Bass.

Kaufer, J. & Katz, J. (1983), Rorschach responses in anorectic and non-anorectic women. *Internat. J. Eating Disorders,* 3:65–74.

Kernberg, O. (1970), A psychoanalytic classification of character pathology. *J. Amer. Psychoanal. Assn.,* 18:800–822.

Kernberg, O. (1975), *Borderline Conditions and Pathological Narcissism.* New York: Aronson.

Kernberg, O. (1976), *Object Relations Theory and Clinical Psychoanalysis.* New York: Aronson.

Kernberg, O. (1977), The structural diagnosis of borderline personality organization. In: *Borderline Personality Disorders,* ed. P. Hartocollis. New York: International Universities Press, pp. 87–121.

Kernberg, O. (1979), Two reviews of the literature on borderlines: An assessment. *Schizophrenia Bull.,* 5:53–58.

Kernberg, O. (1981), Structural interviewing. *Psychiat. Clin. N. Amer.,* 4:1–24.

Kety, S., Rosenthal, D., Wender, P. & Schulsinger, F. (1968), The types and prevalence of mental illness in the biological and adoptive families of adopted schizophrenics. In: *The Transmission of Schizophrenia,* ed. D. Rosenthal & S. Kety. New York: Pergamon, pp. 345–362.

Klein, D. (1973), Drug therapy as a means of syndromal identification and nosological revision. *Psychopathology and Pharmacology,* ed. J. Cole & A. Friedhoff. Baltimore: Johns Hopkins University Press.

Klein, D. (1975), Psychopharmacology and the borderline patient. In: *Borderline States in Psychiatry,* ed. J. Mack. New York: Grune & Stratton.

Klein, M. (1930), The importance of symbol formation in the development of the ego. *Internat. J. Psycho-Anal.,* 11:24–39.

Klein, M. (1935), A contribution to the psychogenesis of manic-depressive states. *Contributions to Psycho-Analysis 1921–1945.* London: Hogarth Press, 1948, pp. 282–310.

Klopfer, B., Ainsworth, M., Klopfer, W. & Holt, R. (1954), *Developments in the Rorschach Technique, Vol. 1.* New York: Harcourt, Brace, and World.

Klopfer, B. & Kelley, D. (1942), *The Rorschach Technique.* Yonkers: World Book.

Knight, R. (1953), Borderline states. In: *Psychoanalytic Psychiatry and Psychology,* ed. R. Knight & C. Friedman. New York: International Universities Press, pp. 97–109.

Kohut, H. (1971), *The Analysis of the Self.* New York: International Universities Press.

Kohut, H. (1977), *The Restoration of the Self.* New York: International Universities Press.

Kohut, H. & Wolf, E. S. (1978), The Disorders of the self and their treatment: An Outline. *Internat. J. Psycho-Anal.,* 59:413–425.

Kolb, J. & Gunderson, J. (1980), Diagnosing borderlines with a semi-structured interview. *Arch. Gen. Psychiat.,* 37:37–41.

Kolers, N. (1986), Some ego functions in boys with gender identity disturbance. Unpublished doctoral dissertation, York University.

Kris, E. (1952), *Psychoanalytic Explorations in Art.* New York: International Universities Press.

Krohn, A. (1974), Borderline empathy and differentiation of object representations: A contribution to the psychology of object relations. *Internat. J. Psychoanal. Psychother.,* 3:142–165.

Krohn, A. (1978), Hysteria: The elusive neurosis. *Psychological Issues,* Monogr. 45/46. New York: International Universities Press.

Krohn, A. & Mayman, M. (1974), Object-representations in dreams & projective tests. *Bull. Menn. Clin.,* 38:445–466.

Kwawer, J. (1980), Primitive interpersonal modes, borderline phenomena, and Rorschach content. In: *Borderline Phenomena and the Rorschach Test,* ed. J. Kwawer, H. Lerner, P. Lerner & A. Sugarman. New York: International Universities Press, pp. 89–106.

Kwawer, J., Lerner, H., Lerner, P. & Sugarman, A. (1980), *Borderline Phenomena and the Rorschach Test.* New York: International Universities Press.

Laughlin, H. (1956), *The Neuroses in Clinical Practice.* Philadelphia: Saunders.

Leeuw, P. (1971), On the development of the concept of defense. *Internat. J. Psycho-Anal.*, 52:51–58.

Lerner, H. (1988), The narcissistic personality as expressed through psychological tests. In: *Primitive Mental States and the Rorschach,* ed. H. Lerner & P. Lerner. New York: International Universities Press, pp. 257–298.

Lerner, H., Albert, C. & Walsh, M. (1987), The Rorschach assessment of borderline defenses. *J. Pers. Assess.*, 51:344–354.

Lerner, H. & Lerner, P. (1982), A comparative study of defensive structure in neurotic, borderline and schizophrenic patients. *Psychoanal. Contemp. Thought,* 5:77–113.

Lerner, H. & Lerner, P. (1988), *Primitive Mental States and the Rorschach.* New York: International Universities Press.

Lerner, H. & St. Peter, S. (1984), Patterns of object relations in neurotic, borderline and schizophrenic patients. *Psychiat.*, 47:77–92.

Lerner, H., Sugarman, A. & Barbour, C. (1985), Patterns of ego boundary disturbances in neurotic, borderline and schizophrenic patients. *Psychoanal. Psychol.*, 2:47–66.

Lerner, H., Sugarman, A. & Gaughran, J. (1981), Borderline and schizophrenic patients: A comparative study of defensive structure. *J. Nerv. Ment. Dis.*, 169:705–711.

Lerner, P. (1975), *Handbook of Rorschach Scales.* New York: International Universities Press.

Lerner, P. (1979), Treatment implications of the (c) response in the Rorschach records of patients with severe character pathology. *Ontario Psycholog.*, 11:20–22.

Lerner, P. (1981), Cognitive aspects of the (c) response in the Rorschach records of patients with severe character pathology. Paper presented to the International Rorschach Congress, Washington, DC.

Lerner, P. (1985), Current psychoanalytic perspectives on the borderline and narcissistic concepts. *Clin. Psych. Rev.*, 5:99–114.

Lerner, P. (1986), Experiential and structural aspects of the (c) Rorschach response in patients with narcissistic character pathology. In: *Assessing Object Relations Phenomena,* ed. M. Kissen. New York: International Universities Press, pp. 333–348.

Lerner, P. (1988), Rorschach measures of depression, the false self, and projective identification in patients with narcissistic personality disorders. In: *Primitive Mental States and the Rorschach,* ed. H. Lerner & P. Lerner. New York: International Universities Press, pp. 71–94.

Lerner, P. & Lerner, H. (1980), Rorschach assessment of primitive defenses in borderline personality structure. In: *Borderline Phenomena and the Rorschach Test,* ed.J. Kwawer, H. Lerner, P. Lerner & A. Sugarman. New York: International Universities Press, pp. 257–274.

Lerner, P. & Lerner, H. (1986), Contributions of object relations theory towards a general psychoanalytic theory of thinking. *Psychoanal. Contemp. Thought,* 9:469–513.

Lerner, P. & Lewandowski, A. (1975), The measurement of primary process manifestations: A review. In: *Handbook of Rorschach Scales,* ed. P. Lerner. New York: International Universities Press, pp. 181–214.

Levine, M. & Spivak, G. (1964), *The Rorschach Index of Repressive Style.* Springfield, IL: Charles C. Thomas.

Loewald, H. (1973), On internalization. *Internat. J. Psycho-Anal.*, 54:9–18.

Ludolph, P., Milden, R. & Lerner, H. (1988), Rorschach profiles of depressives: Clinical case illustrations. In: *Primitive Mental States and the Rorschach,* ed. H. Lerner & P. Lerner. New York: International Universities Press, pp. 463–494.

Madison, P. (1961), *Freud's Concept of Repression and Defense: Its Theoretical and Observational Language.* Minneapolis: University of Minnesota Press.

Mahler, M. (1960), Symposium on psychotic object-relationships: III. Perceptual de-differentiation and psychotic object relationship. *Internat. J. Psycho-Anal.*, 41:548–553.

Mahler, M. (1968), *On Human Symbiosis and Vicissitudes of Individuation, Vol. I: Infantile Psychosis.* New York: International Universities Press.

Mahler, M., Pine, F. & Bergman, A. (1975), *The Psychological Birth of the Human Infant.* New York: Basic Books.

Masterson, J. & Rinsley, D. (1975), The borderline syndrome: The role of the mother in the genesis and psychic structure of the borderline personality. *Internat. J. Psycho-Anal.*, 56:163–177.

Maupin, E. (1965), Individual differences in response to a Zen meditation exercise. *J. Consult. Psychol.*, 29:139–145.

Mayman, M. (1964a), Some general propositions implicit in the clinical application of psychological tests. Unpublished manuscript, Menninger Foundation, Topeka.

Mayman, M. (1964b), Form quality of Rorschach responses. Unpublished manuscript, Menninger Foundation, Topeka.

Mayman, M. (1967), Object representations and object relationships in Rorschach responses. *J. Proj. Tech. & Pers. Assess.*, 31:17–24.

Mayman, M. (1970), Reality contact, defense effectiveness, and psychopathology in Rorschach form level scores. In: *Developments in Rorschach Technique, Vol. III*, ed. B. Klopfer, M. Meyer, & F. Brawer. New York: Harcourt, Brace & Jovanovich, pp. 11–44.

Mayman, M. (1976), Psychoanalytic theory in retrospect and prospect. *Bull. Menn. Clin.*, 40:199–210.

Mayman, M. (1977), A multi-dimensional view of the Rorschach movement response. In: *Rorschach Psychology*, ed. M. Rickers-Ovsiankina. Huntington, NY: Krieger, pp. 229–250.

McMahon, J. (1964), The relationship between "overinclusive" and primary process thought in a normal and a schizophrenic population. Unpublished doctoral dissertation, New York University.

Michaels, M. (1983), Plenary address. Presented at the symposium "Distortions of Personality Development and Their Management." Toronto, Ontario.

Modell, A. (1963), Primitive object relationships and the predisposition to schizophrenia. *Internat. J. Psycho-Anal.*, 44:282–292.

Modell, A. (1975), A narcissistic defense against affects and the illusion of self-sufficiency. *Internat. J. Psycho-Anal.*, 56:275–282.

Modell, A. (1978), The conceptualization of the therapeutic action of psychoanalysis: The action of the holding environment. *Bull. Menn. Clin.*, 42:493–504.

Murray, J. (1985), Borderline manifestations in the Rorschachs of male transsexuals. *J. Pers. Assess.*, 49:454–466.

Murray, J. & Russ, S. (1981), Adaptive regression and types of cognitive flexibility. *J. Pers. Assess.*, 45:59–65.

Nifakis, D. (1989), Victims of father daughter incest: An investigation using object relations theory. Unpublished doctoral dissertation, University of Toronto.

Ogden, T. (1983), The concept of internal object relations. *Internat. J. Psycho-Anal.*, 64:227–243.

Peebles, R. (1975), Rorschach as self-system in the telophasic theory of personality development. In: *Handbook of Rorschach Scales*, ed. P. Lerner. New York: International Universities Press, pp. 71–136.

Perry, J. & Klerman, G. (1978), The borderline patient. *Arch. Gen. Psychiat.*, 35:141–150.

Pine, F. (1962), Creativity and primary process: Sample variations. *J. Nerv. Ment. Dis.*, 134:506–511.

Pine, F. & Holt, R. (1960), Creativity and primary process: A study of adaptive regression. *J. Abnorm. & Soc. Psychol.*, 61:370–379.

Piotrowski, Z. (1947), *A Rorschach Compendium*. Utica, NY: State Hospital Press.

Piotrowski, Z. (1957), *Perceptanalysis*. New York: Macmillan.

Piran, N. (1988), Borderline phenomena in anorexia nervosa and bulimia. In: *Primitive Mental States and the Rorschach*, ed. H. Lerner & P. Lerner. New York: International Universities Press, pp. 363–376.

Piran, N. & Lerner, P. (1987), Piagetian cognitive development and ego development: A study of anorexic patients. Unpublished manuscript, Toronto General Hospital, Toronto, Ontario.

Piran, N. & Lerner, P. (submitted), Borderline phenomena in anorexia nervosa and bulimia.

Piran, N., Lerner, P., Garfinkle, P., Kennedy, S. & Brouillette, C. (1988), Personality disorders in anorexic patients. *Internat. J. Eating Disorders*, 7:589–600.

Piran, N., Lerner, P., Garfinkel, P., Kennedy, S. & Brouillette, C. (submitted), Personality organization in restricting and bulimic anorexics.

Prelinger, E., Zimet, C., Schafer, R. & Levin, M. (1964), *An Ego-Psychological Approach to Character Assessment*. Glencoe: Free Press.

Pruitt, W. & Spilka, B. (1964), Rorschach empathy—object relationship scale. In: *Handbook of Rorschach Scales*, ed. P. Lerner. New York: International Universities Press, 1975, pp. 315–323.

Pruyser, P. (1975), What splits in splitting. *Bull. Menn. Clin.*, 39:1–46.

Rabkin, J. (1967), Psychoanalytic assessment of change in organization of thought after psychotherapy. Unpublished doctoral dissertation, New York University.

Rapaport, D. (1950), The theoretical implications of diagnostic testing procedures. *Congres International de Psychiatrie*, 2:241–271.

Rapaport, D. (1958), An historical review of psychoanalytic ego psychology. In: *The Collected Papers of David Rapaport*, ed. M. Gill. New York: Basic Books, pp. 745–757.

Rapaport, D., Gill, M. & Schafer, R. (1945–1946), *Diagnostic Psychological Testing*, 2 Vols. Chicago: Year Book.

Reich, A. (1960), Pathologic forms of self-esteem regulation. *The Psychoanalytic Study of the Child*, 15:215–232. New York: International Universities Press.

Reich, W. (1933), *Character Analysis*. New York: Farrar, Straus & Giroux, 1972.

Ribble, M. (1943), *The Rights of Infants: Early Psychological Needs and Their Satisfaction*. New York: Columbia University Press.

Rinsley, D. (1979), The developmental etiology of borderline and narcissistic disorders. *Bull. Menn. Clin.*, 44:147–170.

Ritzler, B., Zambianco, D., Harder, D. & Kaskey, M. (1980), Psychotic patterns of the concept of the object on the Rorschach test. *J. Abn. Psychol.*, 89:46–55.

Robbins, M. (1976), Borderline personality organization: The need for a new theory. *J. Amer. Psychoanal. Assn.*, 24:831–854.

Roland, C. (1970), Anorexia nervosa: A survey of the literature and review of 30 cases. In: *Anorexia and Obesity*, ed. C. Roland. Boston: Little Brown, pp. 45–60.

Rorschach, H. (1942), *Psychodiagnostics*. Berne: Hans Huber.

Rosenthal, D. (1975), The concept of schizophrenia disorders. In: *Genetic Research in Psychiatry*, ed. R. Fieve, D. Rosenthal & H. Brill. Baltimore: Johns Hopkins University Press, pp. 199–215.

Russ, S. (1980), Primary process integration on the Rorschach and achievement in children. *J. Pers. Assess.*, 44:338–344.

Ryan, E. R. (1973), The capacity of the patient to enter an elementary therapeutic relationship in the initial psychotherapy interview. Unpublished doctoral dissertation, Department of Psychology, University of Michigan.

Ryan, R., Avery, R. & Grolnick, W. (1985), A Rorschach assessment of children's mutuality of autonomy. *J. Pers. Assess.*, 49:6–12.

Saretsky, T. (1966), Effects of chlorpromazine on primary process thought manifestations. *J.*

Abnorm. Psychol., 71:247–252.

Schachtel, E. (1966), *Experiential Foundations of Rorschach's Test*. New York: Basic Books.

Schafer, R. (1954), *Psychoanalytic Interpretation in Rorschach Testing*. New York: Grune & Stratton.

Schlesinger, H. (1973), Interaction of dynamic and reality factors in the diagnostic testing interview. *Bull. Menn. Clin.*, 37:495–518.

Schmideberg, M. (1947), The treatment of psychopathic and borderline patients. *Amer. J. Psychother.*, 1:47–71.

Schmideberg, M. (1959), The borderline patient. In: *American Handbook of Psychiatry, Vol. I*, ed. S. Arieti. New York: Basic Books, pp. 398–416.

Segal, H. (1973), *Introduction to the Work of Melanie Klein*. London: Hogarth Press.

Selvini-Palazzoli, M. (1974), *Self-Starvation: From the Intrapsychic to the Transpersonal Approach to Anorexia Nervosa*. New York: Jason Aronson.

Serban, G., Conte, H. & Plutchic, R. (1987), Borderline and schizotypal personality disorders: Mutually exclusive or overlapping? *J. Pers. Assess.*, 51:15–22.

Settlage, C. (1977), The psychoanalytic understanding of narcissistic and borderline personality disorders: Advances in developmental theory. *J. Amer. Psychoanal. Assn.*, 25:805–833.

Shapiro, D. (1965), *Neurotic Styles*. New York: Basic Books.

Sharpe, E. (1940), Psycho-physical problems revealed in language: An examination of metaphor. In: *Collected Papers on Psycho-analysis*, ed. M. Brierley. New York: Brunner/ Mazel, 1978, pp. 155–169.

Shevrin, H. & Schectman, F. (1973), The diagnostic practice in psychiatric evaluation. *Bull. Menn. Clin.*, 37:451–494.

Siegman, A. (1954), Emotionality—a hysterical character defense. *Psychoanal. Quart.*, 23:339–354.

Singer, M. (1977), The borderline diagnosis and psychological tests: Review and research. In: *Borderline Personality Disorders*, ed. P. Hartocollis. New York: International Universities Press, pp. 193–212.

Singer, M. & Larson, D. (1981), Borderline personality and the Rorschach test. *Arch. Gen. Psychiat.*, 38:693–698.

Small, A., Teango, L., Madero, J., Gross, H. & Ebert, M. (1982), A comparison of anorexics and schizophrenics on psychodiagnostic measures. *Internat. J. Eating Disorders*, 1:49–57.

Smith, K. (1980), Object relations concepts as applied to the borderline level of ego functioning. In: *Borderline Phenomena and the Rorschach Test*, ed. J. Kwawer, H. Lerner, P. Lerner & A.Sugarman. New York: International Universities Press, pp. 59–88.

Spear, W. (1980), The psychological assessment of structural and thematic object representations in borderline and schizophrenic patients. In: *Borderline Phenomena and the Rorschach Test*, ed. J. Kwawer, H. Lerner, P. Lerner & S. Sugarman. New York: International Universities Press, pp. 321–342.

Spear, W. & Sugarman, A. (1984), Dimensions of internalized object relations in borderline and schizophrenic patients. *Psychoanal. Psychol.*, 1:113–130.

Spear, W. & Schwager, E. (1980), New perspectives on the use of psychological tests as a measure of change over the course of intensive impatient psychotherapy. Paper presented at meeting of Society for Personality Assessment, Tampa, FL.

Spitzer, R., Endicott, J. & Robbins, E. (1975), Research Diagnostic Criteria (RDC). *Psychopharmacol. Bull.*, 11:22–24.

Stern, A. (1938), Psychoanalytic investigation of therapy in the borderline neurosis. *Psychoanal. Quart.*, 7:467–489.

Stolorow, R. & Lachmann, F. (1980), *Psychoanalysis of Developmental Arrest*. New York: International Universities Press.

Stone, M. (1980), *The Borderline Syndromes: Constitution, Personality and Adaptation*. New

York: McGraw-Hill.

Strober, M. & Goldenberg, J. (1981), Ego boundary distrubance in juvenile anorexia nervosa. *J. Clin. Psychol.*, 37:433–438.

Sugarman, A. (1979), The infantile personality: Orality in the hysteric revisited. *Internat. J. Psycho-Anal.*, 60:501–513.

Sugarman, A. & Lerner, H. (1980), Reflections on the current state of the borderline concept. In: *Borderline Phenomena and the Rorschach test*, ed. J. Kwawer, H. Lerner, P. Lerner & A. Sugarman. New York: International Universities Press, pp. 11–38.

Sugarman, A., Quinlan, D. & Devenis, L. (1982), Ego boundary disturbance in anorexia nervosa. *J. Pers. Assess.*, 46:455–461.

Teicholtz, J. (1978), A selected review of the psychoanalytic literature on theoretical conceptualizations of narcissism. *J. Amer. Psychoanal. Assn.*, 26:831–862.

Thompson, A. (1986), An object relational theory of affect maturity: Applications to the Thematic Apperception Test. In: *Assessing Object Relations Phenomena*, ed. M. Kisson. New York: International Universities Press, pp. 207–224.

Tolpin, R. & Kohut, H. (1978), The disorders of the self: The psychopathology of the first year of life. In: *The Course of Life. Vol. 1, Psychoanalysis and the Life Cycle*, ed. G. Pollock & S. Greenspan. Washington, DC: NIMH, pp. 425–458.

Tuber, S. (1983), Children's Rorschach scores as predictors of later adjustment. *J. Consult. Clin. Psychol.*, 51:379–385.

Tuber, S. & Coates, S. (1985), Interpersonal modes in the Rorschach of extremely feminine boys. *Psychoanal. Psychol.*, 2:251–265.

Urist, J. (1973), The Rorschach Test as a multidimensional measure of object relations. Unpublished doctoral dissertation, Department of Psychology, University of Michigan.

Urist, J. (1977), The Rorschach test and the assessment of object relations. *J. Pers. Assess.*, 41:3–9.

Urist, J. & Shill, M. (1982), Validity of the Rorschach Mutuality of Autonomy Scale: A replication using excerpted responses. *J. Pers. Assess.*, 46:451–454.

Van-Der Keshet, Y. (1988), Anorexic patients and ballet students: A Rorschach analysis. Unpublished doctoral dissertation, University of Toronto.

Wagner, E. & Wagner, C. (1978), Similar Rorschach patterning in three cases of anorexia nervosa. *J. Pers. Assess.*, 42:426–433.

Watkins, J. & Stauffacher, J. (1952), An index of pathological thinking in the Rorschach. *J. Proj. Tech.*, 16:276–286.

Weisberg, L., Norman, D. & Herzog, D. (1987), Personality functioning in normal weight bulimia. *Internat. J. Eating Disorders*, 6:615–631.

Wender, P. (1977), The contribution of the adoption studies to an understanding of the phenomenology and etiology of borderline schizophrenia. In: *Borderline Personality Disorders*, ed. P. Hartocollis. New York: International Universities Press, pp. 255–269.

Werner, H. (1940), *The Comparative Psychology of Mental Development.* New York: International Universities Press, 1957.

Wilson, A. (1985), Boundary disturbance in borderline and psychotic states. *J. Pers. Assess.*, 49:346–355.

Wilson, A. (1988), Levels of depression and clinical assessment. In: *Primitive Mental States and the Rorschach*, ed. H. Lerner & P. Lerner. New York: International Universities Press, pp. 441–462.

Winnicott, D. (1953), Transitional objects and transitional phenomena. *Internat. J. Psycho-Anal.*, 34:89–97.

Winnicott, D. (1960), The theory of the parent-infant relationship. *Internat. J. Psycho-Anal.*, 41:385–395.

Winnicott, D. (1961), Ego distortion in terms of true and false self. In: *The Maturational*

Processes and the Facilitating Environment. New York: International Universities Press, pp. 140–152.

Witkin, H. (1950), Individual differences in ease of perception of embedded figures. *J. Pers.,* 19:1–15.

Wright, M. (1981), False self development and the role of the alter ego. Paper presented to the Toronto Psychoanalytic Society, Toronto, Ontario.

Wright, N., & Abbey, D. (1965), Perceptual deprivation tolerance and adequacy of defense. *Percept. Mot. Skills,* 20:35–38.

Wright, N. & Zubek, J. (1969), Relationship between perceptual deprivation tolerance and adequacy of defenses as measured by the Rorschach. *J. Abn. Psychol.,* 74:615–617.

Young, H. (1959), A test of the Witkin's field-dependence hypothesis. *J. Abnorm. & Soc. Psychol.,* 59:188–192.

Zilboorg, G. (1941), Ambulatory schizophrenia. *Psychiat.,* 4:149–155.

Zimet, C. & Fine, H. (1965), Primary and secondary process thinking in two types of schizophrenia. *J. Proj. Tech. & Pers. Assess.,* 29:93–99.

Author Index

283

Subject Index